PHIL SAUNDERS

This Club Could Be Your Life

Copyright © 2022 by Phil Saunders

All rights reserved. No part of this publication may be reproduced, stored or transmitted in any form or by any means, electronic, mechanical, photocopying, recording, scanning, or otherwise without written permission from the publisher. It is illegal to copy this book, post it to a website, or distribute it by any other means without permission.

Phil Saunders has no responsibility for the persistence or accuracy of URLs for external or third-party Internet Websites referred to in this publication and does not guarantee that any content on such Websites is, or will remain, accurate or appropriate.

Designations used by companies to distinguish their products are often claimed as trademarks. All brand names and product names used in this book and on its cover are trade names, service marks, trademarks and registered trademarks of their respective owners. The publishers and the book are not associated with any product or vendor mentioned in this book. None of the companies referenced within the book have endorsed the book.

Advance apologies: My memory is terrible. I am already mortified that I have undoubtedly forgotten someone special. I am already gutted that I will have forgotten a great story. Also, the swearing, sorry Mum.

First edition

This book was professionally typeset on Reedsy.
Find out more at reedsy.com

Contents

I   INTRO

For The Kids	3
Prologue	4
Anatomy of a Clubnight	6
2004	13
Who The Fuck Is Phil Saunders?	16
Boro Needs A Rock Night	20

II   SUMO

The Johnny Cash Club	25
Sumo DJs	29
Haxed Forum Announcement	33

III   THE CORNERHOUSE

A Legendary Labyrinth	37
Area 2	40
Launch Night	42
The First Sumo Setlist	46
The Ceiling	50
All Downhill From Here	51
Two Thousand Free Drinks	53
1977 (The One With The Haircuts)	55

The Fluffgirl's Bucket	58
MySpace	61
A Cornerhouse Playlist	65
Paparazzi	66
To Hull and Back	70
Sumo Tattoo	72
Good Fridays	74
Little Tokyo	77
Tell Your Mates Who Don't Like Metal	81
Can You Do 600?	85
Booking A Band	87
Area 2 Take 2	89
Bands Bands Bands	93
Behind The Curtain	96
Training Day	99
Planet Dare	105
Friday Afternoons	108
Punching A Skeleton To Pieces	111
Sumo Room 3	114
He Pushed His Fingers Into My Eyes	118
Bring Me The Horizon, Malpractice and My Wife	121
A Set List from December 2006	124
Men, Women And Children	127
Some Sumo Stuff From 2006	130
Black Jack Rabbits	132
Sorry, You're Not A Winner	136
A 2007 Rock Room Set List	139
A 2007 Indie Room Setlist	142
A 2007 Room 3 Setlist	145
Chop Chop	147
I'm Sad I Missed The Wedding	149
I'm Ron Burgundy?	152
Sumo Durham	154

My First Frank Turner Story	160
Goodbye Durham	162
My Noisettes Story	164
My Sheilas Story	166
Once Upon A Time In Hartlepool	169
Kev Sumo	173
Skid Row	175
The Glory Years (2008 - 2009)	178
Like A Motherfucker From Hell	180
The ID Problem	182
A Bit About Saturdays	184
Where Is Gary Numan?	188
Bad Medicine Rock Club	189
Ain't No Party Like The Sumo Xmas Beach Party	194
Uncle Alberts	199
Loving The Haters	201
The Battle For Thursdays	204
Bring Back The Good Old Days	210
Rock Box Boy	212
My First Jedward Story	216
Raptastic In The Powder Room	220
Joey Jordison And The Guy From Boyzone	222
A 2010 Rock Room Setlist	223
The Great One Pound Sumo Disaster	226
The Final Sumo At The Cornerhouse	229
A Cornerhouse Epilogue	231

IV THE EMPIRE

The Gold Standard	235
I've Not Made An Empire Map	238
Sumo Is Moving	240
The Sumo Empire Launch Party	242

Pound Sumo Part 2	247
An Empire Playlist	250
A New Ten Feet Tall Office	251
My Other Jedward Story	254
Two Bands One Stage	257
Big Barry	261
Middlesbrough Music Live	266
Mosh Or Die	271
Xmas In July	272
Letlive	275
Animals V Machines	278
The Empire Run	283
Let's Put A Skate Ramp In The Club	285
Sumo Sunderland	288
A Live Music Empire	293
May The 4th Be With You	294
Zombie Survival Sumo	296
Sumo Darlington	299
Styrofoam Crucifixes	302
Sumo Was Seven	305
Empire Sumo In 2012	308
The Art of Partying	310
Bands That Want Drugs	312
Silent Sumo	316
One Pound Fish	319
Cannonball Claire	320
Empire Sumo In 2013	324
Rick Sumo	327
The Real Cost Of Halloween	332
Twenty Four Seven	335
Schooled By A Strobe Light	336
A Bit Of A Blur	340
New Years Eves	342

Sumo WK	347
Sumexico	348
Jake Radio	352
Baby Godzilla	359
What's The Matter With Kids Today?	362
Empire Sumo in 2014	365
Definitely Too Old For This Shit	368
Sumo Air Guitar	371
Grand Theft Sumo	372
The Class of 2005	376
Cat Sumo	380
Sumo41 and KazSumo	383
Empire Sumo in 2015	384
Conspiracy Theory	387
Golden Hour	389
An Arctic Monkey	392
Twenty Sixteen	395
The Apprentices	398
Korn Again	402
Farewell AVM, Enter Holy Shit	405
Disco Load Outs	409
Double Dad	418
The Graduates	419
Mrs. Sumo	420
Mrs. Milk	424
I'd Rather Smash My Face Into That Wall	427
Sumo Sauce	428
Toxicity	430
OK, Time For Plan B	433
The Unicorn	435
Two Weeks In The Wilderness	437
I Look Like I Feel	440
Into The Upside Down	443

I Quit	447
This Is My Last Sumo	449

V THE END

Life After Death	453
Meanwhile In Team Sumo	457
The Last Of The Gang	459
Some Kind Of Meeting	460
Here We Go Again	464
We The Rats	466
Reflection	469
Sumo Sumo	471
What's In A Name	475
It's Fang Now	476
Sumo On Ice	478
Job Done	479
Conclusion	480
Epilogue	482
TL:DR	483
Thanks	487

I
INTRO

For The Kids

For Sydney and Piper.

Prologue

Perhaps at some point in your life or past life, you have frequented or ended up in a Rock Night. The venue will usually be very dark, possibly dirty, and the music will be fucking LOUD.

You'll meet some of the friendliest, most wonderful people in the world at a Rock Night. And if the promoter has done their job right, you'll have had a damn good time. You'll be tipped out onto the pavement at around 3am, sniffing around for the nearest pizza or kebab, with your ears ringing and your clothes soaked in VK and Brown Ale from the mosh pit on the dance floor.

I spent almost fifteen years of my life running the best Rock Night within miles and miles. It was called Sumo. As I am writing this down, today is August 12th 2020. Today would have been Sumo's 15th birthday.

Many have told me, with great drunken enthusiasm, that Sumo was the greatest Rock Night in the UK, if not the world. So that's the story I'm going to try to tell. How I'll get fifteen years into one book, I don't know.

I'm writing this book for a few reasons. Mainly because I think it's a good story, with great characters, tall tales and a few plot twists that will hopefully entertain anyone that's stumbled in or out of a club in their lifetime.

Perhaps this book will serve solely to make my kids cringe as they read about what daft old Dad got up to in the good old days.

Another purpose for this book could be to serve you, dear reader, as an instruction manual.

Like the Once-ler handing down the last Truffula seed to the hero in the final pages of The Lorax, you may study this tale as a handbook of sorts. Take it, and use it to create your very own Rock Night. Because we did it so well and got it dead right for so long. And the world's going to need another great Rock Night.

Good luck.

Anatomy of a Clubnight

'What's a clubnight?' - my parents would ask, as I left my job in local government with the alleged best pension in the land.

I don't know if Clubnight is a term that I'd ever heard myself until, in 2004, when I entered that world. Is there a dash or a hyphen? Is it one word or two? I don't really know. I've never Googled it.

Hang on; I'm going to Google it.

Ok, so Google, and all of its assorted dictionaries, want to direct you to what a Night Club is. I'm talking about *Clubnights*. As I write this word into my Google doc, I'm getting a red squiggly line under the word *clubnights*. I swear it's a real thing. Maybe we invented them?

When I say we, I mean he. By he, I mean Graham.

Ok, I'm jumping too far ahead.

A clubnight is an event, one-off, weekly, monthly, you decide. This event is typically hosted by a nightclub. The clubnight sits within the nightclub, yet it is its own separate entity.

A clubnight has its own identity, look, feel, and even name. The nightclub is the walls, the bricks and steel. The clubnight is the idea, the creative being that can extend and transcend the walls of its host. The clubnight is a brand, a t-shirt, a badge, a slogan, a zine, a music policy. The clubnight is the sum of all those parts. The clubnight could be defined by any aspect of itself. Maybe the clubnight is defined by the people that attend it. There are thousands of clubnights hosted by nightclubs across the world. I've been to hundreds personally, and I promise some of the best were in the North East town of Middlesbrough.

The Venue

I've put events into around thirty different venues across the UK, and these venues are, in some ways, the same. A real set of characters. The management, the bar staff, the glass collectors, the cleaners, the door staff. If you can find a decent venue to host your clubnight with a great tight-knit family of grafters, you're probably set for a fun and rewarding ride in clubland.

The symbiotic relationship between venue and clubnight, in my experience, goes as follows; The venue and its manager look after the running of the venue. It sounds simple, but there's a whole world there that you, as the promoter, don't want to get too caught up in.

The bars, the bar staff, the drinks, how to make a cocktail properly, how to wash a glass properly, the security, how to remove a drunken idiot properly, the lights, the power, electricity itself, business rates, business tax, barrel tax, cellar systems, the ice machine is broken, the roof is leaking, the delivery guy only brought us four cases of Smirnoff ice and forgot the Red Stripe, the milk we bought last week for the White Russians is now off. It's 10pm, and tonight's special is White Russians. Someone needs to run to Tesco…

This, and a whole world more, goes into running a venue. It's a mind squishing headfuck in its own right. I'm not surprised that any venue would happily hand off the promotion and the problem of putting people inside the place, to an entirely different person, or team of people. That's where we come in. We're the promoters.

The Promoter

Some venues hire a promoter to promote the venue. We operated entirely externally to the venues we worked and collaborated with. They were the landlords, but we were very much the party's hosts.

As promoters, our problems and tasks are thankfully far less mundane than making sure the ice machine was working.

To over-summarise at this stage, the promoter decides what's going to happen; they then tell as many people as they can what's going to happen. Then many people turn up and enjoy the happenings, and everyone's happy.

Venues and Promoters, IDST

Suppose you can find a venue with a phenomenal team of hard-working people that make everything just right, the perfect host, with a watertight environment in which to allow a promoter to come in with complete creative control and execute their vision. In that case, everyone concerned can have a bloody good time for years. And dare I say, make a few quid along the way.

The Cast and Crew

First disclaimer: I want to get this clear from the off. Sumo wasn't just me; it was a We. Throughout this story, you'll see me say that We Did This; We Did That. It was always the gang of us. We never had job titles, and no one was really above anyone else. I was uncomfortable for a long, long time about morphing into someone who was becoming the gang leader, but that's what happened.

Sometimes I think it was just that I managed to stick it out longer than anyone else - Who else was going to fly this crazy plane? It was never my intention to end up "in charge". Friends eventually told me I was too modest and should just accept it. Then they told me to shut up and write the book.

The clubnight called Sumo belonged to a family of events, all created and run by a small company with a little office in Middlesbrough - a town we will sometimes refer to as 'Boro', throughout this book. This Boro events company was called Ten Feet Tall.

Ten Feet Tall

The company was founded by Graham. A fiery, passionate, immensely driven Scotsman who found himself in Middlesbrough in the early nineties. He filled Middlesbrough with clubnights, comedy events and live music. Years before I knew what Ten Feet Tall was, I was barely legally attending Graham's events; watching the likes of Oasis and Asian Dub Foundation at Middlesbrough Arena or Coldplay and Catatonia in The Cornerhouse. Graham and the Ten Feet Tall team launched a myriad of events over the next twenty years. Some of Ten Feet Tall's greatest hits, in no particular order, include;

Sixty Nine
    Thursdays at The Cornerhouse in Middlesbrough

Play: Rock n Roll Disco
    Saturdays at The Empire in Middlesbrough

Cherry Jam
    Mondays at Moby Grape in Stockton

Lifesize

Tuesdays at Moby Grape in Stockton
+ Saturdays at Jax in Hartlepool

Sweet n Sour
Thursdays at The Welly in Hull
/ Saturday's at Hull University

Sumo
Fridays at The Cornerhouse in Middlesbrough
/ Fridays at The Empire

Metropolis: The Greatest Show on Earth
Saturdays at The Empire in Middlesbrough
/ relaunched as **MILK**

Bad Medicine
Wednesdays at Spensleys Emporium / Secrets in Middlesbrough

Cannonball
Wednesdays at The Keys in Yarm

Sumo Durham
Fridays at Studio in Durham

Betamax
Saturdays at Studio Durham

Sumo Sunderland
Fridays at Independent

Sumo Darlington
Thursdays at Inside Out

All of this was ran successfully and simultaneously by an amazing squad of promoters, photographers, stage managers, sound techs, lighting techs, bar teams, and venue managers. Even the cleaners in the venues were superstars, funny, smart, and damn hard working.

What made this circus all the more fun was that the clubnights were just one faction of the business. There was a constant stream of one-off gigs, world-class touring bands to look after, tons of local band showcases, and a whole other world of live stand-up comedy.

There were monthly comedy clubs in five different towns across the North East, usually sold out, always a riot to work - plus the ongoing task of bringing the household names into town. Jimmy Carr, Sarah Millican and all the rest were regulars at Ten Feet Tall comedy events.

All these plates were simultaneously spinning at all times. It was commonplace to run three events in one day. We'd spend a day setting up a clubnight in Middlesbrough, then run over the road to soundcheck a band in a second venue, and then you'd be driving over to Stockton or Saltburn to get a seating plan right for a comedy club. Then... get the early doors comedy crowd in, get the acts fed and watered, hop back to Middlesbrough to make sure doors were open for the gig, then when those early events were done and dusted, you'd run back to the nightclub for 11pm doors and start that event up and running. Whizz about the club, making sure everything ran just right... Then, it's 2am. Get cashed up, sink some beers, and it's hometime around 4am. Easy.

Another disclaimer: Before my time, during my time, and after my time at Ten Feet Tall there were some real heroes and legends who sadly don't get much of a mention across the pages of this book. I've chosen to focus my story on Team Sumo, and the Friday's at Cornerhouse and Empire that occurred between 2005 and 2020. This omits many people - as they were busy doing everything else. People like Robin, a bear of a man who was always a safe rock in the storm -

the most reliable gentleman alive. People like Ted and Martin who had such a passion for the local music scene. People like Stevie and Jamie Wisdom who worked all the hours under the sun to make wonderful things happen. People like Jess and Laura who would turn their hand to anything we threw at them. People like Charlie and Claire who would literally make the most amazing props, costumes and decor. People like Peter who booked hundreds of world class comedians to fill Teesside's venues with laughter, and Carmel that helped organise the mountain of stand-up shows. People like Marty and Pop who ran the none-stop design and print factory. People like Debby and Charlotte who ran the day to day office so damn well.

These people really mattered and these people will have more great stories to tell. I just can't fit it all in. So it's not a Ten Feet Tall book. It's a Sumo book. I hope you lot don't mind.

2004

To reignite your memory and get you locked into the ride we're about to take - you need to put yourself in 2004.

You might be in a trucker cap or a slouchy beanie. Your jeans will be baggy. Really baggy. Your feet are in Converse, Vans or maybe some super fat DCs or Etnies. We all watch and quote Peep Show non-stop. Shameless on Channel 4 is genuinely shocking. We all watch Green Wing and Scrubs. We only *just* got introduced to brand new shows; The X Factor and Hells Kitchen.

No one really cares what they look like, and hardly anyone has any tattoos. Everybody smokes, wherever they want to.

No one has Facebook, and no one has Myspace. No one has an iPhone. These things don't really exist. I honestly believe the people of 2004 are far less self-aware than the people of 2020. I'm not saying that's a good or a bad thing. People seemed to care a lot less. About themselves, about anything. People were pretty carefree.

In 2004 we still bought a lot of our music on CD, although we had began trading mp3 files we'd downloaded on Limewire or Napster. We discovered new bands because our mates told us about them, they'd send us a file on MSN, then we couldn't wait to request that tune in the local nightclub.

Daytime radio in 2004 plays Destiny's Child, Usher, Nelly, and Girls Aloud, but you may have a slightly different taste if you're reading this book. I'm going to pigeonhole you; The Streets just released Fit But You Know It. Avril Lavinge and Green Day punctuate the radio waves, and The Killers, Eminem, The Vines and McFly are releasing bangers. Gwen Stefani has flown solo from No Doubt. The Beastie Boys release To The Five Boroughs. Slipknot released Duality. Blink 182 go dark and just released I Miss You.

It's 2004 and life is peachy.

Teesside in 2004 was especially great, I was back from University, jobless and happily bored, and I was partying my way through every rock and alternative night I could find.

The weekend started on a Wednesday.

Wednesdays were Blackout at The Dickens Inn, a harder mix of metal, rock, electro bits and gothy moments, with DJs Lauren and Stubbsy. More on him later.

Thursday's were Blaises, what some consider the original and greatest Boro rock event. There's a great Blaises experience built in Minecraft on YouTube if you want to experience what I lived through every Thursday. When Blaises sadly dwindled and closed, The Crown gave Thursdays a great rock and metal event with a dedicated live music slot early doors too - the brainchild of DJs Knightsie, Tubby and pals.

Friday's at The Arena were called Trashed - DJ'd and championed by Ashe and the moderators of a local online forum known as Haxed. If we wanted to stay closer to home in Stockton, we'd often spend Fridays nights at The Georgian Theatre, with local legend DJ Mal providing the heaviest mix in an absolute diamond of a venue.

Saturdays were always for Empire. My pals and I discovered this club after spotting a flyer that read 'Indie Funk Soul and Punk'. The word Punk lured me in. There was a tiny room at the top, top floor of the Empire known as The Gods where DJs Dave and Lauren would play pretty much the same records in the same order every Saturday – but we fucking loved it.

I was a regular at them all, and I guess this was my schooling in clubnights.

Who The Fuck Is Phil Saunders?

I'm not sure how or why I ended up where I ended up. I didn't plan on it. I didn't set my sights on running a world-class rock clubnight. I just somehow found a path and almost unwittingly followed it. Maybe the path found me.

I think I can pinpoint the exact moment that I discovered the path.

When I was eight years old, I decided to organise a bike race. At the top of the road where I lived was a college with a vast field with a dirt running track. I had a rather smart Parker pen that my Dad had given me as a Christmas present. It came in a very fancy looking box and seemed the poshest item I owned. I decided this would be the first prize for whoever won the bike race. I drew a poster in my bedroom with the headline WIN THE RACE, WIN THE PEN. I walked to Billingham town centre, to Miles's The Newsagent, photocopied the poster ten times, and sellotaped it to various shop windows and lamp posts. Four people turned up to the race. The kid that won had a mountain bike with about twenty gears. Me and the other guys on our BMXs didn't stand a chance. I gave the winner the Parker pen.

I have absolutely no idea why I did that or what motivated me to organise that Billingham bike race.

Maybe it was a TV show I'd seen? Perhaps I just wanted some new friends?

God knows. For some reason, or perhaps for no real reason, since the age of eight, I've found myself organising events, promoting shit, telling people,

"Hey you! You should come and do this; it'll be fun!".

Another random one;

In the last week of primary school, I organised an American Football tournament. Me and my friends were eleven years old; we had no idea what we were doing or what the rules were. We threw our football up and down the school field each playtime, yelling stuff like *"TWELVE! TWENTY FOUR! HUT HUT!"* I still don't know the rules for this game, but an eleven-year-old me told all the guys at Pentland Primary School that we were doing a proper tournament.

I'd told everyone the Miami Dolphins were coming.

Word spread like wildfire. The field was packed. What the hell was I thinking?

Typical promoter bullshit.

One more then;

I was named the Student Entertainment Officer at sixth form college, given a small office, a pile of sharpies, a ream of A2 paper, and a budget for college parties. We hired The Arena, my bands and mates' bands played live, and the events were always packed out.

My college pop-punk band Helter Skelter had been given a crate of about two hundred tapes by the local radio station. Each tape was 6 minutes long and contained radio jingles. We painstakingly taped four of our band's songs onto these cassettes (two on each side) and handed them out in college so when the parties came along, and everyone knew the words to our songs.

This was my event's CV. I don't know why it started. I don't know why I chose that path.

I went away to Uni, came home broke and moved back in with my parents in a nice house in the aforementioned town of Billingham in Teesside. I'd been in bands since I was 15, and following a deal with a Los Angeles based company called Prestige Management, Helter Skelter had spent the best part of the past seven years courting record labels and ultimately getting nowhere. Prestige had a few acts under its wing, the three best being Helter Skelter, Johnny Panic, and Busted. One of us made it. That's another story.

So, after having 'Musician' as my job title for so long, I'd finally entered the rat race and grabbed the first super-easy office job I could find. I was now officially a Payroll Clerk for the local authority. I got paid £11,500 a year salary to literally shuffle paper. Plus, my Dad told me I had The Best Pension In The Land.

I managed to withstand around two years in this job. I went out partying five nights a week, and I played in three fairly active bands, No School Reunion, Burnout In The Capital and Exit By Name. My job was such a breeze I could get the day's work done in a couple of hours, which left me plenty of time to book tours, photocopy flyers (for free on the office machine) and ultimately chase down a record deal for Exit By Name. So I was back to being a wannabe rock star, and a Payroll Clerk.

My bands had played a load of shows for this guy called Graham, we always pulled a crowd, and he'd give us decent slots supporting some pretty big names. Graham's promotions company, as you know, was Ten Feet Tall.

One night after a packed gig at a pub on Linthorpe Road called The House (now a Wetherspoons), Graham asked me what I did during the day when I wasn't gigging. I told him I was a Payroll Clerk. He told me his payroll clerk had just quit, so he needed one. He invited me for a job interview.

I met him at The Hog's Head, a pub in the middle of Boro town centre, which is now a Tesco. I didn't own a suit, so I wore my Dads. It was way too big for me, and there was a total downpour of rain, so I arrived looking ridiculous in this giant suit, soaked to the skin.

After asking why I was wearing a suit, Graham told me his payroll and admin took about two days each week. He was looking for someone part-time. I explained that with student debt, I'd need to work full time; two days a week wouldn't work. He told me he could maybe hire me full time and that he'd *"Figure out some stuff to fill the rest of the week"*.

When I look back, I think it's weird that I didn't talk about my previous experience in events. I could have told him the 'Win The Race, Win The Pen' story.

Despite not mentioning any of that, I got the job.

Boro Needs A Rock Night

I got stuck into my new job at TFT and never looked back. The payroll did only take a day, and I busied myself with the other admin and paperwork tasks, which included chasing in money that the company was owed. These guys were owed a lot of money. When you're having fun putting on gigs, comedy festivals, club nights and thinking up new ways to party, no one can be arsed to look after the books.

I created endless spreadsheets, forced everyone to begrudgingly keep receipts and hand them over, and drove around Teesside, knocking on doors and chasing venue owners to hand over cheques for owed door takes. The cheques would bounce. So I'd drive back, get another cheque, and repeat that process until everyone paid up, and the books and the admin were to a gold standard. No one wanted these crappy admin jobs, but I lapped them up.

It earned me the affectionate title of Office Bitch from chief band booker and Saturday night superstar DJ Stubbsy.

Stubbsy was an enigmatic legend who worked from home in York but drove up to Middlesbrough to play the tunes at 'Play', the huge Saturday night at the Empire of which I'd been a regular for some time. He was also in charge of booking bands for Graham. If you saw a band you loved in Boro, it was probably due to Stubbsy and Graham getting them in front of your eyes.

The TFT office was on the top floor of a building known as The Old Scientific Institute. Google it; it was an amazing building, sitting at the top of Corporation road. This massive historical building was owned by Big Barry, who owned the Empire nightclub, and he rented us the whole of the upstairs. It was freezing, took an age to heat and the heating always broke. The two huge rooms that filled the first floor served as TFT's home. We all sat in one of the rooms on desks with ancient PCs, while the other room was used for storage, whizzing around on Segways, and for me, post-5pm band practice.

As I got my admin jobs down to a day a week, I was paired up with the more indie side of the business and kept away from the pop, house and Rnb events. I assisted Ted, Stubbsy and Stevie, who were the main players in TFT's guitar-based businesses.

Pretty soon, I got out of the office and spent my days and weekends assisting with the clubnights, gigs and other events. Hull was up and running, so I'd drive down there first thing on a Saturday morning to stand in the rain outside HMV looking for indie kids' to give them a flyer for TFT's new indie venture known as Sweet n Sour. Saturday Nights, I'd be alongside the team at the Empire, taking on any task that was thrown my way.

In the Summer of 2005, the Middlesbrough Cornerhouse, located right underneath the train station on Albert Road, was thriving with two jam-packed weekly events. They had the Pop/Rnb/Indie Thursdays courtesy of TFT known as Sixty Nine and the town's only dedicated gay night, 'SaturGay' every Saturday.

The venue was owned by Ladhar Leisure, which had a large collective of bars, hotels and strip clubs in Newcastle. The Cornerhouse was one of the company's first venues.

I remember the day weirdly clearly. Mr Ladhar himself paid a visit to the

TFT office in Middlesbrough. There were rumours abound that The Arena was about to close down, the owner, known only to me as Edzy, was moving to London. I'd heard this, and I think I'd guessed why Mr Ladhar was paying us a visit. He wanted a Friday at The Cornerhouse, everything he'd tried hadn't worked, and with the news about The Arena, he thought the masters of Indie Rock n Roll (Ten Feet Tall) would be able to help.

The conversation took place only with Graham, and perhaps it was due to the fact we had Indie in The Empire on a Saturday and an Indie room in Cornerhouse already on a Thursday, but a Rock Night was Graham's suggestion. I don't think Mr Ladhar was too keen; Rock didn't sound like it would deliver any decent numbers. Graham called me over, and I talked through the Arena's Friday, how Blaises was a still big loss for Boro, and I told them that although there were a good few rock nights, I felt like there was space for a new one. So I agreed with Graham that Rock was the right move. As the only mosher in the organisation, it was handed over to me to assemble the team, prepare the launch and get ready for Boro's brand new rock night.

Not bad for the office bitch.

II

SUMO

The Johnny Cash Club

Graham asked us all to submit our lists of name ideas for the new rock night.

Ten Feet Tall's chief designer Marty had a spreadsheet with a bunch of clubnight name ideas on it. His favourite name suggestion for our new event was Sumo. Marty wouldn't give Graham his list – *"Why would I give you the list, I'll just give you the best name, from the top of the list"*.

Despite feeling like I was rightly the best man for heading up this project, and having twenty name suggestions on my list, they were all pretty rubbish. My best effort was The Johnny Cash Club. Or ' The JCC' for short. Looking back, I don't know what I was thinking. That would have been a terrible idea.

So we called it Sumo.

Ten Feet Tall were well known as the clubnight guys, but everything we'd done was pop, RnB, and of course Indie. We were the kings of indie, so we were told.

We knew that mentioning Ten Feet Tall on the Sumo promo might not do us any favours.

A funny breed, us moshers, and I wanted Sumo to feel fresh, new and not give anyone any preconceived ideas or expectations.

We kept it off the TFT website, set up a Hotmail address to put on the posters and flyers and rolled with the story that this was a clubnight set up by me, Phil, and my band. Haxed was a local online scene forum built by a clutch of local tech-savvy kids that was Middlesbrough's main source of news and discussion for gigs and night life. Every venue and every clubnight had a section of Haxed. The guys at Haxed granted me a section for Sumo, which I was allowed to moderate and we set the hype train rolling.

We wanted the posters to look unlike anything TFT had designed before. Marty drew out a single black outline sketch of a Sumo wrestler and we bought a steel stencil of the word SUMO. We spray painted a bright red SUMO across 300 posters of the wrestler. We laid them out across the entire floor space in the office to dry, then made sure they adorned every wall in the North East that we could find. Every shop in town took a poster, and every changing room in every clothing shop was postered. Every shop window, every pizza shop wall, every cafe, anywhere you could imagine had a Sumo poster. We left no stone unturned, we hit dentists' waiting rooms and college cafes. Anywhere that you could attach four little balls of blu tac to, had a Sumo poster. The poster runs on a night would end with us spraying the Sumo stencils onto walls, trees, college car park floors and university building doors. We found canisters of neon pink chalk spray, so the Sumo could be washed away in the rain. This way we hoped to avoid vandalism charges, arguing 'it's only chalk' with baffled policemen who would stop us and ask what the hell we were doing.

We followed the posters with badges, again just the word Sumo for now. I found a guy online, from Leeds, called Luke who had just bought a badge machine and was knocking out cheap badges for bands. Luke would mail us bags of hundreds of badges. (Luke still makes badges, by the way, Google 'Awesome Merchandise'. He did alright did Luke.) We'd split the giant bags of badges into smaller zip lock bags of 20-30 and we would drop them off for friends, people in bands, and anyone I knew that would help get them distributed. I'm not proud of it, but we'd make sure that the other rock nights in town always had Sumo badges out on the tables.

If we were some fancy marketing team, sitting in a big glass office in London, we would, and should, have started our journey by setting out a mission statement. We didn't do that, we were just having fun, throwing parties, putting on shows, and organising stuff we thought would be great. No one really worried about money, it wasn't discussed that much. I guess that's because there was enough of it being made, to keep the wheels turning.

If we did have a mission statement it was to be as good as we possibly could be, and make it different. We were in a town that already had a good clutch of well-attended rock nights. Our's would have to stand out if we were to survive long term and win over the fickle crowd.

Once we got rid of all our teaser posters and the few thousand badges, everyone in town was now asking what Sumo was, so we put our launch date on Haxed's forum and made new flyers and posters with all our details on them, and got to work replastering the town.

In the spirit of being different and turning heads, Graham spent a crazy amount of time on this print. Even the actual paper that it was printed on was scrutinised, samples were studied, and Graham would pace the office with various different colours and weights of paper stock, slapping his palm with them, folding them into origami shapes, holding them up to the light and even smelling it.

The follow-up poster which revealed our venue and launch date showed a black and white photo of a Sumo wrestler from the back, with his giant muscular arse facing outwards. The paper was yellowed and almost parchment-like as if we'd imported some sort of Japanese scrolls. Marty had been busy folding up bits of paper too and created a small A6 size fanzine, instead of a standard flyer. We ended up keeping the zine format simple, an A4 sheet folded twice, to enable mass production. I set about asking anyone and everyone to submit stories, random reviews, and even hand-drawn cartoons to pile into this 'Issue One' of the "Sumo Magazine.'. It was a beautiful little thing and getting the outside input meant loads of people already felt part of Sumo, and it felt like we'd started a community, without even having gotten to the launch event yet. All this print cost a fortune - it was a way more expensive way of printing, and ironically the more DIY and handmade we wanted things to look, the more they cost.

So we had a venue, a name, a good promo campaign underway and the level of hype that promoters dreamt of. The next thing we needed was what I always considered the most important. We needed music. We needed DJs.

Graham rightly pointed out that every Rock DJ in our town was taken, and if we wanted to turn heads we needed someone fresh in the DJ box. He set me the task of researching rock nights in Leeds, Newcastle, Sunderland, anywhere nearby that could give us a DJ that was great - but that no one would have heard of. I assured Graham that I had exhausted all the leads I had, and had spoken to every decent candidate within 50 miles.

This was a lie, I actually didn't bother, as I knew exactly who I wanted to DJ.

Sumo DJs

I first knew of Craig from the local band scene. He was the drummer in a Hip Hop / Metal cross over act called Sweet Sanity who'd done pretty well, and Craig was found partying hard most Friday nights at Stockton's Georgian Theatre. These Fridays were known as Twisted and later Burn - where DJ Malcolm played a fairly brutal mix of metal, hardcore and punk, mixed with a bit of classic rock, glam and emo too. The G, as I called it, was my spiritual home, a venue I'd started going to aged 14. It's where I bought my first beer, a bottle of becks, for £1.60.

In 2001 Craig had started a band with a few other guys I half-knew from the scene and they needed a singer, or rather a screamer. I auditioned and got in, and since joining we'd become good friends, sharing many stages, van rides and beers. Craig was a little bit older than everyone else we hung around with, and was the only guy I knew that had his own house.

Craig's house was the place where we all started pre-drinking before hitting the clubs, then ended up back there, downing spirits, munching parmo and listening to Craig take charge of the tunes. Craig always had a new band for me to listen to, or had an absolute banger of a song I hadn't heard in ages. In his car on the way to band practice, or in the van on the way to play a gig 200 miles away to no one, Craig would bob his head, sing along, and drum furiously on the steering wheel to a mix CD he'd prepared especially for the journey.

Craig had started filling in the odd Friday at The G for his good friend Malcolm. I thought Craig would be an awesome DJ. He was always more than happy to be in charge of tunes, and although he was only usually playing at a house party or for us in the van, he literally brought the party and made sure the mood and vibe was up there. He was a phenomenal drummer so had the sense of rhythm or whatever it is that DJs need. I asked him, and after we got over the road bump of our mate Malcolm being a little pissed off with us, he agreed.

As ever the wise one, Graham suggested we have two DJs. Long term, having the same guy week in week out was something he thought we should avoid, and he was right.

I'd known my best mate Kev since I was 12 years old, we'd grown up, survived school and college together, and after teaching ourselves to play instruments we spent endless nights in my parents' garage playing Guns n Roses and Alice in Chains songs. We'd graduated the school of life together and in our early twenties had some moderate success in our own bands.

Kev is what I'd consider a musical genius. He is a skilled guitarist and has the ability to listen to a song, and after about an hour, he can play that song. It blows my mind. With over a decade worth of experience playing and creating rock music, being in the rock music industry and also recording rock music, to me I felt like Kev would make a great DJ too, and he agreed to give it a go.

So after lying and telling my boss I'd looked all across the North East for the best DJs, he let me hire my two mates - who had never really DJ'd in their lives.

We talked about the music policy on endless nights out and whenever we were together in the weeks leading up to the Sumo launch party. Craig and Kev were pretty well known locally through our bands and as Kev had spent a bit of time managing the bar at The Georgian.

Craig and I were gigging pretty relentlessly with our band Exit By Name and Kev and I, after the demise of our band Helter Skelter, had started No School Reunion and another band; Burnout In the Capital. We all used our bands to push the Sumo event. Every gig we had we pushed out Sumo flyers and badges. The three of us knew we needed to make this rock night and the music policy somehow better than the other nights in town, or more importantly a bit different.

I noted two things about the other nights in town. Firstly they played wall-to-wall rock music, from 10pm until 2 in the morning, four hours of solid guitars. The second issue was that they all played the same songs. Killing In The Name Of. Walk. All The Small Things. Ace of Spades. Enter Sandman. Down With The Sickness. Halo. Chop Suey. Let the Bodies Hit The Floor.

Doing those two things differently, I hoped, could be our 2 key ingredients to success.

Firstly we'd break up the relentless mosh with curveballs. I'd already printed some flyers with setlists on, and handed out hundreds of mix CDs without consulting Craig or Kev. One day Craig handed me one of my flyers and said *"Why have you put White Wedding by Billy Idol on here?!"*.

No one was playing White Wedding - and it's a banger. So we should play it. Craig and Kev both got it, and we discussed peppering the four-five hour set of guitars with stuff like The Power of Love by Huey Lewis and The News, or The Futureheads' Hounds of Love. It certainly made us nervous, but the idea of following Slipknot with 9 to 5 by Dolly Parton made us laugh out loud, so we figured we should definitely give it a try.

To prevent us having a duplicate rock-night-hits-set that every other club in town was already banging out each week, I asked Craig and Kev to try and play the *second* best song by every great band.

So instead of Walk, we'd play Cowboys From Hell, instead of Killing In The Name, we'd play Bombtrack... etc.

Footnote; There were a couple of things that Craig and Kev would eventually bring to the table that really set Sumo's playlists apart from everyone else and that was their own great tastes in music. Kev's passion for old and new punk rock infiltrated his sets, he'd play tracks by the likes of Hundred Reasons or Jimmy Eat World or classic tracks by Descendents and Bad Religion. Craig brought a heavier edge, and it was the first time I'd heard Norma Jean, Helmet or Chevelle being played in a Boro club. We obviously still played the hits, Chop Suey and the like, it had to be done – but it was clear from the first few weeks that we were offering up something a little different.

Haxed Forum Announcement

July 15th 2005

This is what I wrote, word for word, announcing Sumo for the first time to the world, on Haxed.co.uk - The most important website and social network in Boro in 2005.

SUMO - a night of rock mosh action in boro every friday night

Your venue is Cornerhouse Area2.
After a gorgeous revamp and refurb it's comfy as hell and ready to roll.

It's an enclosed, independent, dedicated rock night run and hosted by people who know the score and actually give a shit. 110% alt-friendly, nice doormen, sensible drinks prices, no dress code (obviously) and a playlist spanning the far corners of rock, punk, metal, hardcore, classic and retro. We just want everyone to have a damn good dance and the best Friday night possible. Our DJs are very friendly for requests, go say hi! or collar a roller girl and make song demands.

£3.50 in / 10pm till 2am / every friday night / cornerhouse2

all that! + surprise bands, secret guests, rollergirl table service, retro gaming, a movie or two, barmy cocktails and all round rock razzmatazz.

for details of Guest DJs/ bar promos / giveaways / occasional bands, keep checkin haxed

III

THE CORNERHOUSE

A Legendary Labyrinth

I like the phrase a Legendary Labyrinth; I used it on many flyers and posters. A nice bit of alliteration and the perfect description, really. The place was a maze. If you check out the website, *thisclubcouldbeyourlife.co.uk*, you can refer to the badly-drawn map I have provided. If you're reading this mapless, try to imagine a linked up multitude of rooms, areas and corridors that formed the rough shape of a giant upside-down horseshoe - with a front door and back door at each end.

The Sumo-era Cornerhouse was made up of the following;

- **Area 2.** What we called The Rock Room
- **Area 1.** What we eventually opened as The Indie Room. Also where we built the stage for most bands
- **Area 3.** What we called Room 3. Home to Pop, Drum n Bass. Burlesque. Also small gigs and acts.
- **The Front Bar.** Also known as Cornerhouse Bar. We would close this area to the public and use it as a dressing room area for artists. Or in later/busy days we opened it up to the public. This bar served cocktails too.
- **Corridor Of Death.** This corridor ran down the side of The Indie Room. The tiled floor was utterly lethal after an hour, the condensation and spilt drinks made it as slippery as an ice rink.
- **Red Corridor.** From entering Sumo using the Area 2 door, you walked

up the red corridor into the rock room. Doormen hated people standing in it, and spent the night hollering and herding folk back into the Rock Room.
- **The Balcony.** A weird balcony area above the Area 2 door. We used it for guest DJs, mini gigs, a DIY casino, and table tennis.
- **The Secret Bar.** Tucked around a tiny corridor, off the weird balcony, this small fire hazard held around 20 people and the barman, usually Karl, would be the fastest place to get served away from the main bars.
- **Little Tokyo.** Underneath the secret bar was another 20-30 capacity room, in which we did some ridiculously small gigs.
- **The Powder Room.** Post-refurbishment the girls' loos got extended to include a small pink pamper room.

Side Note: As a kid, I'd played the venue a few times with Helter Skelter at Bede Sixth Form College parties. It was actually the first time I met Graham, years and years before I became an employee.

Helter Skelter played one hazy teenage night in around 1996-1997, and we packed the place out. After the show, Graham asked us to play The Arena. My girlfriend at the time was having a meltdown, I had spent about half an hour talking to Graham after our set, and when I got back to my girlfriend she was pissed. I remember saying, *"But I've been talking to Graham Ramsay, and he's asked us to play The Arena!"*. To me and my 17-year-old band mates, it was like Bob Geldof had just asked to play Live Aid. She didn't see it that way and didn't talk to me for about a week.

I started regularly going to The Cornerhouse, seeing bands and drinking and dancing the night away at Sixty Nine, the weekly Thursday event. I'd see the flyers and posters for upcoming Cornerhouse gigs; Coldplay, Muse, Catatonia, Cave In, Frank Black, Funeral For a Friend, The Slackers, The Fall, and The Libertines.

I remember being in college and seeing a flyer for a band that had a really daft name, but the flyer hype (one of Graham's) read "The Scottish Nirvana". That was enough to get me and my mosher mates to the gig. The show was incredible. I couldn't believe these three guys could make such a wall of noise. There were about eight people at the gig. The band was Biffy Clyro.

Area 2

We prepared for the grand Sumo launch. We filled the room with shite.

Graham's clubnight Feng shui was to make sure there was nowhere to sit down (so people danced) and any big areas of space where groups of ten or more could disappear, were stacked full of high tables, beer barrels or just draped off. We made the club as claustrophobic as possible, as cosy and intimate as we could. Even if 50 people turned up, it would feel good. We knew that whoever came to the first Sumo, would be the ones that would see our night fly or die. It would be their word on the street, it would be them in college or uni on Monday morning, telling everyone what they thought of our new night.

Scenario 1 : *"It was so busy, you couldn't move!"*

This would mean everyone would want to come to check us out.

Scenario 2 : *"It was dead, it just felt like there was no one there"*

This would finish us. I labour this point because the openness and share-everything lifestyle in which we currently live didn't exist. People talked, people listened to each other. We needed scenario 1, so we literally closed down as much of the club as we could.

Drapes were our secret weapon in the venue, as no one really knew the exact layout, and by night the place was so dark, we were able to staplegun fabric to ceilings in different places, making new areas, or closing old ones as we pleased. This reminded me of an enchanted maze in which the walls kept moving, adding to the sense of confusion week on week.

Even the dancefloor itself wasn't safe from our quest to 'close the room in' and make it as intimate and cosy as possible. We stretched camo net from pillars, and staple gunned it to the wall. This bizarre look created more pockets of darkness for people to hide in.

We hung random stuff from the already low ceiling and we fired projectors at walls to make them come alive. I grabbed a handful of DVDs from the pound shop to project, and we settled on the original King Kong, in glorious sepia, it filled a twelve-foot wall and looked nuts. From The local Cash Converters, I'd bought two TVs and ordered some plug and play Sonic The Hedgehog games. These were tucked in a corner, and strapped down with cable ties and gaffer tape to stop people from stealing them.

We found giant plastic toy robots in Wilkinsons, they looked kind of manga-ish, and somehow they fitted with the style we were going for. We bought the lot and stood them in between the bottles of spirits on the back of the bar. They whirred, flashed and spun in unison, knocking glasses everywhere.

The whole place was finished off with huge correx boards, which we printed with Marty's Sumo artwork in full colour. We'd succeeded in making the venue not look like the venue anymore, it had its own feel and it looked like nothing else.

It looked like Sumo.

Launch Night

Friday 12th August 2005

After spending the last few days decorating the Cornerhouse's Area 2 ready for the Sumo launch party, there wasn't much prep to do. It was around 8pm when everyone from Ten Feet Tall and myself arrived. The venue staff ran around stocking fridges, lighting candles and spraying air fresheners. This underground club had no windows, so airing it out involved opening all the fire doors, spraying four or five cans of Glade, and hoping for the best.

Ladhar Leisure's regional manager Stu asked me to come down to the front door (or back door as it was) and brief the doormen with him. Stu was the only person in the building in a suit, and it felt like Stu didn't come to the venue that often. The door staff gathered around, and he gave them a bit of a speech. I was impressed and chuffed that he did this, and it's a speech that I used myself in the years that followed, when dealing with new door staff, especially at rock nights.

Despite the suit, Stu knew his shit. Probably from his experience of alt nights and bouncers in Newcastle. He explained to the team that the type of people that were coming to The Cornerhouse that night were going to look and act very differently from the people who usually came to the venue. So the door staff would need to act differently too, and treat them in a different way. Clothing policies were out the window, tattoos and piercing were allowed, and trainers were essential. In fact, anyone who looked too smart, sporting crisp ironed shirts and polished Chelsea boots were probably in the wrong place. Stu also explained that many of the crowd will have "a bit of a wild look" - he explained that mohawks, nose chains. T-shirts with abusive slogans, ripped jeans, baggy jeans, skinny jeans, or spray-painted jeans - were all fine. He went through the mechanics of mosh pits, slam dancing, walls of death and headbanging. The ten door staff stood patiently and slowly nodded their heads.

Then he made his final point - and he took his time with this one.

He explained that despite dressing aggressively, acting aggressively and dancing aggressively; *"These kids are the most sensitive souls you will ever encounter. You must be very respectful with them, even with banter. If you make a joke about their haircut or make a wisecrack - telling them to pull their jeans up; it will finish this night off, they will not come back"*.

He was right, the alternative scene was a close-knit group and rightly protective of each other. All the hard work in promoting an event, decorating a club, and making sure the music was spot on, can be undone in the blink of an eye, by a bouncer saying or doing the wrong thing.

Back in the rock room, the sound system had been fired up and Kev was getting set up.

Danielle (more on Danielle later) and her friends who had been brought in as roller skating hostesses were whizzing around, getting the feel for the floor. They had little waitress pads and pencils, ready to take song requests from people, then glide the suggestions over to the DJs. That was the idea anyway.

I'd loaded the 156 batteries into our Japanese robots on the bar back and flipped the on switches. It was looking ready to go. Out the back of the venue, we'd found a full-size fibreglass horse. I've no idea where it came from, but we'd painted it white, and hung it from the ceiling. We killed the house lights and fired up all of our projectors, including one that hit the horse. The place looked absolutely awesome.

It was at this point that Graham called me over. He stood, arms folded, looking at the dance floor. He tilted his head, and paced the room, looking at this twenty-metre square space from four or five different angles.

"It's too big," he said. "We need to close it down somehow."

There was less than half an hour until doors opened, and I wasn't sure if we had the time to solve this, and also I was pretty sure this was unnecessary. Graham and I headed out into the back rooms of the venue, to see if there was anything kicking around that could help. Graham spied four large stage blocks. Each block was about six feet square, and about a foot high. We dragged them into the club and flopped them onto the dance floor. Danielle skated by and told us, *'you're mad putting them out'*. But Graham was adamant they should stay.

We opened the doors at 10pm. The night itself is a bit of a blur; I don't have too many memories, other than I just never stopped moving, my feet barely touched the floor as I flew from one situation to the next. I did a lot of talking, I thanked a lot of people for coming, and I dished out many free shots. Schmoozing aside, a clubnight rep spends his/her time fixing stuff. From physical fixes such as saggy banners, dropping drapes, or wonky projectors to other types of fixes, daft door lads forgetting the brief, tills out of change, bar staff making cocktails wrong.

As the creator, curator and ultimately the host of the party, you spend your whole night making sure everyone's having the best time, and the place is looking tip top. That's the only way I can describe the job I did for all those years.

We had 410 people through the door, and with a capacity of about 300, the place felt insanely busy, probably too busy. Plus, those dancefloor stage blocks were a fucking nightmare.

They were black, in a dark club that was filled with smoke from a smoke machine (and the smoke of 400 smokers who all smoked inside). People tripped on the blocks, fell over them, fell off them, bashed their ankles on them, and generally suffered many injuries on these stage blocks. Around 1am, we managed to slide them into the corners of the room, but it was just too busy to flip them up and remove them.

They never returned after week one, but those stage blocks were all anyone talked about for about two months.

The First Sumo Setlist

Friday 12th August, 2005.

As a setlist, looking back, I think it's a really funny one. It's definitely self-indulgent in parts.

We played two songs by Helmet. I think Craig, Kev and I were three of about six people in Teesside that listened to Helmet. Helmet are great.

About 70% of the tracks were requests. We hung a clipboard and an A4 pad of paper on the DJ box door, along with a pile of pens, and we openly welcomed requests. We'd always try and play as many requests as we could, and it being launch night, I think we actually played them all.

As time went by, the lads soon learned that they knew best, and in terms of keeping the dance floor packed and keeping people moving, they realised their judgement was their compass.

Paying too much attention to the requests pad and going with every crazy whim from the customers would often clear a dancefloor. As much as it hurt, we learned to start saying no.

The launch night set is a setlist with multiple personalities and I think you can see we were maybe still finding our feet. I didn't mind we didn't get too many curveballs in. Our plan to smash Dolly Parton on right after Slayer had to be put on the back burner. This was launch night, and we had every single type of mosher along to check us out, to see if this was the night for them. We had punks, goths, 17-year-olds with good fake IDs, 30-year-old ska guys, thrash metalheads and MySpace emos.

We tried and maybe failed, to impress everyone. But it didn't matter, we stuck to our guns, just playing great songs by bands we loved.

Some reflections from Kev - Sumo DJ since 2005;

"I had the 1st hour so I think I had the easier job and possibly got to be a little bit more self-indulgent. I think you can probably see the point in the set where I finished and Craig started.

In the early days, I was probably known as the more punk/emo guy and Craig as the more metal guy. But I think that difference worked well and we influenced and learned from each other. I definitely picked up a lot more of the metal stuff from Craig and I think he probably picked up a lot of the pop-punk/emo stuff from me.

Looking back on that setlist now though, had I known this was going to be the 1st night of Sumo's long journey, I maybe would have chosen a more iconic song to start it off with."

Sumo Launch Night Setlist;
    Horrorpops – Miss Take
    Senses Fail – Lady in a Blue Dress
    The Movielife – Jamestown
    The Get Up Kids – Holiday
    Copperpot Journals – Atlas & I
    Reggie & the Full Effect – What the Hell is Contempt?
    Alexisonfire – Accidents

Thrice – Silhouette
Fightstar – Palahniuk's Laughter
Brandtson – Who are you now?
Alkaline Trio – Private Eye
Rancid – The 11th Hour
RX Bandits – Sell You Beautiful
Motion City Soundtrack – Everything is alright?
The Used – I'm a Fake
Brand New – Sic Transit Gloria
Weezer – My Name is Jonas
Taking Back Sunday – Cute Without the 'E'
Helmet – Unsung
Metallica – Master of Puppets
Trivium – Light to the flies
Bullet for my Valentine – Four words to choke upon (r)
FFAF – Streetcar (r)
Glassjaw – Ry Ry's Song (r)
3 inches of blood – deadly sinners (r)
Pantera – 5 minutes alone
Weezer – Beverly hills
Jay Z & Linkin Park – POA, 99 problems
NERD – Lapdance
MCR – I'm not Ok (r)
Atreyu – You give love a bad name
Head Automatica – Beating heart baby (r)
Rancid – Ruby Soho (r)
Motley Crue – Kickstart my heart
Mighty Mighty Bosstones – Impression that I get
Flogging Molly – Drunken lullabies (r)
Goldfinger – 99 red balloons (r)
Lost Prophets – Shinobi v Dragoninja (r)
Everytime I Die – Ebolarama
Poison the Well – Nerdy (r)

THE FIRST SUMO SETLIST

Will Haven – Alpha Male (r)
Helmet – Tic
System Of a Down – BYOB (r)
Audioslave – Cochise (r)
Deftones – Back to School
36 Crazyfists – Bloodwork
Foo Fighters – All my life
Lynyrd Skynyrd – Sweet Home Alabama
Kiss – Crazy Crazy Nights (r)
Dog Eat Dog – No Fronts
Snoop Dogg – Gin n Juice
RATM – Sleep now in the fire (r)
Life of Agony – Weeds
Hed Pe – Bartender (r)
Incubus – Hot Dancer (r)
Motley Crue – Girls Girls Girls (r)
Queen – Don't stop me now
Feeder – Just a day
Pantera – Walk (r)
Van Halen – Jump
G'n'R – Paradise City
Ice Cube – You can do it
Queen – We will rock you

The Ceiling

This was a total pain in the arse but we managed to keep it up for the first few weeks of Sumo. We'd string 100 things up to the ceiling.

A joiner had installed 100 hooks up there, so Fridays afternoons were spent up ladders with fishing wire and our 100 items. The quest to have a *different* thing each Friday soon became pretty tricky. As soon as the doors opened, the first few people through the door would have leapt up and swiped our props, but that was fine and became part of the fun.

On week two we had mini watering cans. This was the level of crap that we'd hang - it had to be something we could find for about 50-75 pence max, otherwise the 'ceiling of things' would be a pretty expensive way to blow money every week.

Still, it was £50 - £75 a week but people seemed to love it. The week we had the watering cans up there, people carried them around all night like trophies, using them as vessels for DIY cocktail kits. I watched as people experimented with VK flavours, beer, shots, anything and everything went into the watering cans and the crowd slurped them joyfully for the entire night.

All Downhill From Here

From the excitement and elation of having over four hundred people at the launch night, we plummeted down in numbers, it was soul-destroying, crushing.

On week two we had a couple of hundred, then at the end of August, on the Friday of that bank holiday about eighty people were rattling around the club, it was shite.

Looking back, and having learned this in future years, I can't believe I took it so hard when it was bloody Leeds Festival. Over the next ten years we always took a kicking on our numbers that weekend - but in 2005, not knowing what the hell we'd done wrong, the team and I were miserable.

I slowly paced up and down that long red corridor between the front door and the bar hoping another fifty people would wander in from somewhere. Every time I passed my mates Simon or Bex who were working at the bar, or Danielle at the door, they offered me a weak smile; but we were all thinking the same thing - we've fucked it.

Sixty minutes down the road in Leeds, every mosher in the North of England was wrecked in a field enjoying some once-in-a-lifetime live sets from the likes of Iron Maiden, Pixies, Foo Fighters, The Killers, Marilyn Manson and QOTSA. Of course, Sumo, and Boro in general, was bound to be dead for the night.

I trudged across the sparse dancefloor to deliver the news to the DJs that no one else was coming, as a young lad was thoroughly enjoying himself to Memphis Will be Laid to Waste by Norma Jean at 150 decibels. He executed a perfect spin kick (the hardcore scene dance move not an actual assault), that I walked right into. He connected with me just above the knee and practically broke my leg. I winced and as my watering eyes met his, he began to apologise profusely, he was mortified. I waved him away, fake-laughing as I limped to the DJ box, I sank twenty beers and thought about how black and blue my thigh would be the next day

Two Thousand Free Drinks

It's Sept 2005

We all felt pretty shitty about the numbers we'd done at the end of August after such an amazing launch, we knew we needed something pretty crazy to get people through the doors. We'd had so much hype in the lead up to launching Sumo, and I was scared it was about to fizzle and we'd be gone and written off as a flash in the pan.

I knew rock nights inside out, I knew this one was better than any that had existed before it, and I hated those people who had been along for the first night, trash-talked it online, and not come back. I knew we were good, we just needed to reach more people, get more people to come and sample the goods, and they'd be hooked, surely.

After discussing various bands, scams, competitions, and guest DJs, I repeatedly told Graham that the only things people cared about were cheap drinks or even *free* drinks. People would do anything for a free shot, or a two-for-one beer. Of course, you can't give away free drinks. Or could you? That was the puzzle we needed to crack.

The answer was The Roulette Table. We'd give everyone that came in a free spin on the table, people would play in pairs, and bet red or black. The winner would be handed three drinks. The idea was that anyone getting handed three drinks would surely hand the loser one of them, thus every single person through the door is getting free drinks, everyone's happy, happy people have a happy time, and tell their friends. We knew this was going to be a winner. Sumo Roulette saved our arse, it was the talk of the town.

We spared no expense and hired a joiner to make a huge wooden replica table, strong enough to withstand drunken moshers climbing on it. We bought a professional roulette wheel from an online casino supply store that sat as the centrepiece. This wheel itself weighed a tonne, and cost £350. To me at the time, I thought that was a crazy amount of money.

That was in the days before I was cashing up takings from 1000 payers at £6 a head each week.

We ordered makeshift croupier outfits, those daft green visors, and custom printed Sumo poker chips to act as "Spin Tokens' - everyone that came in got one (or three) and they could exchange their chip for a spin. We had about a hundred buckets filled with ice, Coronas, VKs, Smirnoff Ice, allsorts - and as people won - we just lashed them out. The venue didn't mind, the place was packed. We gave away about 400 bottles and everyone left with a big fat smile on their face.

It was so successful we decided to re-run the roulette night and give away 400 bottles, every week, for 5 weeks. We printed posters that just said TWO THOUSAND FREE DRINKS in massive letters, and plastered the town with them.

The other clubs and bars in town must have hated us, but it secured Sumo the numbers we needed in the early days. The free drinks were handed out and necked within 15 minutes, and we gave them the best tunes, the best club and all the Sumo trimmings for the rest of the night to make sure they had the best time, and would keep coming back for more.

1977 (The One With The Haircuts)

Friday 30th Sept 2005

Night club promotion tactic number 1. If you can get the cool kids in, everyone else will follow. Honest to god I didn't run this as a tactic, I didn't know this *was* a tactic, but we stumbled across it.

As cringe as that is, it's true. Graham used to call them The Haircuts. The kids from the local art college, CCAD, were the coolest kids in town, and they all had the wildest hairstyles.

I'd become friendly with a local barber called Martin Fox. Foxy had the coolest salon in town. He'd also been the rapper in Sweet Sanity, who I'd seen a few times, and we shared a common pal in Sumo DJ, Craig. So, Foxy was up for helping Sumo, and Craig out in any way he could. Foxy cut all the cool kids' hair.

I'd had an idea to flavour Sumo up with some music themed nights. Not wanting to change the music completely, but to keep the curve balls flying, I wanted to do a 'Time Travel Trilogy' of events called 1977 (we played punk / The Clash / the Pistols etc for the 1st hour), '1986' (we played classic rock like Kiss and Motley Crue for a bit) and '1992' (Grunge basically).

We'd add some relevant party props, a fancy dress competition as per each decade, and we'd have some easy parties.

'1992' and '1986' were actually shite, despite the bar staff all rocking full Kiss make up, but '1977' was an absolute beast, people were totally into it, it was totally rammed.

The poster was Pistols-pink and yellow and we announced that as well as punk tunes and 70's cocktails, the star addition to the show was that Foxy and friends from the salon would be in Sumo 'cutting punk mohawks, or whatever you want'.

Despite being a former rock star, MMA black belt, a cage fighter and being tattooed head to toe, Foxy is one of the most laid-back, lovely men you'd ever meet. Nothing phased this guy. I don't think he even took a fee for doing it. The buzz online for these free haircuts was raging, it became the only thing people talked about, so we zeroed in on that, asking people what they were getting done, offering free drinks for anyone getting a proper mohawk, and double daring everyone online to fuel the hype.

Foxy and company rocked up ten minutes before doors with two giant barber chairs, lamps and their kit, we gave them some earplugs, some drinks and left them to it. I must have checked on him twenty times, to ask if he was ok, and did he want to finish yet, as it got well into three hours of him working his way through the line of about fifty people that queued up, in a line that snaked around the whole venue and across the dancefloor.

He spiked mohawks, shaved portraits and names into the backs of people's heads, and delivered open blade undercuts to drunken moshers.

It maybe doesn't sound all that crazy but it felt like we'd done something that no one had done before and people genuinely stood with jaws on the floor as their mates got half their locks carved away in front of them.

Side Note: In 2020, fifteen years later. I'm in a business meeting, in a room of 30 and 40-year-old executives, we stumbled onto the subject of the local bars and clubs of Boro and, as sometimes happens, a colleague points out that "Phil used to run Sumo!".

One of the forty-year-old suits looks up and says, "Sumo? Was that the place where that barber came in and shaved people's heads yeah?"

I said Yeah, that was the place.

The Fluffgirl's Bucket

A Saturday in 2005

It was my third ever shift running Play Rock n Roll Disco at the Empire.

As the kid that has only run events for a month or so, and those events mainly being under-attended little rock nights, running the show at the 1200 capacity Saturday was a trial by fire and every weekend was a steep learning curve.

On this particularly packed Saturday night, Ten Feet Tall had booked The Fluffgirls Burlesque Troupe to come in and perform their outrageous show on the big stage. Burlesque was something totally new to me, and as far as I can recall this was one of the first times Middlesbrough had seen a large scale burlesque production.

The quartet of Canadian girls wowed the crowd and eyes popped out of heads as the practically-naked ladies ran through their set pieces on stage, accompanied by Stubbsys deafening rock and roll soundtrack that boomed through the Empire's huge sound system.

As the first half of the show concluded, the girls sat splashing around in paddling pools on the stage, as the crowd whooped and cheered them on. I watched from the wings of the stage, trying to remember where I'd seen some towels that I could use to dry up the stage before the second half of the show began.

We closed the Empire stage's huge red curtains and the girls scattered up to the dressing rooms while I dragged paddling pools into the wings and dried up. It was around 1am at this point and I made my way down the stage steps and into the main hall and grabbed a beer.

Graham was at the clubnight, as he usually was in those days, and I assured him everything was going well.

The curtains cracked open momentarily and we were surprised to see the Fluffgirls coming down from the stage into the crowd, holding glittering golden buckets. Painted on each bucket was the word "TIPS". These six-foot-tall drop-dead gorgeous models began to work the room, saying hello to their fans and shaking their buckets for coins.

Graham leant in to me, pointed at the girls and said;

"Tell those girls I'm paying them a thousand pounds for this show and there's no way they're tapping up our punters for more money, that's not on. Get it stopped"

I was mortified. I waved to one of the girls to follow me to a quieter corner of the dancefloor where I explained we needed them to stop the bucket shaking. I think she could see how embarrassed I was, and despite being twenty-six years old at this point, I was wet behind the ears and it probably showed. She rounded up the girls, they retreated to the dressing room and dutifully bounded out on the stage ten minutes later to deliver a spectacular second half.

They obviously didn't hold it against me. As 3am rolled around, the venue emptied out and the Fluffgirls packed their bags to head over to their suite at the Thistle Hotel.

They asked me if I was going to come over with them, but I politely declined and headed to my girlfriend's house where I was staying. I'm pretty sure Stubbsy enjoyed a wild night drinking into the morning with the Fluffgirls; I'm still a bit gutted I sat that one out.

MySpace

Mike Todd, a local punk hero, phoned my mobile to tell me to get my band a MySpace.

Mike was, and is, one of the loveliest guys, and played a phenomenal part in the Teesside music scene, mainly through his label Toddler Records. Throughout 2003 and 2004 he orchestrated the release of albums from the likes of Mad Flower, Stories and Comets, The Hitchers, Jeniferever, The New Lev Yashin and Burnout In The Capital.

Mike was still working closely with Middlesbrough Rockabilly punk survivors The Hitchers as they gathered momentum, they were getting some European shows and gearing up for the release of their next album. Mike told me that MySpace was the number one thing in the band's arsenal and he was using it for booking shows, talking to fans, making announcements and even streaming songs online (that was a pretty new thing, Pure Volume was the main alternative). Mike talked feverishly about how this website was replacing the Forums, Blogs, Mailing Lists, and even printed promo that the band previously did.

He told me that my band, Exit By Name, should really get on this, as brand new bands such as Pen Knife Love Life and Bring Me The Horizon were having major success with MySpace as a tool.

I thanked Mike for his call, we caught up, and I said bye and went back to my desk.

I sat there surrounded by posters, flyers, badges, and even stencils and spray cans. I logged on to the site and created a MySpace for Sumo.

I didn't realise this at the time, but I think that this MySpace was ultimately the tool that took Sumo from a couple of hundred people a week to the raging beast that topped a thousand regulars throughout 2008 and 2009.

I didn't know everyone, and my town was bigger than I'd imagined.

We'd spent weeks standing outside bars and clubs handing out Sumo flyers with frozen fingers. We'd cable-tied planks of plastic sprayed with SUMO onto roundabouts in the middle of the night, and chalked slogans and song lyrics on the walls of colleges and universities. We'd waded in the murk of local forums and e-noticeboards, trying to get our message out amongst every other band, artist, nightclub and promoter. MySpace gave us a place where we could build a dedicated online community, display hundreds of photos and share the music we loved.

Virtually everything in the Sumo world was a team effort, I can't stress that enough, and I can't alone take credit for the thing being as successful as it was. But to be fair to myself, this MySpace world I built for Sumo, was fucking perfect.

Before things such as algorithms existed, and the stream of online information that you got was so saturated, anything you signed up for or interacted with online, you got it lock stock and barrel.

Once a person had 'Made Friends With' ClubSumo on MySpace - they saw every single thing we put out there. And we were the kings of content.

All of the crazy stuff we were doing inside Sumo, was now on our MySpace.

My weekly MySpace bulletins, which went directly into everyone's inbox, were a blow by blow account of everything brilliant that you'd missed from last Friday's adventures. Setlists, photos, gossip, who did what, it was all in there - plus a round-up of what was coming up this Friday and beyond. We could hype the event like never before. People lapped it up, there was a never-ending stream of questions, comments and interaction. We could now take song requests, shoot the breeze or even destroy haters publicly within seconds. Rumours could be shut down, or emblazoned for publicity. We had the ability to reach, inform and hype like never before, and the number of 'Friends' we had on MySpace rocketed by hundreds each week.

Our lead designer Marty was producing Sumo artwork that was absolutely next level, now that was reaching ten times more eyeballs than ever before.

Later down the line, our other designer Dani, who had done some techy degree at Teesside Uni, had the skills to re-code our MySpace so it looked way better than anyone else's, with slick custom backgrounds, fonts and colours that no one else had.

We had the biggest following of any local club or event. Our blogs and bulletins were read by hundreds of people and the photos and flyers we shared online had thousands of views.

I'd regularly show Graham this mini online empire we'd created, with great pride.

To his credit, he insisted we kept up the physical 'street promo', so the badges kept getting made, fanzines kept getting printed and folded, flyers were still pushed under everyone's physical nose as well as into their online world.

Eventually, the time would come when the numbers were so great and so regular, that we shifted our focus (and the spending) onto what was happening inside the club, but for now, in these early days, the amount of promotion Sumo got was crazy.

Now the people of the North East didn't just see Sumo on the Pizza shop wall, or on the side of the college Coke machine, they had it on their computer screen. We were now a twenty-four-hour, seven days a week onslaught on people's minds.

A Cornerhouse Playlist

Paparazzi

The first clubnight Paparazzi I knew was Lomas. Before I joined Ten Feet Tall, my mates and I would often end up at the Empire's massive Saturday night which was called Play. Play was, what some might say, Graham and Ten Feet Tall's finest clubnight. Lomas was a tall handsome South African curly haired fella, who always sported double denim, with his blue shirt unbuttoned a little way. With his massive camera slung around his neck, he'd waltz around the club taking photos of the crowd. Lomas did something that I've never seen another clubnight photographer do. He would approach his subject, take them by the arm, put them up against a wall, and literally put them into the pose he wanted. Like an artist arranging the limbs of a wooden manikin before sketching it on paper. It was quite something to watch and I imagine he didn't do it to everyone, and probably quite a few people told him to fuck off. But when he did it, and people allowed it and went with the flow, the results were absolutely mint.

The Play paparazzi photos were uploaded every Monday to the Ten Feet Tall website. In those days, of course, there was no social media. I remember being 16 or 17 and gathering around one of the computers in the IT suite of my sixth-form college and clicking through the album of photos on the website. You had to put your email in and a password to access them. My mosher mates and I usually didn't make the cut to be in Lomas's photo set, but I still loved flicking through them. It was a work of art, and it 'sold' the dream that Play was the utterly coolest place to be.

When it came to our Sumo photos, our resident photographer Danielle did an absolutely amazing job of capturing the madness and atmosphere of Sumo every week with her photosets. I'd got to know Danielle vaguely from The Arena, where she sometimes DJ'd the downstairs room of 'Trashed' and played an eclectic mix of Nirvana, The Breeders, Pixies, and Jon Spencer Blues Explosion. Frequently dressed in something outlandish like a pink PVC nurse's uniform, with bright blue dyed hair, none of my mates dared approach her to request a song, so I would be nominated to head over and submit our requests.

Danielle had also booked a few bands for the Arena - I recall standing in a tiny cramped corridor watching a french solo artist who played a drum kit, through guitar pedals. It sounded insane and was one of the best gigs I'd seen in Middlesbrough. The act was booked by Danielle but the club owners had decided that the act couldn't play in the main rooms of the club, so a fuming Danielle had to showcase the guy in the corridor between the rooms. I thought it was totally intense and totally unique. It definitely worked way better there in that confined space - and I think it probably planted a little seed in my head to try and put 'bands in small odd places' years later, which I often did...

When we were assembling the Sumo team, and the recently shut down Arena's team was available, I was buzzing when Danielle said yes to my request to come on board. She became our paparazzi photographer, and also entertained the various other jobs which we threw her way.

As Sumo was still hidden from the indie-pop-Ten-Feet-Tall-ecosystem of events, we couldn't put our pics on the TFT website, so instead, we used Haxed, the local alt forum to upload and showcase Danielle's Sumo pics every week. The problem was, there was no way to moderate comments on the pics. As always with the internet, the comments could be savage.

Danielle had a refreshing approach to photos' - almost the opposite to

Play and Lomas's policy of showcasing the beautiful people. She would photograph everyone, and everyone made the cut. No one was deemed unfit for the photo set, Danielle crowned everyone worthy, everyone was beautiful just as they were. I loved that policy and when we got her photos on a Monday morning, we'd add a little Sumo logo and upload the lot.

Every so often a Haxed forum user would leave something mean, cruel, or damn right racist as a comment on one of our photos, and we hated it. We could delete the comment, but unless we monitored every pics 24hours a day, the comments would often get seen by the Sumo goers before we saw them. We worried about this affecting our reputation, and we worried about people getting hurt.

Moving the photos to MySpace was the obvious move, but we knew if we had a dedicated website to host all our photos, we could collect Emails, and all the web traffic from people coming to see the photos' would drive the site and give us a place to promote events.

This was a long time before SEO, or before E-marketing existed, but we knew hundreds of people would want to see these photos.

The meeting took place in Marty's little side office. We brainstormed an idea for a website that would host all the photos, and our idea was to get people to log in, somehow create a profile for themselves, and to interact with the photos. We wanted a way for people to be able to claim and take the photos of themselves, and the more they went to Sumo, the more photos' they'd get, and they could maybe create an online photos album. We knew it would be cool for people to somehow point out or 'tag' their friends in other photos, and we wanted to facilitate a way for people to create conversations around the images, start threads, notify friends in comments and pick their favourite photo as their profile picture.

We'd basically just invented Facebook before the UK had heard of Facebook.

After a few more meetings about this mini-paparazzi-photo website, we all agreed that we didn't have the tech skills to build this thing, and MySpace could pretty much do everything we wanted. Graham seemed a bit gutted that we went with MySpace to host our photosets. I remember him saying *"I've got a feeling we're missing a trick here you know"*... As usual, he was right. But we went with MySpace, and it did the job well enough.

To Hull and Back

In the madness of getting Sumo going, some other plates being span included; Saturdays at the Empire, the ever depressing attempt to start a party in Hartlepool, and also Sweet n Sour, in the city of Hull

Ten Feet Tall had launched Sweet n Sour in 2004, at The Welly Club. In terms of cementing the clubnight as the ultimate place for post-millennial indie heads to gather each week, Graham had ploughed a crazy amount of time, energy, and cash into getting the thing going.

Bands we'd showcased there in the first year included: The Cribs, Maximo Park, The Glitterati, Bloc Party, Hard Fi and Boy Kill Boy, The 5678's twice, Har Mar Superstar three times, and Kasabian four times.

I'd drive down with Ten Feet Tall's Ted on a Thursday morning and we'd stand in the rain outside Hull HMV trying to spot the cool kids and give them a soggy flyer. Then come 8pm I'd be into my crash course in how to run a club night. We'd run around the place throwing up decor, cable tie-ing props to the ceiling, draping walls and shoving furniture around while that week's band soundchecked. I'd blink and it would be 3am and we were heading to the bed and breakfast where we usually crashed. The place was a small quaint eight bedroom house run by an elderly lady who had decorated each of the bedrooms in their own unique garish theme.

I'd usually stay in The Jungle Room, and Ted would be in The Seaside Room or "Egypt".

I remember packing the club down, boxing up our Sweet n Sour decor and teetering on step ladders grabbing our banners at 3am, as Ted sat banging a tambourine along with Carl Barat who'd acquired an acoustic guitar and a small crowd of punters who had been blessed with an intimate lock-in session. Carl played Yellow Submarine to these twenty drunks for about two hours straight.

We were up first thing Friday and back on the road, back to Boro, back for Sumo.

These Thursdays at the Welly blew up so big that Hull University offered TFT the Saturday nights - which we took. A bigger, better room, with the best night of the week. We thought ditching Thursdays for Saturdays, and being in the heart of the University would be a genius move. We found out later, that it wasn't.

So Ted could get the Saturday job done in Hull, I was thrown into Play Empire Saturdays. Play was Graham and Ted's baby, and I was happily chucked in at the deep end, fumbling my way around, solo, learning how to be a stage manager and trying not to have bands like The Music, Doves and We Are Scientists walk all over me.

Hull didn't quite work out in the end. But Ted met a lovely Hull girl and moved down there. He left TFT and never looked back. I think he's still there, living his best life.

As much as I loved being involved in the Empire and that monstrously-attended Saturday, it always felt like the Empire as a venue had a lot of control and called many of the shots. I still preferred my first love, Fridays at The Cornerhouse, mainly because they left us to do whatever the fuck we wanted.

Sumo Tattoo

In 2006 no one had a tattoo. Well, I don't mean *no one*. But compared to these days, where *everyone* has between two and twenty tattoos; in 2006 very few people had them. It's probably hard to get your head around but even of our Sumo regulars, only a handful of these folks had ink. A few tribals, a couple of flaming skulls here and there. But there were certainly no necks, faces, no sleeves. This was a small poor town in the North East and there weren't even that many Tattoo shops in town.

In our quest to be cool, be seen and be talked about, I posted a MySpace Bulletin declaring that anyone who got a Sumo Tattoo, would get free entry for a month. I knocked this little blog up without much real thought, I just threw it up one morning at the office.

It only took about an hour, and the internet went fucking crazy. We had hundreds of comments, shares, and dozens of Emails to our hotmail account asking how big these tattoos had to be, could we recommend a tattoo shop, and double checking that we'd honour the offer because these people were serious.

I also had five missed calls from Simon, the operations manager for Ladhar Leisure, the owners of Cornerhouse. I called Simon back and he was in a blind panic. The owners had seen our Sumo Tattoo offer and tasked Simon with getting it shut down immediately. They wanted all traces of this tattoo deal removed from the internet as soon as possible. I was gutted, embarrassed and fuming. I was also scared that Graham was going to kill me.

He didn't, but Simon and Graham explained their worries to me.

"All it takes is some daft 17-year-old to go and get SUMO inked across their arm, and then we've got a furious Dad on the phone to the Evening Gazette telling the world why our club needs to be shut down".

The front page of the Evening Gazette sounded like great publicity to me, but I went with the elders and removed all traces of Sumo's offer.

Good Fridays

Sometime in 2006

Sumo was regularly filling the back half of the venue, known as 'Cornerhouse Area 2'. The front half of the venue, which was accessed from a different door and operated entirely independently from Sumo, saw a few different promoters come and go, but nothing seemed to work or stick in this space known as 'Area 1'.

There were raves, reggae nights, gigs, but what usually happened was, people wandered in that half of the building for a while, then came out, and wanted to be in Sumo. Sometimes we'd make them pay again to join our event, but mostly we'd let them in free, to show them what a party we were having.

One event that took place monthly in Area 1, was Brighton Beach. I don't know where these promoters came from but it wasn't Brighton, and they did draw a decent crowd with their sixties, mod, Britpop and indie events. The Cornerhouse team hated the event, they disliked the promoters and the DJs and often told us horror stories of them not paying their rent and leaving pints of piss in the DJ box at the end of the night. Nice.

Things came to a head when the Brighton Beach team had booked Pete Doherty's band to perform. Pete was at the height of notoriety, he was post-Libertines and in and out of Babyshambles touring. He'd recently been arrested and let off without charge when he announced the one-off show at the Cornerhouse.

The sold-out gig in the 300 capacity room took place a few hours before we opened up Sumo, and as we arrived to get our party ready to open up around 9pm, the gig was drawing to a climactic finale. I stood at the back of the room and watched the last few songs, cringing as Pete proceeded to smash every light in the lighting rig during his last song. He just whacked each light using his microphone, like a toddler, smiling, wide-eyed as each bulb shattered, one after another.

The Brighton Beach team and Cornerhouse staff were left with 300 chewy punters who all wanted to meet Pete while they attempted to mop up the broken glass from the stage and dance floor. That side of the venue was clear by about midnight that night, the band, customers and Brighton Beach team had all gone home - leaving a few pints of piss in the DJ box as usual for the venue to sort out.

The following morning we got a phone call from the Cornerhouse to say Brighton Beach was out, and they wanted us to replace it with a weekly Indie Friday clubnight.

We said yes, and 'Good Fridays' was born. Awful name, but a decent night. Graham's mate Russel DJ'd it and played a retro mix of indie bangers. We kept the tunes a bit old school, to keep things different enough to 'Play' so as not to upset our pals at Empire.

'Trying not to upset Empire' became a bit of a running theme over the years, but they were more worried about Sumo's growing popularity than this little Britpop night that we'd chucked into the mix.

Good Fridays were pretty good(!) and pulled a crowd of about 150 each week. The problem was that halfway through the night, the crowd would all want to be next door, in Sumo.

By 1am the Good Fridays crowd would have all drifted outside, and blagged their way into Area 2, where they'd pester Sumo DJs Kev and Craig for indie tunes.

"But you can get that next door in Good Fridays" Kev would say.

"Yes we know, but we want you to play it in here" they'd reply.

It of course set a precedent for things that would eventually come.

Little Tokyo

February 2006

The actual Cornerhouse runs deep under Middlesbrough Train station. The venue is a confusing mash-up of different rooms connected by corridors. Behind the venue as we know it, there's even more rooms and tunnels that lead back deep under the train station. These spaces were inhabitable mainly due to water leaks, unsafe floors or ceilings. We used these rooms for storage, and they were a good space to sit for ten minutes to get away from the relentless noise of the club.

One thing we discovered about the venue is that even at the front-facing side of the venue, there were rooms still to be discovered.

Just near the back door to the club, under Albert Bridge, which we confusingly used as Sumo's front door, we discovered a small room, about six metres by eight metres in size.

The venue hadn't used the room in several years and the manager's theory was that it used to be an office. It was barely big enough to hold 25 people but we thought it would be a brilliant idea to use it as part of Sumo. We were constantly looking for new talking points, daft things to turn people's heads, and this seemed like the ideal place to cram a little sideshow. We announced a new club-within-the-club, a micro event that could only be witnessed within Sumo, for 60 minutes only. The room would open at midnight, showcase something, and then close at 1am.

Marty christened the room Little Tokyo and set about making some printed propaganda which we handed out in the venue in the weeks leading up to Little Tokyo's launch party. There was a decent buzz, and the people of Boro seemed genuinely excited as if a new clubnight was opening up. The clever thing was, that this new clubnight was inside our clubnight.

We treated Sumo as a multidimensional being, a place where you could explore, get lost and - should you get bored - there was something totally different to discover literally around a corner.

Local DJ and occasional collaborator Bobzilla once said Ten Feet Tall created "Tesco style" clubnights. I don't mind that. They had something for everyone, they had everything you needed, and they were fucking massive.

Little Tokyo hosted many madcap events. They were notoriously epic, because the room was just so small.

We launched with a Noodle Bar. We rigged up a PA system that was far too big for the room and blasted Show tunes, Sinatra and musical soundtracks from an iPod while Gary and I served everyone boxes of noodles. This makeshift street kitchen was basically the office microwave and pile of ninety nine pence noodles packets from the local cash and carry. People queued up all the way through the venue just before midnight.

Once people were served, they dispersed throughout the Cornerhouse - and as news spread that there were free noodles on the go, a couple of hundred people queued up to squeeze into Little Tokyo to get fed.

After giving the noodle splattered room a good clean we followed this launch party with a succession of gigs from thrash metal, to hardcore punk, all ending in carnage as everyone in the whole building tried to cram in to catch a glimpse of the mayhem.

A Teesside band that had done really well in terms of releasing a few albums, getting some international acclaim and building a great local following were The Hitchers. I'd got to know Mike, Rich and Greg well from growing up gigging alongside them at The Georgian Theatre and the Riverside festival scene in Stockton. I remember the show well, as it was one of the first times that Graham from TFT had been along to see Sumo in action since the launch.

He'd very much left things to me and the team, but wanted to come to see how Little Tokyo was shaping up. The Hitchers had loaded in around 8pm and despite being a three-piece outfit, they already seemed to fill the room, with Greg's massive double bass eating up about a third of the floor space. The band sat with their friends drinking beers in the locked room until midnight when we unlocked the door and let the queue of Sumo-goers pile in to see the show. The Hitchers play a perfect punked-up mix of rockabilly, surf and rock and roll. As always, Little Tokyo was packed tight, about a hundred degrees and a sea of moshing, pogo-ing and crowd surfing. Graham and I managed to push ourselves into a corner for a few songs. He was absolutely buzzing and I remember him screaming at me over the music;

"It's like something out of a movie, it's fucking crazy in here".

One of the last shows we crammed into Little Tokyo before the novelty wore off was a double bill of Pig Latin and The Fifteen Minute Society. Both bands were essentially the same members, and both had a well-deserved place in Teesside band folklore as being utterly insane live prospects.

Their enigmatic frontman 'Pop' had always done a fantastic job flyering and promoting Sumo, and actually became a full-time member of Ten Feet Tall staff in later years - and had the job of drawing many Sumo designs and decor pieces. If you ever remember the twenty-foot cartoon penis that spelled SUMO in the Empire foyer, Pop drew that.

Back in the Cornerhouse's Little Tokyo, as the final feedback-drenched chords rang out to announce the end of The Fifteen Minute Society's show, amps began to topple, guitars got smashed up and I noticed Pop had begun dowsing the drum kit in lighter fluid. I began pushing through the crowd towards the exit door, with my arms outstretched trying to scoop up as many humans as possible. I'd gotten everyone about two metres back from the ethanol-soaked drums when Pop tossed a lit lighter onto the mess, the drum kit lit up gold and blue and the crowd behind me roared in approval. It was an explosive end to Little Tokyo's reign and the coolest thing we'd done to date.

Tell Your Mates Who Don't Like Metal

April 2006

We'd tried and pretty much failed at establishing a stand-alone Indie night in the front half of the Cornerhouse. Good Friday's, ironically, just wasn't good enough. Especially with Boro's best clubnight right next door.

The Sumo rock night and the Indie night next door were linked by a small dark three-metre long corridor - a link that we had blocked off every Friday night, by locking the huge black doors at the corridor's mouth.

Graham threw the idea up of opening the corridor; *"What do you think would happen if we just opened those doors, and had that corridor open, for everyone to just walk to and fro as they wished?"*

I offered my considered reply that the following would happen;

1. Moshers would hate us, we'd be turning their exclusive intimate rock clubnight into a big fat commercial sell-out. Our core fanbase would rebel and not turn out. We'd lose hundreds of heads.
2. The corridor that would connect both rooms, plonks moshers directly onto the Indie Room dancefloor. Similarly, anyone wandering from the Indie Room, would be walking blindly straight into a circle pit. Joining these two entities at the hip would not be subtle.

3. There would be fights - We'd created a safe space for alternative culture to reside at the far end of town, far enough away from any other clubnight, and now we were going to ruin it.

My concerns were not altogether ignored and I was tasked with schooling the doormen to ensure the wrong type of people didn't get let in. I was able to help curate the playlist and keep it alternative enough to actually add to the Sumo experience musically. We set a precedent that musically we'd play new, fresh, guitar indie and avoid all traces of the retro classics that Good Friday's and Brighton Beach had relied on.

Once we'd ironed out the kinks we went head first into a promo campaign for the 'New Sumo Indie Room'.

We went with the slogan Tell Your Mates That Don't Like Metal. It seemed to roll off the tongue, and get our message across pretty well. We plastered the venue, and the town with this message and got the hype train well and truly fuelled. The date was set, Friday April 28th, 2006, the grand opening of Sumo's brand new room. We'd killed off Good Fridays a couple of months earlier to let that memory fade, and everyone was psyched for the new room opening.

As fate would have it the legendary Electric 6 frontman Dick Valentine was doing a run across the UK, playing solo acoustic versions of the band's hits such as Danger! High Voltage and Gay Bar. The act suited Sumo's tongue in cheek pastiche and having the main man from a band that crossed over well between Sumo's (now) multiple genre offering, actually worked really well.

The night rolled around and we had an extra hundred people pile into Sumo that night, all still through the back door down under Albert Bridge. We had Dick, real name Tyler, set up on a makeshift stage at the far end of our new Indie Room.

To access the indie room you had to navigate your way through the many corridors, twists and turns of the venue, and, as was my worry, you had to literally cross the rock room dancefloor to get to the indie room. To my pleasure and surprise everyone just got on with it, indie kids and moshers mixed fine, no one wanted to kill anyone else, no one hated us for introducing the new room, and all my fears were waylaid.

It turned out, moshers have loads of friends, who don't like metal.

So now they could all attend, and all party together. It also turns out that moshers, once drunk, love to jump around to indie bangers. Conversely, indie kids, once drunk, love to throw themselves about to Sum41 and Slipknot.

Our new resident indie DJ was another Arena DJ that we were lucky enough to scoop up in the fallout from that venue closing down. Burnsey was a young fresh faced talented DJ that was totally passionate about getting the room busy, and keeping everyone bouncing until they dropped. To pour more praise to my friend Burnsey here, one thing he always did with great gusto was promote Sumo. He did a fantastic job online and would happily swing by the office to collect a bag of flyers, posters and badges.

Burnsey had his dance floor packed right from the off and I actually started to worry that bringing a guy out on stage at 1am with an acoustic guitar was going to kill the feverish launch party vibe we'd whipped up.

Tyler however did not let us down. At 1am Dick Valentine strode onstage, guitar in hand, in a full Middlesbrough FC kit, and had the crowd going bananas to hit after hit of his Electric Six catalogue. Once he'd exhausted the crowd with a ten minute singalong version of Gay Bar, Burnsey returned to the decks for a triumphant last set of wall to wall anthems. He seamlessly blended the likes of The Libertines and Arctic Monkeys into harder dance anthems from the likes of Prodigy and Pendulum, and even threw in plenty of his own curveballs, Sweet Dreams, Mr Bluesky all had the crowd going absolutely mad for it. There was a decent dance-rock uprising at this point so his sets were peppered with the likes of Klaxons, Bloc Party, The Rapture and other disco beat bangers that really kept the energy levels up.

The Sumo indie room had landed with a bang and we'd unlocked the path to getting significantly more people into the clubnight. We were still only using two-thirds of the Cornerhouse at this point. We were bringing people in through the back door, giving them the rock room and indie room, but there was still a beautiful front room to the venue - a room we currently used as a Backstage dressing room area for the acts we had play our new indie room.

At this point we never talked about money, we were never fixated on attendance figures or scrutinising costs, we were just throwing the best party we could and we were just so happy with the fact that people were loving it.

Can You Do 600?

June 2006

In June 2006 Graham and I were asked to come to The Cornerhouse for a meeting with the owners, Ladhar Leisure, to discuss the Fridays. We hadn't really heard from these guys in almost a year since we'd started Sumo.

When the big boss men want a meeting with the promoter you can assume it's about one of the following things;

1. They're going to want to add a few pence to all the drinks they'd been selling so cheaply.
2. They're going to want a few pence from your juicy door take.
3. They're going to suggest that you'd get more people coming in, if you didn't play that god awful rock music.

Thankfully It wasn't any of those reasons, they actually just wanted to tell us how pleased they were with Sumo. They told us that they'd never have expected us to be doing 400 people each week, and was there anything they could do to help?

We thanked them for their help so far, we told them we'd still needed 100% of the door, as we were ploughing every penny back into promo, and that the cheap drinks they were providing were really helping draw a crowd.

They told us to keep up the good work, that 400 heads was great, and as we all shook hands and stood up to leave, they said;

"So I guess the next plan is to get to 600 regulars right?"

We told them yes. Yes, Sumo would do 600 a week.

As Graham and I walked back up Albert Road to the office, we didn't really talk much. I think we were probably both wondering how the hell we'd get 600 regulars into Sumo.

Booking A Band

I was initially absolutely terrible at booking bands. I'd pick a band I liked, for example Reuben, then I'd get a phone number from wherever I could, and then I'd phone them, and ask them to come and play Sumo.

Me – "Hi, is that Barney?"

Reubens manager Barney – "Er, yes?"

Me – "Barney, I was hoping to get Reuben to play a rock club night in Middlesbrough. It's called Sumo and it's really good, packed each week, I think they'd go down a treat"

Barney – "I mean, erm, when? And er what sort of fee do you have in mind?"

Me – "They could play any Friday they want, and we've got £500"

Barney never called me back to confirm a show.

To be honest, I don't know why I tried, we had Bryan, and I soon learned that if I wanted a band for Sumo, I went to Bryan and his little black book of contacts and agents. I'd call him at his house in York, and ask him for a band, for example Capdown or Enter Shikari, and he'd calmly shoot me down instantly.

When do you want them? Are they in the country? Are they even touring? They're not going to drive all the way up to Middlesbrough for a daft one-off are they Phil?

I learned to do my homework, stalk bands, make sure they were likely to be available, know what size venues they were playing, and generally be way savvier.

Then I could give Bryan all the details he needed, prove I'd done my homework and he would then proceed to email and negotiate with agents for a date.

We got Capdown and Enter Shikari and loads more, mainly thanks to Bryan.

Cheers Bryan. Boro owes you one.

Area 2 Take 2

In June 2006 Ladhar Leisure told us they were closing half the club down, to give it a refit.

This stressed me out and pissed me off for a few days, while I rearranged all of our events, and shifted bands and acts. I didn't see the need for the refurbishment, but I guess the place had made some decent money from their new Fridays doing decent numbers now.

It was also a little heartbreaking to close the Indie Room just as we'd got the thing established in Area 1, but we needed to put the moshers in there until the refit was done. After months of telling people Area 2 was Rock and Area 1 was Indie; now Area 1 was Rock, but only for a while. It was confusing.

There was a particularly messy night where we'd crammed the Indie room into Cornerhouse's 'Room 3', then had Rock back in Room 2 and Room 1 got patched up by the builders. Also, I had to somehow accommodate two of my mates' post-hardcore bands from Leeds, Hot Prophecy and Diagoro. We squeezed the bands in a corner through a tiny PA and hoped for the best. It was a totally confusing night, with rock kids, indie kids and people trying find a gig, all wandering around the club, lost as fuck.

We soon got on board with the refit, once we'd seen the fancy plans for how Area 2 and the rock room would look - and we started the hype.

My current Ten Feet Tall partner in crime on Fridays was Jamie. Jamie had done promo work like flyering for ages for Ten Feet Tall and also started doing some DJ sets in The Empire, up in The Gods. Jamie's a stone-cold grafter, has the driest sense of humour of anyone I know. He's also a wicked drummer. He and I played in a few bands later down the line, but at this point in 2006, our main job was to keep people interested in Sumo Fridays and we used the refit as our new promo story.

We'd booked raggapunk legends Skindred for Friday July 7th, as we were reliably told the new rock room would be ready. They decked the place out with a new bar, loads of nice dark wood and red LED lighting, plus the new Function One sound system was absolutely insane. They added a powder-room next to the ladies toilets with giant mirrors, pink padded seats and created a totally over-the-top place for girls to do their makeup. I thought this new powder room would be a great place for a gig, the Cornerhouse guys shook their heads and said that *'over their dead bodies'* would I be putting a gig on in their fancy new powder room.

The rock room did look totally kick ass now, but they did keep the same shitty disco lights which was a shame.

Jamie and I asked Danielle to come down to the club a couple of nights before the grand reopening. For some reason, we hired gorilla suits and wore lab coats and posed as mad ape scientists. It was probably Marty's idea; he loved an excuse to pay homage to Planet Of The Apes. Danielle shot the ape scientists in various positions and poses as they inspected the venue and we published a report deeming the venue now *'fit for human occupation'*. I know this makes no sense, and it didn't make any sense at the time, but that's what we did.

The photos gave everyone on Myspace and Haxed a laugh, and we had the buzz of Skindred too, plus everyone wanted a nosey at the new look of the place.

On the eve of the grand opening, Jamie and I were at the venue from about 4pm, we'd prepped the place for Skindred to load in. The dressing room was set, the rider was on ice, the place looked immaculate, and of course, Jamie and I had built the heavy steeldeck stage at the far end of the room.

Any Cornerhouse regulars may recall the steel pillar that stood smack bang in the middle of the room, and when that stage was built, that pillar was front and centre stage, much to the annoyance of any lead singer that came up against it. As it was a supporting pillar, there was of course nothing anyone could do about the situation.

Benji, the enigmatic frontman of Skindred, arrived on show day, and figured he could solve the pillar problem.

Benji spent a few minutes walking around the steel deck stage and studying its construction. Nine pieces of 8-foot by 4-foot deck came together with bolts and cable ties, up on five foot legs. This metal rectangle slotted perfectly between the back wall, and the Cornerhouse's infamous steel pillar.

"We can make this stage work way better here, lads" proclaimed Benji in his wonderful Welsh accent.

Jamie and I assured him that the stage only really fitted in one way, and that's the way it was. Benji said he had a plan, and he'd like us to help him, take apart and rebuild the stage, his way.

We insisted we'd built this stage in here, week-in-week-out, for almost a year. We'd tried it every way possible, and that it definitely did not fit any other way.

Benji was, and still is, a formidable force, and we weren't winning this argument.

He got his way, and Jamie and I dutifully took apart the eight sections of heavy steel deck. We followed his instructions and built the stage in his new vision.

It didn't fit.

There was no budging the Cornerhouse's walls or supporting pillars. Even when you thought the thing would fit - if you could squeeze it an inch or so - you discovered that steel doesn't squeeze. It is what it is. After about an hour and a few different permutations of this gargantuan Tetris puzzle, Benji suggested that we *"probably should just put it back how we first had it"*.

So when the night finally got underway, we had a packed out rock room in Area 2, Skindred smashed it, followed by a mega indie room homecoming from Burnsey and it was another landmark moment in Sumo becoming the beast it inevitably became.

We all started to believe that we *could* do 600 a week, as we'd half promised the owners of the venue. We still didn't realise at that point, just how far we would take it.

Bands Bands Bands

I loved putting on bands, and I'm glad we did it so often. The reason it was great, at first, was because we had a captive audience. Even if a local band only had ten mates, they still got to play to a packed room, and that usually made them play better. The regulars were getting some entertainment and seemed happy to wait until the band were done before they got their fix of their fave songs from the DJs. There are people in Boro who are purely live music promoters and have done a phenomenal job of supporting and promoting the local music scene in the town. I always felt like I wasn't exactly part of that gang, but I was putting every and any local band I could on that Sumo stage. I felt like it was kind of my duty. Plus I'd been in bands myself for so long, I knew how important it was to let the locals get up and perform.

The by-product of this process was that the band members became Sumo fans, and their mates and fans became Sumo fans. Little by little, it helped our cause and helped our numbers. That (believe it or not) never seemed like a goal, but that's what was happening.

The same went for the touring bands and breaking bands we showcased, only a good handful of people were buzzing that The Datsuns, or whoever, were in town, but the place was packed anyway. Clubnight shows, as we called them, were every band's favourite show. Booking the bands as part of Sumo gave us fresh news, and it meant we always had something to shout about.

Then a problem started. As the gigs went on, over the years, I started noticing something - most people started to turn up *after* the bands had played. The Sumo kids who just wanted the DJ to play the hits, no longer wanted to stand through the 'next big thing'. Unless they knew at least three songs by a band, they actually avoided the place like the plague until the band were packed up and off. They figured out that they could sit in the pub until about midnight and roll up into Sumo when it was in full swing.

It was a frustrating thing, and it's something we fought against for years to come. We'd offer cheaper entry if people came in earlier, even cheap drinks before a certain curfew. It became a bribery game to get people down to see a band. We were paying money out for the band, money on extra staff, money for PA systems and lights, and then charging less for people to see the act. As bizarre as it is, that's what we did because we always made the coin back when 600 people showed up later on. After the cash was counted up at 3am, the costs didn't matter. That was the best time at Sumo, when no one worried about money; money wasn't an issue because there was plenty of it.

For me, I never thought about the money, I just thought about making the event as good as it could be; that's what mattered in those early days.

So, still, we soldiered on with bands. Despite the extra costs, the heavy steel stage that almost didn't fit and crowd apathy, we kept on keeping on.

We'd even host annual 'Sumo Fest' events. We'd open early, and stick bands in every corner of the building, three stages, fifteen or so bands, running from around 8pm until midnight, then roll into the DJ sets. We continued this madness throughout the history of Sumo, and right up until the final few events in Empire. Some might say, a colossal waste of coin, pushing the live element that essentially only a handful wanted.

Side Note : Here's some bands that played at Sumo between 2005 and 2009;

Nick Oliveri, Skid Row, Little Boots, Enter Shikari, The Cribs, innerpartysystem, Airborne Toxic Event, Fei Comodo, Dan Le Sac Vs. Scroobius Pip, Men, Women and Children, The Sheilas, Electric 6, Jonah Matranga, Skindred, The Automatic, The Departure, Devil Sold His Soul, The Chapman Family, Capdown, Heads We Dance, The Karoshi Bros, Daughters, The Ghost Of A Thousand, Haunts, Frank Turner, Throats, Poison The Well, Beatrix Von Bourbon, Johnny Panic, Gallows, Lethal Bizzle, Rumblestrips, Bullets N Octane, Fuel Girls, The Big Pink, We Fell To Earth.

Behind The Curtain

October 2006

When the bands had finished playing their sets, in the Indie Room, we'd throw up a big black curtain in front of the stage, so that the bands could pack down in peace, and Burnsey could get the bangers on and get the party started on the dancefloor.

The audience who had watched the band could literally go from clapping the band off stage, to being plunged into darkness and hit with a stone-cold dancefloor filler. That's how we orchestrated it, no room for dilly-dallying, just non-stop partying - keeping energy levels as high as we could for as long as we could.

The black curtain trick also meant that the crowd couldn't see the stage filled with roadie's bum-cracks and mardy sound engineers, breaking down mic stands or wrapping cables for an hour.

Once a band had finished, myself and Jamie or Gary would pop up two step ladders and work our way from the venue's wall, inwards towards the centre of the room, along the front of the stage, with a piece of fabric that fitted perfectly from floor to ceiling and wall to wall.

We used a heavy black flameproof theatre cloth which we'd buy from a warehouse in Bradford in twenty metre rolls. We used it all the time in venues to hide areas we didn't want people to see, or to create fake walls and extra corridors where we needed to filter people at an event.

The Cornerhouse's 'Stage Curtain' was a piece of this fabric, about twelve metres wide, and it was attached to the ceiling with a staple gun.

Once the band had packed their gear away, the PA company had rolled their sound system out the fire doors into the street, the next job was dismantling the steel deck stage itself. Steel deck was a lot cheaper to buy than its expensive and lighter cousin, aluminium deck. This shit was *heavy*. Each 2-metre by 3-metre piece would be flipped onto its side, then slid across the venue's ice-rink-like tiled floor out into the street, dragged by hand down Albert Road, past loitering revellers, and into a storeroom at the back of the venue. It was a brutal task, undertaken every time a band played, at about 1am. Many fingers were nipped, toes were crushed, blood was spilled.

Once all of this dragging, humping and flexing was done with, we were now left with a jam packed Indie Room, and it was time for the stage curtain to be taken back down. As crazy as that sounds, after all the effort of putting the thing up, by this time in proceedings, we needed the space.

A few sharp tugs on the tough fabric was enough to pull the staples out the ceiling and, like some kind of bizarre Vegas magic act, the few hundred punters who were happily dancing away, were now presented with a huge empty space where a band on a stage had once been. They would flood into the space, spreading themselves out, and enjoying the extra freedom of movement the larger area had brought them.

Our big black stage curtain was getting pretty frayed from the constant stapling up and ripping down, so I wanted to take the thing to get hemmed and eyelets stitched in. I'd fitted a row of hooks along the ceiling in Cornerhouse, and I figured hooking the thing up each week would give the fabric a longer lifespan.

One Monday morning, I bundled the giant ball of black fabric into a huge bag, and carried it to a place called Stitches, a dressmaker shop, which was located 2 minutes walk from the venue. I entered the shop and explained what I needed to the lady who owned the place, who seemed to just about understand. She said she could sort it for me, but could we spread the fabric out on the shop floor so she could measure up, and also requested I show her where these eyelets would be going.

As I emptied the fabric out of the bag, I was mortified as two half-full VK bottles rolled out, spilling pungent alcopop onto the floor. I quickly scooped them up, and apologised. However, the worst was still to come.

As we unfurled the sinister black bundle, we revealed a huge splurge of vomit that ran from top to bottom of the curtain. Someone had puked their guts across the front of the curtain, and as I'd pulled it down and wrapped it from the other side, I hadn't seen the offensive mess that was now laid out on the floor of Stitches shop floor. The three-day-old vomit, having been wrapped tightly in the fabric and left in the cold venue, had been pretty well preserved and was still nice and fresh.

The lady from Stitches put her hands on her hips, and said;

"Well, I'll wait for that to dry, scrape it off, get them hem and eyelets in, and have it ready for you by the end of the week. It'll be £20 if that's ok?"

I was stunned by how casually she just accepted the task in front of her, and despite my embarrassment, I went back to collect my curtain at the end of the week.

I also insisted on paying her £40.

Training Day

There was no training or manual. All of us learned everything as we went along. There's a hundred stories to highlight this. I won't tell you them all. We'd throw ourselves or anyone on the team into the deep end every weekend. It's how I learned, and it's how everyone learned. If there was something we hadn't done before, we didn't Google it, and we just winged it. We were the kings of wing.

Random example; On Hannah's first day in 2015, we had a dilemma. We had a sold-out show about an hour down the road at The Cluny in Newcastle, with cult blues stalwarts Nine Below Zero literally loading in. The guy we'd hired as a stage manager had pulled a sickie.

Hannah overheard us chatting through options. *"I guess... I could go try and help?"*. So she got in her car, drove to Newcastle, stopped at Tesco on the way for some beers and sandwiches for the dressing room, and managed a sold-out blues show. And so, by midnight on her first day, Hannah knew how to be a stage manager.

That's how it was, all of us winging it, picking it up day by day.

Another day;

Our apprentice-turned-full-time-grafter Jay loved live comedy and could run a comedy club with his eyes closed, and often did. He'd not run a live music event before, but - as we told him - *how different could they be?*

We sent Jay to ARC in Stockton to run a capacity show for Limehouse Lizzy, a well respected tribute act and awesome touring show in their own right.

When Jay arrived, he was presented with a boxed up drum kit and asked by the band's drummer to set the kit up. I know that's pretty unusual, but this was just Jay's luck. Having never really paid any attention to any of the fully built drum kits he'd seen in his life, Jay had a good go at guessing how the kit should go together.

With the tom toms facing flat up to the ceiling and the cymbals plopped aloft cymbals stands, set as high as they could possibly go, the kit looked virtually unplayable.

This particular incident is worth mentioning because the band's drummer sound checked and then later played the three-hour show with the kit exactly how Jay had set it up. I still sometimes wonder why he did that?

Jay said watching the guy having to reach ridiculously far every time he wanted to hit a cymbal looked positively painful, but the guy just went with it for some reason.

So back to 2005;

...after I'd been with the company for about eight months, I had the pleasure of running a show for Flogging Molly, who we'd booked to play Legends in Newcastle. We'd talked to Legends about putting a rock clubnight in place for about a year, and we'd never followed through with it. They were owned by Ladhar Leisure who owned Cornerhouse and I guess we just got too busy with Sumo to take on the city of Newcastle's alternative scene. We did, however, put a good handful of bands into Legends.

Looking back, I don't know why we did it. The load in was horrendous, down fifty steps into the vast basement club. Plus we had to bring fresh PA and lights in, as the club sound system wasn't up to task. The stage was tiny (much to Flogging Molly's horror, they barely fit), and there were no dressing rooms.

I learned a lot about prepping and advancing shows, stage managing shows and keeping bands happy on these gigs. Fozzy, VNV Nation, The Undertones and Flogging Molly have all braved the little stage at Legends through a Ten Feet Tall booking. All were haphazardly stage-managed by me.

On this particular day, Flogging Molly had arrived at 9am to load in down the fifty steps into the darkness of this battered nightclub that we'd decided would be a great place for them to play. I'd 'created' a dressing room by commandeering a small balcony area of the club. The band wearily trudged into the club, muttered a few expletives about the tiny stage, and headed for the 'dressing room'.

The tour manager, who looked slightly familiar to me, sized me up as a rookie instantly, and he sat me down to explain everything that was wrong with this show. I was shitting my pants. It was only 9.30am.

The TM was in fact, Joe Gittlemen, the bassist in legendary bands The Mighty Mighty Bosstones and Gang Green. Joe had recently taken on a role at Side One Dummy records and had somehow ended up looking after Flogging Molly for the short run of UK shows. I learned everything I needed to know about stage management, running a rock show, and looking after a band from Joe that day.

Here's a few hot takes.

- Breakfast - When a band is crawling into a dark venue at 9am, they should be presented with breakfast. Not asked, *"Would you like any Macdonalds?"* - They should be presented with cereal, fresh milk, fruit, a toaster, plus bread and spreads. I hadn't prepped well enough, I assumed Maccies would be OK, it wasn't.

- A lockable dressing room - Every band wants and needs this. My roped off balcony area was not a substitute. Joe explained I could replace the non-existent locking door with a 'big ass security guy'. A few phone calls later, and fifty quid lighter, I'd sorted this one by the time doors opened.

- A Drum Mat - In hindsight, I'd have thought a band of Flogging Molly's calibre would have had a drum mat with them. But they didn't, so not-having-a-drum-mat becomes my problem, not theirs. For those of you who don't know why this is an issue - essentially, if you set up a drum kit, and hit it, it will slide forwards. If you're playing on a carpet, this doesn't happen. Wooden stage floors, vinyl floors, concrete floors - your kit is going to be inching away from you as you play.

Some drummers carry a drum mat, about 3 metres by 4 metres in size with them. These guys didn't. Some venues have a house drum mat, or a £30 Ikea effort lurking in a cupboard for this very purpose. This venue didn't. Soundcheck proved that the absence of a drum mat would seriously affect the show, as the drum kit hopped about the tiny polished wooden stage, despite the ample amount of gaffer tape I'd applied to the situation.

So I walked out onto the rainy streets of Newcastle to find carpet. The nearest music store didn't sell drum mats. Determined to be unbeaten by the situation, I walked from shop to shop, cafe to cafe, premises to premises, literally knocking on every door in Newcastle city centre, asking the same question. 'Do you have a piece of carpet or a large rug I can buy or borrow?'.

A small cafe just off Grey Street saved my day. The request was bizarre enough to pique the owner's interest and he asked me to explain why I needed a rug. I explained, and, making it sound as though this guy could save Rock n Roll by helping me, he dutifully walked me to the back of his shop where he had a small makeshift office/store room.

He asked me to help him push his desk to the side, we stacked piles of paperwork up onto shelves and we literally ripped up the carpet from the floor. He wished me luck with the show and I bid him farewell as I triumphantly strutted back to the venue with this roll of carpet on my shoulder.

- Drinks, on ice - I always did a decent job of getting riders, I always left the house on show day nice and early so that I could get to Tesco or whatever and take my time getting the band pretty much everything they had asked for in advance. I was careful to buy the right beer, but in my formative years, I never thought about drink temperature.

If you have a band from the United States, you *have* to get their drinks cold, they will be pissed about warm drinks. No one wants to drink warm beer, or room temperature water, especially Americans. In the club on this particular day, all the venue fridges were stocked and locked, and dragging a fridge up to this balcony area would have been a nightmare. Joe had warmed to me a little and I think he enjoyed the task of schooling the rookie.

He asked, did I have ice? - Yes. I had a fuckload, as the venue had a great ice machine.

Did I have some clean buckets? No.

I offered to go buy some, but following the drum mat episode, he didn't want to lose me for another hour.

He asked me if I had gaffer tape, bin liners, and empty cardboard boxes. Like a good pup, I returned from a quick venue scavenger hunt with the items Joe had requested. He pulled the top off each box, and gaffer taped the bin liners inside. *"Here you go, ice buckets".*

I began pouring ice into our new receptacles.

"No!" Joe yelled – *"Drinks FIRST, Jesus Christ man!"*

Beers first, then water bottles, then ice on top.

I learned so many other things that day, but those bits stuck with me – and every band I looked after following that show had ice cold drinks, a secure dressing room, and drum mat.

Planet Dare

If I played the role of the Mam and Dad at Sumo, running around making sure everything was just so, doormen were being polite, the money was right, wristbands weren't being put on too tight or whatever... then Danielle was everyone's super-cool older sibling.

Danielle partied *hard* alongside the punters, getting the shots in and essentially getting paid to have a damn good night and make sure everyone else did too.

Danielle was asked to join the team from the first ever night, where she roller skated round the club, taking song requests and attempting to deliver drink orders. As you can imagine, roller skating around the dark club was soon knocked on the head and she took over paparazzi duties, capturing the madness and energy of Sumo for years and years. She also occasionally manned the reception, giving everyone the warm welcome they needed, and she kept the money and doormen right while she was there.

As we got into our second year of Sumo, Danielle wanted to find a way to make the photos a bit more interesting. I guess she did it to make her job more of a laugh too, but certainly, we needed a way to spice up that first couple of hours in the club where everyone was too shy. I wanted people partying harder, and she wanted to avoid having the same set of posed photos every week, pics of many of the same people.

If you Google *nightclub photos* from any place in the world, from Los Angeles to London to Middlesbrough, almost every single set of fifty to a hundred pics are always the same.

Everyone wants a nicely posed shot for the socials, so you can end up with quite a sterile set of nice pics. We wanted people to get loose, and go wild, and get them snapped doing so.

Danielle came up with the idea of giving the Sumo-goers dares and challenges, in exchange for rewards. She curated a list of dares, and respective rewards and she named it Planet Dare (a homage to the B52's song Planet Claire).

- "ROBOT" - Wrap your mate in tin foil for a free shot.
- "BRA" - Bring us 3 bras - not your pals' for a free Sumo pass
- "PIT LICK" - Lick an armpit, not your own, for a free beer
- "PUSH UPS" - Drop and give us 20 for a free badge
- "LEMON" - Eat this raw lemon for a bottle of fizz
- "DARE BURGER" - Eat our house special for a King Dare trophy

There were dozens of Dares and that's just a few. A Dare Burger consisted of a large floury bap stuffed with Marmite, Red Hot Chilli Sauce, Garlic, Fish Paste and of course, half a can of chunky dog food in jelly from the pound shop.

Danielle captured everyone's antics on film, and they made the photos utterly spectacular. She and her pals Trudie and Kathryn ran the Dare Zone, managing the masses of Sumo-goers that all-too-eagerly licked pits, snogged strangers and wolfed down burgers. It was carnage. As people ran around the club waving bras, wrapped in foil, the girls somehow managed the madness and got everyone well and truly drunk.

Danielle had a special dare called "Moustache". Two strangers would be paired up and encouraged to draw a moustache on each other's top lips with a bottle of squeezy ketchup. Then, both victims were blindfolded and asked to lick the others moustaches off. I stood and watched all this unfold, and marvelled at how everyone just *did* every dare. They just cracked on. In 2006 anyone would do anything for a free shot.

We'd bring Planet Dare back a few times a year, eventually with Rick or Eddy filming the madness too. We incorporated the I'm a Celebrity Get Me Out of Here craze into Planet Dare and had people chomping through freeze dried locusts and scorpions.

I loved Planet Dare and I love Danielle for bringing it to the table. Even after hanging up her camera and leaving Sumo, she encouraged us to keep the dare parties going. I just don't think there are many rock nights doing that sort of shit.

Friday Afternoons

The Thursday nights in Cornerhouse, known as Sixty Nine, were a legendary proposition. They were infamous, and they were huge.

Pop, 'R n B' and Indie, with their own daft fun and games, they attracted crowds that ran well over the 1100 capacity every week. Sixty Nine was the reason people called the venue The Sauna House, as on a Thursday, steam billowed from the venue from the cracks in the fire doors, and everyone left the place soaked in sweat.

So every Friday daytime, the Sumo team would enter the venue and try to put the place back together. The cleaners had done a thoroughly half-arsed job and I guess about half of the sick, broken glass and blood was gone. Sumo was a very different beast in terms of numbers and vibe, so we'd rearrange all the furniture to create a cosier venue for the few hundred customers we had at that time. The half-knackered sofas and splintered tables weighed literally nothing and slid easily around the venue that had a notoriously slippery floor. It didn't take too long to rearrange the place. Everything we moved would reveal a pool of puke or a stack of half-drank VK bottles that had been slung behind a table or couch.

We discovered that if we flipped every couch over a few times, about £5 in change fell out of the cushions. So our Fridays usually began with the bizarre ritual of cartwheeling furniture around the club. This amassed about £30, which I took to Subway to get everyone lunch with. We'd sit and chomp through Footlongs and mountains of cookies, before powering on with the rest of the set up.

Our next task was to remove all the Sixty Nine branding and decor, posters and whatever else they'd strung up on the walls and pack it all away in the bowels of the venue.

Then, with our blank canvas of the Cornerhouse set ready, we could begin the task of making the place into Sumo.

Our favourite material was Correx. A thin, lightweight plastic material, the same stuff estate agents use to make For Sale signs. We used local printers to print huge sheets of this stuff, printed with full colour designs that Marty had created. We covered the flaking cracked walls in giant Sumo logos, random collages and whatever else had sprung from Marty's mind. We wallpapered the toilets and corridors in posters, mainly for people to steal and take home, and we decked all the backs of the bars with huge colourful menus. Our drinks offering was unique to Sumo, we had drinks that no one else had, and cocktails that no one had heard of - mainly because I'd make them up, off the top of my head.

Graham had a penchant for projectors, and his absolute favourite decor piece was to set up a projector and fire it onto a wall, playing some trippy visuals that Marty would create. Over the years, this practice became a perfected fine art in its own right. Graham would buy up to ten projectors and have them firing at every part of the club.

We'd break out the step-ladders, fishing wire and cable ties and hang our random crap from the ceiling and we'd be almost ready to go. This whole thing took about five hours with three of us scurrying around the venue. We wanted to make Sumo look and feel unlike any of the other nights in the venue, or in the town, and I think we did a bang-on job.

As the place closed at 3.30am and an army of glass collectors made their way through the venue with giant brushes and mops, me and the Sumo team would carefully flip out our ladders and begin the task of taking everything back down and packing it away.

Thankfully, putting it all away only took about an hour. So by 4.30am we were done, and free to escape into the night, usually to find a gaggle of Sumo-goers outside plotting which after party to head to.

Punching A Skeleton To Pieces

The thing about the DJ boxes in Cornerhosue is that they were fucking gross.

They were disgusting, and I spent a good hour every Friday afternoon making them somewhat habitable for our Sumo DJs. The venue wouldn't allow the cleaners into the DJ boxes, for fear of them breaking the DJ equipment. This was a bit of a joke in itself as the decks were usually coated in vodka and beer and really messed up from the night before's partying. I don't think the cleaners giving them a wipe over would have been a bad idea.

I'd remove bottles and trash from the DJ boxes and the venue manager Jonny would give the decks a test, blasting a half-hour of hard house, probably just to affectionately annoy us moshers as we worked.

The lighting rigs in the Cornerhouse were another broken joke. The lights themselves looked like they came from Argos or Maplin, and they probably did. A spaghetti junction of cables led to the DJ boxes and culminated in a small black lighting control box that had about 6 buttons on it. These buttons weren't labelled, and it was a skill in itself for the DJs to mash the buttons to make the lights creak their way around some kind of lighting pattern.

The equipment in Cornerhouse was the main frustration, of the DJs that played Sumo. Their anger and disdain for the gear was only born from their love of the event and the fact that they wanted things to be perfect. They'd be playing to a packed crowd, having a blast and whipping the crowd up into a frenzy; then the music would skip, the lights would freeze or flood the room with bright white light. On some nights, the whole power would just cut out for 10 minutes.

It was ridiculous, and the DJs got more and more frustrated that they couldn't do the job they loved to the best of their ability due to the dilapidated kit they were given.

This came to a head one Friday night in 2008 - Burnsey was doing a stellar job as usual ramping up the indie bangers. He had the crowd giving it big guns, it was a proper hands-in-the-air bouncy night, he had them in the palm of his hand. I was squeezing my way through a jam packed dance floor, when simultaneously the music froze, and the lights jammed on bright white, then started strobing to the silence. It was super awkward. Not knowing the Cornerhouse kit was to blame, the crowd started booing Burnsey. Luckily it only lasted 20 seconds or so, the lights kicked back into a dark red wash, and Burnsey dropped the next track. Everyone just got back on with bopping away, but I knew this would have hurt his DJ pride.

As I walked up into the DJ box with a couple of cold Red Stripes for him, I could see Burnsey was fuming. I glanced down to see both his hands were bleeding; his knuckles looked really sore. On the floor was a big pile of plastic bones - the remains of a plastic skeleton. It had been a good few weeks since Halloween and this full size prop hadn't been packed away when it should, and it had felt the full force of Burnsey's frustrations. I was lucky I'd made a trip to the bar before going in, otherwise I fear I may have met the fate that the skeleton did.

The key thing I want you to take away from this random tale about shitty lighting desks is this; The Sumo DJs were intensely passionate about the event, the product and the night. More so than I realised until years later (we'll come back to this).

These DJs put their hearts and souls into Sumo. Despite the themed parties, daft props, the bands and acts or the cheap drinks - there was one thing that was more important than anything else in making Sumo the huge success that it would become, and that was the music. The team that played the tunes at these events, I believe, were the single most important people in the equation, and without them and their fierce passion, Sumo wouldn't have lasted as long as it did, or outlasted everything else that came close.

Sumo Room 3

We grew and grew through 2006. We got to the point where we had outgrown the two-thirds of the venue that we now continually rammed to the point of daftness.

It was time to open the last segment of the venue. This enabled us to spread the Sumo-goers out, and add a third element to the fun and games, another music policy, more DJs and another space to shoehorn bands. It meant we'd lost our makeshift dressing room for bigger touring bands, but we just needed the space to house the partying public by this point.

If you referred to my makeshift map on the website, you'll see that we'd created a system of rooms that now ran as Room One (The rock, punk, metal one), Room Two (the Indie/pop one) and our new room that we obviously christened Room Three.

It created a confusing scenario for newcomers, as we could now use the venue's proper front door rather than the back door. So we now used the Cornerhouses' traditional corner door which led you into Room Three as the first room you encountered. You then had to work backwards through Room Two to finally get into the last room of your journey, Room One. I'm probably overthinking it. However, I wanted to mention this, as it was such a headfuck explaining to people where things were.

We'd often draw maps, print them as posters, hand them out, and cover the walls in giant arrows and signposts. Sometimes it helped, but we'd still find people utterly confused and lost.

"*How do I get back upstairs?*" people would ask me. The venue was all on one level.

So now our new Sumo Room Three was here and having covered all the music that I wanted to with the first two areas, Room Three was tasked with becoming an eclectic space where we could play fast and loose with music policies. We adopted an anything-goes attitude that served us well.

We created a rotating calendar of events where four semi-regular guests would do their thing roughly monthly. There was, and still is, a wealth of talent in Middlesbrough. 2006 was chock full of DIY promoters, gigs and events organised by people that were usually our mates. We offered the space out to a few of the best.

Our first Room Three special guests were - Black Jack Rabbits.

Black Jack Rabbits was a burlesque-meets-freakshow carnival of weirdness, hosted, DJ'd and curated by Danielle, our photographer. Sword swallowers, topless opera singers, knife throwers and tripe eating contests. More on that later. It deserves its own chapter.

Our next Room Three guest was - Pop Disco.

I'd known Henry a while; a fantastic DIY gig-putter-onner from Guisborough, my bands had played dozens of his shows. Henry in 2006, alongside the likes of Glen from Open Season, was bringing some very cool names to town, including Aconite Thrill, This Girl, Meet Me In St Louis and Martha. Henry also played the drums in The New Lev Yashin. He later became a proper pop star as the guitarist in DARTZ!. But right now in our timeline, Henry was tasked with playing some big fun pop songs. He curated what he called 'Pop Disco', sorted his own promo and posters, and played a mix of music that somehow resonated immensely well with the die-hard moshers. Pop Disco appealed to everyone's pop heart and everyone's dancing shoes. Imagine the last power-hour from a wedding DJs set, Henry managing to skate the fine line between cult pop and cheeseball shite. Moshers say they want to hear Cute Without The E, or Walk With Me In Hell, but by 2am after nine cans of Red Stripe, they just want You Can Call Me Al.

Cue the air trumpets.

Week three, Room Three - Maison De Varietes.

Fashion Fil was a local DJ who had cut his teeth at the Arena, becoming a bit of a cult face as the DJ in the Arena's back room, aka The Purple Room. Fil was also a decent graphic designer and had a wealth of promo ideas, and he'd later go on to play at the 'Kaboom' clubnight at Empire and perhaps his lasting Boro legacy is that he launched and single handedly brought 'Creeps' into the world - a Thursday Night event that's ran for over a decade to date. But back in the day, Fashion Fil played some funk, soul and very cool pop in Sumo's Room Three. He called it Maison De Varietes.

The last Friday of The Month in Sumo Room Three - Tubbyphunk.

A long-time Ten Feet Tall collaborator was Robert, aka Superdeejay Bobzilla. Bob and his pals played a heady mixture of Drum n Bass and breaks. Bob's DnB was brilliant to me, it was different to everything else we were doing, not just for the lack of guitars, but the thunderous beats and breaks literally shook the walls as it bellowed out of the Cornerhouse's ridiculously large sound system. I do think it all went over most people's heads. We'd always played a few very commercial DnB tracks, Roni Size, Pendulum and Freestylers, in the Rock Room and it properly set people off. However, four hours of the hottest new cuts just didn't quite work. Despite attracting a die-hard following of about twenty heads, we knew it needed a little something.

Bob had an idea, and that idea was The Blacklight Mega Rave. I loved the name and the concept. We simply turned all the lights off in Room Three, and hired giant 400 watt UV blacklights to give the room an eerie deep purple glow. We added glow sticks, UV face paints, white gloves, and we discovered a whole world of UV crap you can import to give your DIY rave an uber-kitsch vibe. We even bought a UV bubble machine, which people soon pulled down, and smeared UV bubble fluid all over themselves. Under the blacklights, everyone looked bonkers, and it was a wild vibe.

Side note : In addition to this revolving door of DJ talent in the Cornerhouse's third big room, we'd started putting an array of entertainment onto a small mezzanine area that sat above the back door.

From the aforementioned casino table and ping pong, we'd also showcase gigs and guest DJs there, too – to a crowd of about twenty people, all the balcony could hold.

Notable riotous shows included – a DJ set from the Rock n Rose girls Emily and Jess, and a Black Jack Rabbit's live rockabilly spin-off show. The highlight of this was BBC presenter and local legend Bob Fischer playing an acoustic set, accompanied by Russell from Russell and the Wolves on a washboard.

He Pushed His Fingers Into My Eyes

Friday 19th August 2006

It was around 1am, on a typical Friday Night.

The venue was pretty full, all the dancefloors were at a decent capacity, and it was an unremarkable night as far as Sumo's would go.

For some reason - such as getting more change for the front reception till - I was making my way back into the behind-the-scenes chambers of the Cornerhouse, through an internal fire escape door, into one of the dimly lit corridors that led to the back office.

As I left the deafening noise and smoke-filled air of the Rock Room and the fire door clicked shut behind me, I was presented with a hunched figure leaning against the wall in front of me. Akin to the final scene in Blair Witch, a random person stood, facing away from me, seemingly propped up against the wall by their forehead.

The maze of back-corridors of the Cornerhouse rarely had anyone loitering in them, the staff that used these shortcuts would whizz through them fetching stock, ice, glasses or whatever was needed as the night progressed.

This was definitely a drunk punter, and I gave him a semi-friendly but authoritative *"Mate, you can't be back here"* which I suppose I intended to be enough to get the lad moving back into the club.

He half spun around, pivoting while propped against the wall, and revealed he was pants down, dick in hand, and was continuing his drunken piss. He just about managed to mumble, *"fuck off"*.

I should have walked away.

Years later, things like this rarely bothered me, but at this point in my Sumo journey, I felt very personally offended by this. It was like finding someone pissing in your house. Sumo, at that time, was my personal weekly house party. I (thought I) knew everyone who came along on a Friday night for a lovely time. This guy was not welcome, he's broken an unwritten rule in my mind, and I saw red.

I ran at him, not thinking, and attempted to spin him around, to frogmarch him through the external fire door that he was just a couple of yards away from.

Unfortunately, this was not the drunken oaf I expected, he came alive, and now standing upright, he was a damn sight bigger than me. I realised in an instant that I'd bitten off more than I could chew.

He wrapped his fat fingers around my head and pushed his thumbs as hard as he could into my eye sockets. His hands felt unbearably strong, and I could feel and smell the warm urine that soaked his hands.

I suppose I should have kicked him in the balls or pushed hard forward, slamming him into the wall. Since I was sixteen, I'd spent over a decade in nightclubs, and I'd somehow avoided any kind of fight or scuffle. I was utterly useless.

I screamed, yelled and thrashed helplessly until this guy dropped me and ran for the exit. I must have shouted pretty loud as a small battalion of doormen had appeared out of nowhere and surrounded me to ask what was going on. I pointed at the open fire door and exclaimed something along the lines of *"He's poked my fucking eyes out"*. The doormen streamed out the fire door into the street and to be honest I've no memory of what happened after that.

There's a lesson for anyone who stumbles across any beef in a nightclub. Go and get security. That's what they are there for.

Next time, and every single time from then on, that's what I did.

Across a dark room, filled with smoke and dazzling lights, you never know what you'll come up against if you dive in headfirst. People are stronger than they look, people carry weapons, people pump themselves full of drugs; people pee on their hands and then wrap them around your face. So always get an actual adult involved, someone who knows how to handle situations like that.

Bring Me The Horizon, Malpractice and My Wife

On Dec 1st 2006, Lost Prophets headlined Middlesbrough Town Hall, supported by Bring Me The Horizon. We at Sumo took the opportunity to brand our party that night as the 'Unofficial Aftershow Party'. We made the word *Unofficial* nice and small on the flyers, and rumours soon went round the town that Lost Prophets, and more importantly, the up and coming Bring Me The Horizon, would be at Cornerhouse, partying after the show. With 1200 moshers at the sold out gig, we did pretty well off the back of that and Sumo was packed out by midnight.

I missed the Town Hall gig that night as I was setting up for Sumo, but I recall seeing the Bring Me The Horizon lads leaving at the end of the night. Oli Sykes was being carried out by some helpful regulars, as he was so drunk he couldn't walk.

On this same night, Bryan had booked a band to play Sumo - something we probably didn't really need that night, after all, anyone interested in watching a band was at the Town Hall. But he was offered Malpractice, and assured me it was too much of a star turn to turn down. The band was only available on this particular date, and he and Graham felt it was a very cool booking so we'd put it in.

Malpractice were a self-monikered Metal Supergroup, fronted by Adam

Fenton, aka Adam F. The actor, film composer, globally renowned DJ and drum n bass/hip hop producer was returning to his first love of singing. After all, he was the son of scouse pop legend Alvin Stardust. No, I'm not making this up.

Under his Adam F producer alias, he'd worked his magic for global superstars including David Bowie, Pet Shop Boys. De La Soul, LL Cool J and Redman. So I guess he was worth booking in for a Sumo show. His live band was made up of the guitarist from Brit-rock stalwarts "A" and the former Killing Joke drummer. Ok, the credentials checked out.

In an extra twist, Bryan had asked Adam if he'd like to DJ for an hour in the Rock Room, following Malpractice's set. He agreed, so we had the additional buzz that night for the drum n bass fans, that this world renowned DJ would be taking to the decks from midnight until 1am.

Sometimes it was hard to fit all of this on one poster, but this was our event, the "LostProphets-and-Bring-Me-The-Horizon-Unofficial-Aftershow-Party-starring-Malpractice-(feat. Adam F, plus members of 'A' and Killing Joke)-plus-Drum-N-Bass-Adam-F-set-in-the-Rock-Room-from-Midnight"

There was also one other thing going on that night in Sumo.

We had started a little initiative whereby we were recruiting people to DJ the first hour of the night. A notoriously quiet part of any clubnight is the first hour, so we'd offer up a crate of booze for anyone who fancied jumping in the DJ box and having a go. These warm-up DJ's brought a little bit of a new flavour to the night, they also usually brought all their mates in earlier, after all, no one can drink 24 bottles themselves, so they passed them round, and everyone had a nice time.

We took sample playlists through MySpace and vetted out any weirdos.

Tonight's guest DJ was a girl called Claire. I'd known Claire from nights out, and generally always seeing her at Empire, The Georgian Theatre and gigs. She worked at HMV and had a cool haircut. By my standards, this made her a decent DJ candidate.

So as midnight rolled around, Claire was finishing off her set, and finishing her drinks with the Sumo DJs Kev and Craig, and they were welcoming Adam F and his DJ Kit into the tiny DJ box. Adam definitely took a bit of a shine to Claire and I think the main focus of his DJ set was trying to impress her with his mixing and beat matching skills. His set bombed, as the crowd patiently waited out the bludgeoning Drum n Bass, in favour of Craig and Kev getting the rock and metal 'Regular Sumo' tunes past 1am. Claire was having none of Adam's advances and he joined his band to load out the back doors of Cornerhouse and disappeared into the night.

I was fairly oblivious to all of what was going on to be honest, I was too busy trying to spot members of Bring Me The Horizon, and ensure we got some photos of them for use on future promo. I have the details of Adam's romantic pass, because many years later, Claire became my girlfriend, and eventually my wife. But that's another story.

A Set List from December 2006

Here's a list of songs that Craig played, one Friday in 2006.
.

Abominable Iron Sloth – Hats made of veal and that new car scent
Botch - O'Fortuna
Chris Cornell – You know my name
Incubus – A kiss to send you off
Lost Prophets – Can't catch tomorrow
Paramore – Emergency
Cave in – Inspire
Will Haven – I've seen my fate
Exit By Name – Keep my Distance
The Bled – Sound of Sulphur
Bloodsimple – Path to Prevail
Norma Jean – Blueprint for future homes
Taking Back Sunday – Make Damn Sure
Dashboard Confessional – Hands Down
Finch – What it is to burn
Beyond all Reason – Love crossed pistols
Machine Head – Seasons Wither
Pantera – Walk
Bullet for my Valentine – 4 words to choke upon
Funeral for a Friend – Roses for the dead
Lost Prophets – Last train home
Fall out boy – Sugar, we're going down

A SET LIST FROM DECEMBER 2006

My Chemical Romance – I'm not OK
Metallica – Sad but True
Disturbed – Down with the Sickness
Soil – Halo
Marilyn Manson – mObscene
Stonesour – Come whatever may
Slipknot – Duality
Capdown – Cousin Cleotis
Goldfinger – Superman
Jazzy Jeff & the Fresh Prince – Boom! Shake the Room
Pendulum – Tarantula
Skindred – Nobody
Chamillionaire – Ridin' Dirty
36 Crazyfists – I'll go until my heart stops
Linkin Park & Jay Z – 99 Problems
Limp Bizkit – Break Stuff
Papa Roach – Last Resort
In Flames – Take this Life
Slayer – Raining Blood
AC/DC – Back in Black
Bon Jovi – Livin on a Prayer
Aerosmith – Dude looks like a lady
Queen – Don't stop me now
Tenacious D – Pick of Destiny
Enter Shikari – Sorry you're not a winner
Billy Talent – Red Flag
Head Automatica – Beating Heart Baby
Panic at the Disco – I Write Sins...
Zebrahead – Anthem
Blink 182 – First Date
Good Charlotte – Anthem
Parkway Drive – Romance is Dead
Lamb of God – Redneck

Rage Against the Machine – Freedom
Deftones – Bored
Refused – New Noise
My Chemical Romance – Black Parade
Red Hot Chilli Peppers – Under the Bridge

Men, Women And Children

Friday 8th December 2006

I'll be honest I had no idea who Men, Women and Children were, when Bryan emailed me to say they'd been booked to play at the club. I was psyched to quickly learn that the band was a new project from Glassjaw guitarist Todd Weinstock. I was buzzing on just the idea of having Todd in the building. In these early days I still got pretty starstruck when some of my heroes were in the building and chatted away to me. That feeling waned with time, which is kind of a shame. I became more comfortable with the celebs and rock stars, after all, these people had usually just slept on a bus and all they wanted was a pee and a cup of coffee.

Men, Women and Children loaded into the corner door of The Cornerhouse, and their crew rolled the cases through into the Sumo Indie Room which was that night's stage location. The band members dumped their bags on the Cornerhouse's bar and slumped themselves down into the 3 booths that were situated in the venue's front windows. Todd was on the phone right away, seemingly to a manager or an agent; *"Dude, we're playing a fucking CAFE, what the fuck?"*. He hadn't yet explored the maze of corridors and rooms in the rest of the venue.

Once he'd finished up the call I politely suggested I give the band a quick Cornerhouse tour. They were actually stoked with the 'weird venue' and once I assured them that the whole front bar area was closed to the public, and was their (lockable and safe) dressing room, they chilled.

The show went off without a hitch, as they usually did to be honest. Doors opened at 11pm, the Sumo throng piled in. There was a good handful of people excited to see this new band throw down their unique brand of punk, disco and pop-rock. The band took to the stage at midnight, and once they were done, me and the team did the usual hour-long stage strip, room clear, and by 1.30am the Sumo Indie Room was clear and the clubnight was in full effect.

The band had told me they were planning to stick around and party, so I let them chill in their private chunk of the club while I finished the load out, and went to grab their cash.

I headed through to see them, and was greeted by what was probably the most debauched scene I'd witnessed thus far in my adventures in clubnight world.

I can't say if it was band members or crew, as they had a good few friends and techs with them for the show, but there was basically a sea of white cheeks in the air, and a mini orgy was in full swing. Butts were bobbing up and down in time to the deafening music, which the band had requested be piped through from the main room, into the speakers in the bar. Although the lights were dimmed low, I could make out four girls and three guys hard at it.

Their chief roadie, a Californian Jesus-lookalike named Greg, was slumped over the bar, one eye open, watching a kettle boil. I made a beeline for Greg and gently woke him from his slumber, to let him know the kettle had boiled and that I needed to settle the paperwork. Greg straightened up, nodded to the kettle and said, *"Chocolate Vodka?"*. I hadn't noticed the science experiment that Greg had set up on the bar. The boiling kettle lid was wide open, and inside was a half-full bottle of Smirnoff, in which Greg had stuffed all of the chocolate from the band's rider. If I recall rightly, mainly Mars bars. The chocolate bars had reduced in the vodka, and Greg, with a towel around his hand, pulled the red hot bottle from the kettle and poured us both a gooey molten chocolate vodka, over ice, into two waiting glasses.

He counted the money and signed the receipt as the girls from behind us pulled on their jeans and hurried back into the club. I sipped my drink, shook his hand (and no one else's) and bid them a safe journey into the night.

Some Sumo Stuff From 2006

Here's a list of some of the events we did in 2006. Tick them off if you were there.

Fri 31 March 2006 - Pig Latin + The 15 Min Soc in Little Tokyo

Fri 28 April 2006 - Sumo Indie Room opens, with Dick Valentine

Fri 5 May 2006 - Idiot Savant + Twenty Definitions

Fri 12 May 2006 - Marked For Death in Little Tokyo. Client + Japan for Sega in Rm.2

Fri 19 May 2006 - Oxfam Glamour Models + Dirty Weekend

Fri 2 June 2006 - DARTZ! + Alsatian

Fri 23 June 2006 - Shigeru + Heroes Amongst Thieves

Fri 30 June 2006 - Hot Prophecy + Daigoro

Fri 7 July 2006 - Skindred (Area 2 reopened)

Fri 21 July 2006 - Station Rd + The Howls

SOME SUMO STUFF FROM 2006

Fri 28 July 2006 – Burnout In The Capital + Cantarte

Fri 4 August 2006 – 1000 Battles Lost + The NX

Fri 15 September 2006 – Nick Oliveri, Blag Dahlia, Mayor McCa, High Plane Drifters

Fri 29 September – Brigade + The Scare

Tue 20 October – Howling Bells

Fri 27 October 2006 – Sumo's Wild West with the Johnny Cash Tribute

Fri. 3 November 2006 – The Chapman Family & Get Vegas

Fri 13 October 2006 – Bullets & Octane

Fri 1 December 2006 – Malpractice (Feat Adam F) + LostProphets + BMTH Aftershow

Fri 8 December 2006 – Men, Women and Children

Fri 22 December 2006 – The Sumo Xmas Beach Party

Black Jack Rabbits

Black Jack Rabbits was the brainchild of Sumo photographer and hostess Danielle. She'd originally started the event at The Dickens Inn in Middlesbrough, up in the function room that had formerly hosted the clubnight, 'Blackout' - no relation - one of Bryan's brainchilds. This room, known to some as The Gold Room was a fairly nice gaff, with a slightly grand aura and small stage. It was perfect for the fucked up variety show (her words, not mine) that Danielle wanted to create.

Danielle had brought the idea to the table at Ten Feet Tall and asked Graham for some help, advice and backing. I think she could have pulled the thing off herself but she just needed someone to hold her hand metaphorically through the process of getting the thing launched.

The show was raucous, totally over the top. It was something that Boro had never seen and hasn't really seen since. TFT had hooked Danielle up with gin-drinking Jesus-lookalike and stand up legend Matt Reed to compere. The acts took to the stage one at a time, in between bursts of DJ sets from Danielle's mates, who span the likes of The Cramps, Jon Spencer Blues Explosion, Blondie, and a hundred other unflappably cool records. The acts were a mix of burlesque, bizarre side-show and punk-rock cabaret. Danielle would probably be fine with me describing it as Vic Reeves Big Night Out on crack. I recall a particular madcap bill of a Sword Swallower, followed by a Tripe Eating Contest, with contestants on stage at a long table, forcing a foul feast into their mouths as Matt egged them on over the mic.

After a few sessions in The Dickens Inn's Gold Room, Graham suggested Danielle move Black Jack Rabbits inside of Sumo; another clubnight-within-a-clubnight. I wasn't sure that this was the best thing for Black Jack Rabbits, but at the same time, she didn't seem to mind, and I was buzzing to have this very cool show as part of the Sumo circus.

We crammed the Black Jack Rabbits formula into the third room of the Cornerhouse, with a tiny stage jammed into the corner of Sumo's third room, playing host to the eclectic acts that Danielle and her friends brought to the table. She would usually bring us act suggestions, along with their fees and we'd always say yes.

Burlesque became a popular choice because it drew a big crowd, and it was fairly simple to stage manage (or so we initially thought) in the cramped quarters of Room Three. With no backstage, and no dressing rooms; the likes of Ruby Fortune, Molly Mae and Beatrix Von Bourbon, would graciously get changed and prepped into their outlandish costumes in a corner of the beer cellar. Danielle then guided them through the madness of the Sumo baying crowd, to vault up onto the front of the stage. At the time, I thought this was pretty punk rock, but it soon became apparent that this wasn't fair on the acts. Another issue we had was that the lovely Black Jack Rabbits crowd, who loved to dress the part (three piece suits, corsets, top hats and monocles) didn't actually enjoy mixing with the great unwashed. The moshers and indie kids played nice, but this crowd wanted a nice comfy space in which to appreciate the art. We gave them a beer soaked nightclub with a sticky floor.

Not that Black Jack Rabbits set out to be a pure burlesque event but it attracted that crowd and shared a vibe. I've since been to burlesque events such as The Wet Spot in Leeds, who deliver their event perfectly. Our DIY, punk rock version, was certainly a hell of a party, but I knew it wasn't sustainable. Moving Danielle's exemplar vision into Sumo, just hadn't done it justice, sadly.

On a rainy January night in 2007, we had a packed out event, and I remember an amazing performer who went by the name Meg Lo Mania, who belted out pitch-perfect Soprano style renditions of classic tunes by the likes of Vera Lynne. She did this, practically stark naked, apart from a pair of glittery panties and a feather boa. Meg was incredible, a true talent, but the boys of The Cornerhouse only had eyes for her chest. The entire point of this show of art was missed on the majority of the crowd. Don't get me wrong, the crowd loved Meg, but it felt wrong.

Danielle and I talked about how to make the best of future shows, how to discourage the lads in the crowd, we talked about members cards, restricting room access, or even creating a set of specialist burlesque bouncers, all female, and arming them with super soakers. If anyone dared to leer at the nudity, they'd get a drenching.

And so we took the burlesque out of Black Jack Rabbits and kept the brand going with monthly DJ sets, with Danielle and her friends, Trudie, Ned and Kathyrn all bringing their unique blend of rockabilly, 70's punk rock and B52's kitsch to the Room three dance floor for many months to come.

Before we took the live acts out completely, Black Jack Rabbits went out with a bang. Danielle booked Anna Fur Laxis, and we held her live show in the Indie Room. We gave her the biggest stage we could, which was just as well, as Anna's finale involved her strapping her tour manager and husband to a giant revolving wooden board and she blindfolded herself and threw huge knives at him from about twenty feet away. It was jaw dropping and looking back, it felt like a fitting and spectacular end to the Black Jack Rabbits legacy in Cornerhouse.

I wish we'd carried the show on, found a small intimate venue, perhaps seated, and given Boro the madcap variety show it deserved, it was one of a kind, and sadly, Sumo-ing it, didn't quite work out.

Side note : The great unwashed is a very affectionate term, and included myself.

Sorry, You're Not A Winner

Fri 19th January 2007

I'd seen Enter Shikari play about five times, at some of Teesside's smallest and most DIY shows. Notably, they played at Bar 44, a random top floor dive bar in the quiet town of Guisborough, a show organised by local promoter Weam. My own band had supported Shikari a few times too, and I always knew they'd be massive one day. They were too good, and too unique not to blow up.

It was two months before the release of their debut album, and the height of their initial fame, off of the back of the single Sorry You're Not a Winner. We managed to book the band ourselves for Sumo. This was a massive deal, the band had just graduated to playing Academy's, and tickets to see them were now getting towards £15. We managed to get them to play a show, with a tenner ticket, and we managed to get the licence to do the show all-ages, with a 7.30pm door time. Anyone who was over 18, was able to stay in for Sumo, saving them a fiver entry to the clubnight. It should have been an easy sell, we were very excited to announce it.

This was the first time I witnessed the Boro Apathy for live bands that I came to resent. My unpopular opinion, which was also sadly a true fact, was that there weren't *that* many people in town that would pay to see a rock band. Even though we'd play any one of three Enter Shikari tunes on a Friday night, and 300 people would lose their shit on the dancefloor... no one was buying a ticket to see this band play live.

We had to work our bollocks off to shift the 250 tickets that sold out the room in The Cornerhouse. People complained that it was ten quid. *"We saw Shikari in Guisborough For Four Quid ''* they crowed on Haxed. The regulars and local Shikari fans didn't understand that the band came with a much higher fee these days, and we'd gone out on a limb to bring them this show.

In those early days, we didn't learn, (it took us years and years to learn), that booking amazing hot new live bands was actually a great way to throw money away. We kept booking live shows, hardcore bands, punk bands, metal bands. We gave Boro the absolute finest bands that we could, and we loved it. But I feel we were blind to the fact that only about fifty or so people really gave a fuck.

It never mattered because we'd usually put the bands on as part of the clubnight. So the fifty fans of the act would meld into the other few hundred people who were there to party.

We'd always had top notch bands, and this Shikari show was the first in a long run of epic live shows through 2007 in Sumo. We went in hard, trying to book as many bigger name acts that would consider playing our modest stage within the Cornerhouse. Through Graham and Bryan's booking talents, and our decent relationship with agents from the bigger stages of Music Live Festival and our relationship with the Town Hall and Empire, we had a few agents that would take a chance on our chaotic clubnight show offering.

We followed Enter Shikari with sweaty intimate gigs from The Cribs, Capdown, The Rapture, The View, Howling Bells, Skindred, Daughters, Dan Le Sac and Scroobious Pip, The Noisettes, The Ghost of A Thousand, Frank Turner, Jonah Matranga, Rumblestrips, Little Boots and The Big Pink.

Despite the local apathy and the fact that these gigs were only really turning a few people on, the live bands did give us something new to shout about every week, and slowly but surely, we were winning people over.

I'm grateful for the thousand of pounds Graham ploughed into live bands, as each show dragged fresh faces in, and once we gave them the gig, we gave them Sumo, and they usually came back week on week.

Sumo went nuts in 2008, we'll come to that, and maybe spending all this time, money and graft through 2007 on bands was one of the reasons the night really took it up a notch.

Local Rock Scene Fact : Weam's real name is Dave, and he's a bloody nice guy. Weam stands for Work Experience Administration Man, a role he held at a college for a few years. The nickname stuck.

A 2007 Rock Room Set List

Here's some songs Kev played one Friday in January 2007

Revelation Theory – Slowburn
The Ocean – City in the Sea
Isis – 1000 Shards
A Perfect Circle – Judith
Chevelle – Send the Pain Below
Pig Destroyer – Thumbsucker
Raging Speedhorn – Me & You Man
Useless ID – State of Fear
Slick Shoes – Darko
A Wilhelm Scream – Killing It
The Draft – New Eyes Open
Biffy Clyro – Some Kind of Wizard
Soundgarden – Rusty Cage
Alice in Chains – Man in a Box
Pearl Jam – World Wide Suicide
Stone Temple Pilots – Sex Type Thing
Smashing Pumpkins – Bullet With Butterfly Wings
White Zombie – More Human Than Human
Tool – Sober
Bullet For My Valentine – Tears Don't Fall
Avenged Sevenfold – The Beast & the Harlot
Trivium – The Rising

Helmet – Wilma's Rainbow
Glassjaw – Tip Your Bartender
Deftones – Hole in the Earth
Hundred Reasons – Silver
Thrice – The Artist in the Ambulance
Hell is for Heroes – You Drove Me To It
Weezer – Buddy Holly
Fall Out Boy – This Ain't a Scene….
My Chemical Romance – Famous Last Words
Zebrahead – Anthem
Reel Big Fish – Beer
Jimmy Eat World – A Praise Chorus
Taking Back Sunday – Cute Without the 'E'
The Used – Taste of Ink
Finch – What It Is To Burn
Killswitch Engage – Arms of Sorrow
Stone Sour – 3030150
Slipknot – Before I Forget
Machine Head – Ten Ton Hammer
Enter Shikari – Sorry You're Not A Winner
Funeral for a Friend – Juninho
New Found Glory – My Friends over You
Sugarcult – Bouncing Off the Walls
Lit – My Own Worst Enemy
Sum 41 – Fat Lip
Alien Ant Farm – Smooth Criminal
Good Charlotte – Anthem
Offspring – Want You Bad
Blink 182 – All The Small Things
Less Than Jake – All My Best Friends….
Mad Caddies – Macho Nachos
Goldfinger – Superman
Prodigy – Out of Space

A 2007 ROCK ROOM SET LIST

Pendulum – Slam
Limp Bizkit – Break Stuff
Rage Against the Machine – Bullet in the Head
System of a Down – BYOB
Pantera – I'm Broken
Metallica – For Whom the Bell Tolls
Lostprophets – Shinobi...
Soil – Halo
Drowning Pool – Bodies
Parkway Drive – Romance is Dead
Hatebreed – I Will Be Heard
Throwdown – Raise Your Fist
Comeback Kid – Wake the Dead
Every Time I Die – Kill The Music
Boston – More Than A Feeling
Whitesnake – Here I Go Again
Bon Jovi – Livin on a Prayer
Foo Fighters – Everlong
Fall Out Boy – Saturday
Coheed & Cambria – A Favour House Atlantic
The Movielife – Jamestown
Alexisonfire – Boiled Frogs
Underoath – A Boy Brushed Red...
Panic at the Disco – Camisado
Incubus – A Certain Shade of Green
Red Hot Chilli Peppers – Give it Away
Elvis Presley – Hound Dog

A 2007 Indie Room Setlist

Here's some songs Burnsey played one Friday in January 2007
.

Eskimo Disco – 7/11
The Rapture – Whoo Alright Yeah
Justice v Simian – We Are Your Friends
Eric Prydz V Pink Floyd – Proper Education
Michael Jackson – Beat It
The Gossip – Standing in the Way of Control
Bloc Party – Banquet (Phones remix)
Young Knives – She's Attracted To
Kasabian – Shoot the Runner
Led Zeppelin – Immigrant Song
Automatic – Monster
Yeah Yeah Yeahs – Date With the Night
David Guetta V The Egg – Love Don't Let Me Go
Primal Scream – Country Girl
We Are Scientists – Nobody Move Nobody Get Hurt
Kaiser Chiefs – Everyday I Love You Less & Less
Scissor Sisters – I Don't Feel Like Dancing
Prince V Daft Punk
Hot Chip – Over & Over
Girls Aloud – Love Machine
Lily Allen – LDN
Dizzee Rascal – Fix Up Look Sharp

A 2007 INDIE ROOM SETLIST

Nas - Hip Hop Is Dead
James Brown - Sex Machine
The Coral - Dreaming of You
Razorlight - in the Morning
Interpol - Slow Hands
Housemartins - Happy Hour
The Jam - Going Underground
Zutons - Valerie
Cribs - The Wrong Way To Be
Pipettes - Your Kisses are Wasted on Me
Chemical Brothers - Hey Boy Hey Girl
Bodyrox - Yeah Yeah
Fedde Le Grande - Hands Up For Detroit
Girls Aloud - Something Kinda Ohhh
Rapture - House of Jealous Lovers
Ram Jam - Black Betty
Pendulum - Tarantula
Underworld - Born Slippy
Klaxons - Atlantis to Interzone
Fratellis - Creepin Up the Backstairs
Gogol Bordello - Start Wearing Purple
Pulp - Disco 2000
Kinks - You Really Got Me
The Music - The People
Bob Sinclar - Rock This Party
Jerry Lee Lewis - Great Balls of Fire
Prodigy V Beck
Mylo - Doctor Pressure
Austin Powers Theme
Arctic Monkeys - Mardy Bum
Stevie Wonder - Sir Duke
Rakes - 22 Grand Job
Basement Jaxx - Do Your Thing

Madness - One Step Beyond
Reef - Place your Hands
Fratellis - Chelsea Dagger
Stereokinky - Beatles/Fatboy Slim/Queen
Beatles - Sgt Peppers (LOVE version)
Jamie T - Calm Down Dearest

A 2007 Room 3 Setlist

Here's some songs Henry played in Room 3, in January 2007.

- Huey Lewis and The News - The Power Of Love
- Jazzy Jeff and The Fresh Prince - Boom
- Tears For Fears - Everybody Wants To Rule The World
- Was (Not Was) - Walk The Dinosaur
- Inner Circle - Bad Boys
- Aswad - Shine
- Bomfunk MCs - Freestylers
- Phil Collins - Sussudio
- Madonna - Into The Groove
- Michael Jackson - Thriller
- Coolio - Gangsta's Paradise
- Rednex - Cotton Eye Joe
- Faltermayer - Axel F
- The Four Tops - Loco In Acapulco
- Bugsy Malone - Bad Guys
- Devo - Whip It
- Prefab Sprout - King Of Rock 'n' Roll
- Cyndi Lauper - Girls Just Wanna Have Fun
- California Dreams - Main Theme
- Tiffany - I Think We're Alone Now
- Kelly Marie - Feels Like I'm In Love
- Starship - Nothing's Gonna Stop Us Now...

Michael Jackson – Beat It
Phil Collins – Easy Lover
Kool And The Gang – Jungle Boogie
Starship – We Built This City
Madness – Baggy Trousers
Dexy's Midnight Runners – Come On Eileen
Glenn Frey – The Heat Is On
Men At Work – Down Under
Theme from Ghostbusters
Theme from The Raccoons
Bill Medley and Jennifer Warnes – (I've Had) The Time Of My Life
Survivor – Eye Of The Tiger
Theme from Fresh Prince
Bugsy Malone – You Give A Little Love
Tremeloes – Young Girl

Chop Chop

In March 2007, we launched a rock night at a bar called Blue.

Blue was situated above a club called Basement, which was the old Blaises building. There was a bit of rock heritage there, and we felt that we could surely get a Saturday night going in town, and give Sumo a little brother.

Myself and my Ten Feet Tall colleague Martin spearheaded Chop Chop. Martin was a local promoter who, along with his mates, had been putting some very cool rock shows on in town for a while. Martin had been helping out with Sumo, and the likes of him and Jamie became essential as we were about to begin messing about in Durham too.

Chop Chop looked so fucking cool, it's worth a notable mention, despite the fact it spectacularly flopped after about ten weeks. TFT designer Marty gave the promo a Mexican twist; everything was yellow and red, and the artwork and decor featured luchador wrestlers. We adorned the venue with vaguely Mexican decor, complete with about fifty cacti, which we'd painstakingly arrange on the back of the bar every Saturday before doors. We added some Sumo style pieces and Pac-Man games on mini TVs. Martin set about booking and running plenty of gigs from there. I've no idea how he got Glamour of The Kill and a few other bigger names to play. I hope those bands saw the funny side of playing these funny little bars.

Chop Chop started just as the UK smoking ban came into effect. It's hard to believe that people just smoked inside clubs, at bars, and on dancefloors. I wasn't going to miss coming home stinking of smoke, with fag burns down my arms, but the alternative was possibly worse.

The smoke in the nightclubs was actually blocking out the other smells. Disinfectant and farts. That's basically what nightclubs smell of, and as soon as the smokers were put outside, everyone realised; nightclubs stink.

The venue, Blue, didn't have any sort of decent smoking zone, so the punters were just out the front on the pavement. The venue shared its pavement with the other Saturday event that took place in Basement. This dance and house music night had an older crowd, everyone was sucking on laughing gas balloons, popping pills and generally being arseholes. These two crowds didn't mix well, and the numbers at Chop Chop dropped too low. We canned it before numbers dropped to zero. RIP Chop Chop. I always kind of liked you.

I'm Sad I Missed The Wedding

Fridays were Sumo. That was life. That's what the flyer said. Friday is Sumo Day.

And so, Friday afternoons were Sumo Set Up. If we weren't in the office scheming, or running around the streets promoting, then it was Friday and it was set up day.

We took our time, and for years The A-Team; of Kim, Jamie, Gary, Martin, Rick, Jess, and many others gave up their Friday afternoons to build Sumo up, and make the venue look like a welcome party full of daftness.

I had this great team, but as they'd tell you, I couldn't help myself - and even if there was plenty of them, with a carefully crafted to-do list, I was still usually hanging about, tweaking things, up a ladder with some cable ties, making a dressing room look pretty, or just making lists on my phone of stuff I noticed that needed fixing. We'd usually end up driving to B and Q or Boyes twice on a Friday afternoon to gather supplies and make sure everything was just perfect for the Friday night.

So one Friday, I had been invited to my mates Brian and Sarah's wedding. Now at this point, I hadn't been to many weddings. I had no sense of wedding etiquette that I learned years later. I'd planned to leave the Cornerhouse at around 12pm, leave the team to it, and get myself to the wedding venue for 1pm. Easy.

For whatever reason, sods law, none of The A-Team were available that day to help. The B Team who were helping me that day, bailed. Hangovers, sleeping in, whatever. That's why they were The B Team

With my helpers too hungover to even leave their pits, I was on my own frantically sprinting around the venue setting everything up. 1pm rolled around and I figured I wasn't going to make it for the ceremony so I just kept going and thought I could just turn up for the night-time reception, no one would miss me. So as 7pm rolled around, I was somehow still at The Cornerhouse, finally packing away ladders and finishing things off. I knew I had to be back at Sumo for 11pm anyway, so I decided that going home to eat and shower was what was needed. After all, I had a 6 hour night shift ahead of me. Plus I had a few little finishing touches that I figured, if I got back to Cornerhouse for say 10pm, I could get done before doors.

The window of time in which I could drive over and show my face at this wedding had gotten so narrow, it wasn't worth going at all. I pinged my friends a quick text; "Sorry I didn't make it over guys, hope everyone had a nice day!" and I guessed that was fine.

It wasn't fine. A wedding is the most important day in someone's life, and bailing on it is super-shitty. Sorry Sarah, sorry Brian.

There was one empty seat in the room that day, and all my mates would have looked at it and rolled their eyes. Plus the fact, as I now know, wedding seats are a privilege, and I took a place that could have been someone else's, and Sarah's family will have paid about £50 for my meal, which will have gone in the bin.

Can you believe I didn't just do this once, I did it again, at another mate's wedding, and again, and again. Missing countless 30th birthdays, engagement parties, new years do's, leaving parties and homecomings.

The point here is that Sumo had taken over my life. Sumo wasn't just the number one priority; it was the only one.

I most certainly lost a few good mates, people I'd spent every weekend with since college gradually stopped asking me if I wanted to go hang out. Friday was Sumo day, Saturday became a show day or Metropolis day, or something else. My weekends gradually became a few hours on a Sunday. No violins here, I pretty much loved it for the most part, in the early days.

It feels like I got caught in the moment, and that moment lasted about ten years.

Side Note : Dear Marvin, I know I missed your wedding too. This wasn't Sumo's fault, it was mine alone. When I received your invite, I put the date in my diary wrong. A stupid yet somehow honest mistake. I was so certain it was on a Saturday. Who gets married on a Wednesday anyway? I was in Scarborough with Ian and Kev for a gig with our band No School Reunion. We were supporting The Undertones, we'd just soundchecked and we were getting fish and chips, when people started texting and phoning me, asking where the fuck I was. I'm an idiot.

I'm Ron Burgundy?

A Tuesday in 2007

We booked out a full cinema screen from the local Cineworld, rented Anchorman from the BFI and gave away free tickets to our little movie party, at Sumo.

We billed it as the Sumo Field Trip, and made sure everyone got free sweets and complimentary drinks from the cinema (we pre-paid for about £500 worth). Myself and the team acted as ushers in the foyer, we showed everyone to their seats, and gave them some free Sumo goodies too. We even had DJ Dani there, pushing round the sweets trolley, dishing out bottles of pop. Yet another string to his bow there.

This totally unnecessary party cost us about a grand, and purely served the purpose of entertaining the Sumo tribe, and creating a nice warm feeling. I guess it also made everyone like us, and come give us their money every Friday night too. Naive young me probably didn't see that at the time.

We planned loads more of these Sumo field trips, but sadly never got round to making them happen. As time went on, getting people to the *actual* Sumo became the priority.

Side Note : I distinctly remember Graham walking over to my desk in the office a few weeks after this event and saying he'd just watched Anchorman for the first time, as I'd frequently told him it's the funniest film of all time.

He told me he hadn't laughed once, and that he didn't understand why anyone would think it was funny.

Sumo Durham

As Sumo in Middlesbrough began to blossom into a weekly beast, we found we needed to do less and less in order to keep the massive momentum. It had become a well oiled machine, with Jamie, Martin and Gary from Ten Feet Tall all doing a grand job of steering the Sumo Boro ship, it meant I was free to try and get another Sumo going.

Graham had been scouring other unfashionable northern towns for a place that had no rock night, and a venue that could host one. He found Studio, in Durham, on North Road.

Such were our ambitions and confidence at the time, we figured we might as well get two nights on the go, while we were there in the new city. Friday's were to be Rock and Alt, in two rooms, and named Sumo, with me at the helm. Saturday's were indie and pop, with the TFT indie team taking the lead, and we called them Betamax. We had a new recruit named Jodie in the ranks, and she was tasked with getting these new Saturdays up and running.

We stuck to the formula, and filled the venue with decor, drapes, branding, projections and promised the venue some occasional touring bands.

Our artwork was like nothing the city of Durham had seen before, and there weren't even any other rock nights to compete with. There was a huge university crowd, whom we flyered the life out of, we'd identified a good few sixth form colleges, and we flyered the life out of them too. The promo had Sumo on one side, and Betamax on the flipside. So we were offering something for everyone, and there seemed to be young, cool, clubnight type people on every street, so we assumed this would be a breeze.

We launched in April 2007 and we spent every day for four weeks leading up to the launch night flyering in Durham city centre and on the campuses. We didn't have enough flyer staff to spare for every single day, so we ended up begging and bribing everyone we knew to come and promote with us.

I remember one strange day when Graham had drafted in DJ Munro to come and flyer with us. Munro's a very well respected dance DJ, who has worked with the likes of Beverly Knight and David Bowie. God knows why he agreed to come and dish out Betamax flyers for the day, but I remember his Geordie accent bellowing across the bridge at the throngs of students *"Come to Sumo, take a flyer, free Pot Noodle with every flyer"*.

We didn't have any Pot Noodles, but he seemed to be having fun.

At the time, we also had a girl called Anne French doing some part time work for us in the office, doing some press for the bands we were booking. Firstly, Anne was a great copywriter; secondly, she was a UK Playboy model.

Anne had agreed to work the reception at Sumo in Durham, and she joined Munro and me for the day handing out flyers and putting up posters where we could. With the North East's most famous Rnb DJ, and a six foot tall model by my side, it was certainly the strangest day out promoting I'd had to date.

The team I assembled for Durham starred new fella Dani (as the rock DJ), Kaboom's Fashion Fil (as the room 2 DJ), Trudie (Danielle's trusted bestie on photos), plus two great event reps Cat and Anne to host.

When my future wife and one-off Sumo Boro warmup DJ Claire confessed that she didn't actually own any music and *'just borrowed all my mate's CDs'*, I was introduced to this mate. That's how I met Dani. Dani became a regular DJ at Bar Sumo, the Sumo pre-bar in Middlesbrough, that would soon change its name to Uncle Alberts. Keeping up? Good.

Dani was enlisted to DJ Durham when Kev and Craig said they didn't fancy it. We had a few other DJs on rotation including myself, and a great local lad called Jack. Dani did the majority of the Durham sets, he became a close mate, and (handily) he was a really, really good DJ.

We kicked things off in Durham with a decent start, we'd have about 200 through the door, most people were there for the rock room, and a few were heading up to the top floor for our mash-up of indie, pop and hip hop. Fashion Fil did a tremendous job.

The venue manager was a portly gent called Paul. I've avoided surnames throughout this book, but Paul's surname was Potts. Paul Potts was also the name of a bloke who sang opera who had just won X Factor, the biggest show on TV. I found it hilarious and also a bit spooky that this Paul Potts looked a bit like Paul Potts - and shared the same name.

Paul did not find it funny nor spooky.

Like all the club managers I've worked with, Paul was a proper character. He would constantly ask me what I was doing, standing around, and why I wasn't out flyering. I told him it was 1am, and the promotion had already been done. He seemed to think I could double the numbers of the event if I went out into the night, and dragged people in. Despite pestering locals in places like The Angel rock pub, and flyering a few stragglers outside the forty-capacity Fish Tank venue round the corner, there was not a soul on the streets of Durham. In fact, we would soon discover that 200 people were just about everyone in the whole city that would consider partying with us, but in the early days, we remained optimistic.

The live shows we put on as part of Sumo in Durham went well, the city loved the live band element, and we hosted packed out shows from The Rumblestrips, Kubichek, St Louis rockers Bullets n Octane and even managed to secure a gig with fast rising stars The Pigeon Detectives. The latter band's debut album had just dropped and they were one of the hottest bands in the UK at that time. They arrived in a huge tour bus that we had serious trouble getting parked anywhere near the tiny venue on the narrow cobbled streets of the North Road area. The show had sold out weeks in advance, and Paul Potts told me that he'd taken about a hundred frantic phone calls that day from people begging to buy a ticket to see the band. As the queue started to snake around the venue, it seemed there were a lot of people out there without tickets, hoping to just get a glimpse of the band.

There was a bar underneath the venue that hosted our clubnight, which was also owned by Studio.

Paul had an idea.

He approached me and pitched it; He said he could set up a camera in the upstairs room of Sumo in Studio, where the Pigeon Detectives would be playing. He could feed the video signal down to the bar, and play the gig on the TV screens in the bar. He suggested we could charge £5 a head for people to go in the bar, and watch the show on these screens. I looked at Paul and I was about to laugh, I thought he was joking. He was deadly serious. I asked him how people would *hear* the show, he said that didn't matter.

I politely told Paul that I thought that was something we should not do. He told me to run it past the band. I didn't. I told Paul that I did, and they forbid it. I mean, I assume they would, right?

My weekly trips to Durham were a bit of an endurance test. I'd set off around 6pm to pick up Fil and Dani, load their cases of CDs into my car and we'd head up to Durham for around 8pm. I'd park my car at the top of the hill near the Angel and we'd head down the steep bank past the Fish Tank to Studio.

Dani and Fil would help me set the club up for a couple of hours. Trudie would take the train over and join us around 10pm, I'd jog to the train station to meet her and walk her back to the venue. We'd run our Sumo show, and at 3am, the gang would help me pack everything away and we'd say our goodbyes to the bar staff and Paul who were mopping up and restocking fridges ready for the following night.

Our tired legs would drag CD cases up the cobbled bank, we'd grab some chips from the takeaway, and I'd drive everyone home. I insisted on dropping everyone at their doors, so Dani and Fil would get delivered to Middlesbrough, and I'd take Trudie home to Redcar. Then I'd get back home around 5am.

Saturdays were a bit busier than Fridays, and Jodie had found a new guy in town called Chris who started helping with the Durham promo, and he also did a little DJing too. Chris eventually became very much part of the Ten Feet Tall family and if you've ever been to a jam packed Saturday Night in Middlesbrough Empire, along with thousands of other regulars, it's been Chris on the Decks pretty regularly for the last decade. At this point in his life, he was stomping around Durham with me, sticking Sumo stickers on bus stops.

Jodie and I teamed up on promo missions, her with the Betamax Saturdays stuff and me with Sumo. We spent many a week blu tac-ing posters and stacking piles of flyers into every corner of Durham we could find. We rinsed Durham to death and moved on to Newton Aycliffe, Stanley and Bishop Auckland. We soon realised that the sleepy run down villages were a waste of time, but we felt like we had to do them all, at least once a fortnight, just in case some young restless mosher or indie kid happened to be walking past a butcher shop window in Chester-le-street.

We'd planned to spend the day in Spennymoor, promoting our clubnights, and we quickly discovered that this wasn't going to take a whole day. By 11am we'd got a poster in a guitar shop window, some flyers in the hairdressers, and Spennymoor felt well and truly done. I had a vague memory from my childhood that there was a swimming pool in Spennymoor, with slides and a wave machine. I mentioned it to Jodie, and she insisted we must find it, and go for a swim. We scoured the town for a place that sold swimming kits, and found a local Woolworths. Jodie bought a bright yellow one piece and I found some swimming shorts for a fiver. We bought two towels, and we were in business.

It's no wonder Sumo Durham never worked out, when the promoters spent their days diving into the waves of the wave machine and flying down the waterslides in Spennymoor leisure centre.

My First Frank Turner Story

Friday 10th August 2007

We had the honour of folk rock troubadour Frank Turner playing a solo show at Sumo in Durham. Henry, our Room 3 DJ in Boro, had started doing a bit more work for Ten Feet Tall and was turning out to be a pretty great band booker for us. He also picked out a great local act to support too, The Small Screen Lightshow.

Frank soundchecked around 6pm, and sat drinking tea with us while we set up the club. As we worked he asked us if we had any requests. My good friend Simon was on sound that night and asked for Back For Good by Take That. Probably as a bit of a piss take.

Frank just picked up his guitar and strummed and sang it out, note perfect without missing a beat. He's good like that.

As we hung out, Trudie took a few snaps. There's a great shot of Franks guitar propped against the monitor that she took, which can be seen on the cover of his DVD "All About The Destination".

We had a weekly offer running at Sumo in Durham at this time, it was £2 entry for the first hour, then it went up to a fiver. Of course, this bargain basement price was only for the clubnight and didn't apply to the early-doors gigs.

To cover the additional costs and the artist fees, gigs were priced separately, and this show was a £12 ticket on the door. We had hundreds of people outside, and as doors opened, everyone flooded in, nice and early, to bag a good spot to watch Frank's set.

It was as the room filled up that something awful dawned on me. I hadn't told the girl at the reception the door price.

I raced to the door, and asked her what she'd been charging people to come in.

"£2, same as always, right?".

My heart sank. I had 250 people in, who'd all paid £2 each. So just £500 in the till.

Frank's fee, the invoice for the PA system, and all my staff's wages came in at around two grand. I was fucked.

I called Graham, confessed my sins, and he said don't worry about it, shit happens. We agreed that anything like this would never happen again, and he graciously set about making bank transfers to people. Some bosses would have told me to get my arse to the cash machine, but he just took it on the chin, thankfully for me and my shitty bank balance.

Rock Fact : A very young Matty Vant, who was the singer from The Small Screen Lightshow, is now a successful solo artist, by the name of VANT. you should check him out, he's great.

Goodbye Durham

It was almost a year into our adventures in Durham when we started to realise we just couldn't seem to get more than 150 regulars at either of our weekly events. The Durham university students were too high class to think about coming 'down North Road' for a night out. So they told us. The college kids just didn't seem into it, and the rock fraternity of the city just seemed a little older, and happy in their cosy pub seats. The idea of jumping round to loud as fuck rock until 3am just didn't seem to catch on.

Jodie's Saturdays weren't doing much better and I could see the end was in sight. It was an expensive operation to run, and without more feet through the doors, we couldn't keep going for much longer. This was a shame as there was a new manager at the venue, a young lad called Micheal. He was 25, handsome as hell, a really lovely, funny lad.

It was a Tuesday afternoon and Jodie and I had been up to Durham to do some promotion. I was driving back, when Jodie got the phone call to tell us that Micheal had died.

He'd worked four nights on the bounce at Studio, over the bank holiday. He'd started his Easter run of shifts on the Thursday night, I'd worked with him on the Friday and Jodie on the Saturday. After his shift on the Sunday, he'd driven home at around 4am, and drove his car straight into a roundabout coming off the A1. The theory was, he'd fallen asleep at the wheel.

This rocked us all. We all did those late drives, we all worked daft hours, no one took breaks, and none of us thought something like this would ever happen, but it did.

It affected all of us. He was just like us, and had his whole life ahead of him. We all slowed down a little after that, and took more care of ourselves a bit. RIP Mike, I didn't know you that long, but I often think about what happened..

My Noisettes Story

Noisettes were fucking great. Led by a wild lead singer and bassist, Shingai Shoniwa, they played Cornerhouse in 2007 and then shortly after, played our Saturday night at Empire. The band were ready to go onstage, it was around midnight. You had to go down a flight of steps from the backstage dressing rooms to get on the stage. The guys in the band headed downstairs and walked on stage, but Shingai walked upstairs.

Walking upstairs from the dressing rooms goes pretty much nowhere, to a locked door of a storeroom. But as I followed her up there, she was nowhere to be seen. Like a magic trick, she'd vanished into thin air.

Then I noticed the hatch. The small wooden hatch in the ceiling was open. I hoisted myself up and shone the torchlight from my phone into the darkness.

Shingai had crawled along and found herself inside a gigantic void, above the stage. She sat giggling like a maniac in the dark. She wouldn't listen to my pleadings so I left her to go check on the band. They'd already started the first song and were jamming away on stage.

The guitarist walked over and yelled in my ear as he played. *"Where is she?!"*

I pointed at the ceiling, *"she's in there"*

"*Where?!*" He asked

"*In the walls... like... in between the walls*" I replied.

"*Oh, ok*"

They kept riffing for around five minutes until the star of the show finally appeared in the wings, slightly dusty. She grabbed the mic and tore into the opening number. I mean thank god she found her way out. I'm just grateful I didn't need to crawl in there and get her.

My Sheilas Story

Fri 29th June 2007

When you're a super cool rock clubnight promoter, every day you get Emails from agents, offering you trash pop acts. I'm told it happens to all of us, and I don't know how I ended up on these mailing lists, but these agencies would ping me weekly, with offers of club appearances by faded pop stars, C list celebs and random TV personalities. The type of event these acts get booked for is typically student unions and bars where they show up, mime a few songs, or pretend to DJ for an hour, then pose for photos, sign some autographs then collect their whopping fee.

In my experience, a fantastic up and coming band, who have got a little late night Radio 1 play, a great buzz, and will bring a full-throttle live show to your clubnight will be about £500-700. One of these random celeb appearances will cost two or three times more than that. It just wasn't my scene. However, there's a fine line, where the more random, kitsch or cult celebs are certainly worth a conversation with.

Notably a few years back a promoter I know booked The Chuckle Brothers and then took them on a whirlwind tour around indie nights, rock nights, and clubs across the country. They went down a storm. It just worked.

We'd had an Email letting us know that The Sheila's were doing a tour of the UK. For anyone who has forgotten, The Sheilas were the trio of Australian ladies who sang a song on a UK Car insurance advert. Sheilas Wheels was a women-only car insurance company and the uber-catchy song from the advert went as follows;

> *For ladies who insure their cars,*
> *Sheilas' Wheels are superstars,*
> *Girls are bored beyond endurance,*
> *Payin' too much for car insurance,*
> *For bonzer car insurance deals,*
> *Girls get onto Sheilas' Wheels.*
> *Women make the safest drivers,*
> *We could save a bunch of fivers,*
> *For bonzer car insurance deals,*
> *Girls get onto Sheilas' Wheels.*

We were in the midst of booking a slew of cool rock shows into Sumo, and having The Sheilas on our listings just seemed too funny and too random not to go ahead and do it. Plus, they were only £400.

I mean, why the hell not?

The Sheilas were three of the most friendly, warm and affable people I've ever met. They arrived at Sumo on the night of their show about an hour before doors, pulling three small pink suitcases on wheels, which contained their stage dresses, some hair care bits and make up. We'd constructed a wildly inappropriate dressing room area in the club's cellar and gave them a quick tour of the ratty stage and grungey club in which they were about to perform. They handed us a CD of four songs which made up their set, and they soundchecked, singing live, over the CD. The set started with 'The Theme from Sheila's Wheels', followed by two Motown classics, then ended, ten minutes later, with 'The Theme From Sheilas Wheels'.

We told them they'd be on stage at around midnight, and they headed to their makeshift dressing room to fix their hair and make up.

When we had a band or an act on, I usually had a wingman running Sumo and tonight Jamie was on hand to look after the Sheilas so that I could run about sorting the clubnight stuff, and he could ensure the girls were happy, got on stage on time, got paid and got out unscathed.

I witnessed The Sheilas set, and they went down a storm, it was the perfect show for Sumo. It was very loud, very pink and very daft. We should have done more shows like this one. It wouldn't have harmed us, it would have worked.

When I'd finished shoving the stage away and helped pack up the PA system, I went to check on Jamie to see if he'd paid The Sheilas. The girls were sitting drinking champagne with Jamie and a big gang of regulars. They seemed to be having a whale of a time. Jamie was covered in red lipstick and blushing. He explained that when they came off stage, one of the girls had some texts from Pete Waterman, confirming details of a record deal they were negotiating. The legendary trio of hitmakers Stock, Aitken and Waterman had just announced they were regrouping, and their first project upon reuniting was going to be The Sheilas.

This was probably the absolute pinnacle of that group's success and undoubtedly will have been the single most important text message of their entire careers. I'm glad Jamie (who co-ran Sumo with me for years in the early days) was there to celebrate with them in style.

Once Upon A Time In Hartlepool

Throughout my time at Ten Feet Tall, there were plenty of clubnights that we tried and failed. For every roaring success, with weekly crowds, there were a good few duds, some of which only lasted a few weeks.

Right before we launched Sumo at The Cornerhouse, we had a proper good go at cracking Hartlepool.

It was June 2005, and we'd hoped that Hartlepool, with its multiple colleges, must surely have a few hundred 18 to 19 year olds up for a party on a weekend. We'd discovered Jax Bar, a quirky venue with a large upstairs room that was off the beaten track and seemed to serve well as a place we could house a DJ and some live bands too.

We set our stall out as Fridays being Rock, and Saturday being Indie, and in true TFT fashion, we threw everything at all. We posted our plan all over Haxed, we tried to get the internet excited, and we papered Hartlepool with Posters and flyers. There was nowhere near the buzz that we experienced with Sumo, but we went in guns blazing anyway.

For this first clutch of Hartlepool Fridays, we booked a string of decent bands and local rock DJs that thought would do the trick. I had an absolute trial by fire for a few weeks learning to be a stage manager as I went along. The crowd was super-apathetic, usually sitting around, arms folded in baggy jeans with beanies and baseball caps pulled down over their eyes.

Everyone in this town seemed to wear a hat. There were a handful of punks and emos and some skaters, no real metalheads to be seen. We grinned and bared it through sparsely attended shows (which were fucking great) by The Sound Explosion, DARTZ! and Reggie and The Full Effect. The latter show was particularly bizarre, with the band playing to around 15 die-hard fans, who obviously could not believe their eyes that Reggie and The Full Effect were playing in their hometown of Hartlepool.

We'd also successfully booked the latest MySpace hype band, Bring Me The Horizon to come and play. At 5pm on the day of that show, as I waited for the band to arrive from Sheffield, their singer Oli text me to say sorry, they had a flat tyre, so they wouldn't make it. I phoned Henry, and asked his band to fill the slot. So the Hartlepudlians got DARTZ! instead of BMTH that night. No one seemed to mind.

Jax Bar was situated on the corner of a shopping centre, and the only way to load into the room where the stage was, was to follow a maintenance path up to the actual roof of the shopping centre and load in through a fire door near the ventilation turrets. It was a surreal experience putting the band's kit back in the van and looking out across the rooftops of the town and its new marina in the distance.

On one of the last Fridays we bothered with in terms of the rock night, we'd booked Radio One's Mike Davies to see whether a credible celeb DJ would drag the moshers of Hartlepool out the house and get up for a dance. We were very, very wrong.

About ten kids showed up for Mike Davies' set. We had a warm-up DJ cover the early part of the night, and Mike and I sat in a suitably dire dressing room chatting shit until it was time for his set. Walking Mike Davies to the tiny DJ booth, to play System of a Down songs to ten people who were sat down, was a career highlight. I can't even remember what we called that Friday night clubnight. It was embarrassing, and I'd kind of erased it from my memory until it came to writing this book.

Saturdays at Jax however, we're banging. A slew of packed sweaty intimate gigs from the likes of Revered and The Makers and The Pigeon Detectives had set the bar pretty high and we had TFT's finest DJs playing to a decent crowd every Saturday. We'd arranged some celeb DJ sets, despite the Mike Davies incident. Maximo Park's Paul Smith came and did a set, and the town was especially hyped by our latest booking at the time - The Libertines' Carl Barat was set to play, and I was put in charge of making sure Carl was well looked after for the duration of the event.

I pulled up at The Grand Hotel, where Carl was booked in for the night, to collect him and take him to the venue for a soundcheck. I rang the phone number I'd been given, and a lady answered. She explained she was Carl's girlfriend, Annalisa, and that she DJ'd with him, and I was probably best dealing with her. I had my current girlfriend with me along for the ride. She was a big Libertines fan.

My girlfriend and I walked in the hotel foyer and met Annalisa, she said Carl was around somewhere, and we should grab a seat. There was a wedding in full swing at the hotel, and Carl had joined in with their celebrations. He was having a whale of a time chatting with the bride and groom, entertaining guests regaling some tales of rock and roll and enjoying a bottle of red wine. As Annalisa pulled Carl away from his fans, we jumped in my 1994 Honda Civic and drove to Jax.

When we got to the venue, my Missus showed Carl to the dressing room while Annalisa gave the DJ equipment a good check over and blasted out a few tunes. On returning to the dressing room, Carl was getting stuck into the rider, and as no one was DJing until past 11pm, we all sat, chatted, and drank. I never hung around in dressing rooms with acts, but Carl and Annalisa said we should stay, and tell them about the local area, and insisted we help them drink through the generous pile of beers and spirits that Ten

Feet Tall had supplied.

As the driver, and on a promise by my boss to deliver Carl safely back to his hotel at 3am, I couldn't help demolish the drinks. Annalisa also took it easy, as DJ duty awaited her. My girlfriend and Carl got absolutely smashed. When the time for the DJ set came around, I helped Carl fight his way through 300 pairs of grabby indie fan hands. The Hartlepool indie boys really really wanted to touch Carl. He smiled, signed stuff, posed for photos and shook all 300 hands over the next hour or two. No wonder his lady friend had to take on the job of swapping CDs every 3 minutes.

Side Note : I'll be honest, I have a very sketchy memory, and I had to fact-check this on online and with friends multiple times – I have memories of all this happening at Jax bar in Hartlepool, but I can't believe it happened right before, and during, us launching Sumo. They seem like totally separate worlds in my memory, not one. I guess when Sumo took off in Boro, and Hartlepool wasn't really doing the numbers, Hartlepool just got forgotten, and dropped.

Kev Sumo

I'd like to take this moment to mention Kev Sumo. As you know, Kev, along with Craig, was one of the two original Sumo DJs. He's a quiet lad, he doesn't go wild on social media, and as a DJ he stays very focused on the job in hand; playing the very best mix of songs to get a dancefloor, and *keep* a rock dancefloor raging. It's a talent.

You know those DJs in clubs, that are wannabe MCs, that get on the microphone and chat shit, shout out to birthday people, introduce songs, and generally ruin the whole night by yelling stuff like;

"Put your hands in the air and scream! You having a good time tonight?! This tracks gonna blow the roof off, come on guys, ARE YOU WITH MEEEEE?!".

Well, Kev is the literal opposite of that DJ.

Perhaps because of his so-laid-back-he-is-horizontal demeanour, he has occasionally slipped into the background of Sumos' life story, which is something I needed to rectify. For reasons that will become apparent later on in this epic story, I need to say that Kev (along with Craig and Dani) has very much shaped the core of Sumo, with his musical selections since the very first day. He was the DJ at the first Sumo, he was the DJ at the last Sumo.

When I was running around launching Durham, Sunderland, AVM, Bad

Med, or having children, and generally "not being there" for Sumo in Middlesbrough, he was a constant rock in the storm, always having his eyes open, and always in my ear, keeping me right.

Every stupid idea I had for Sumo, I ran it past the calm, collected brain of Kev first. And when I literally bailed and quit Sumo in its final years, Kev stayed on and, with a few other crewmates, helped steer a ship when it had no captain, or probably felt like it didn't even have a rudder.

When Sumo was at its lowest points and sailing so close to sinking, he kept it afloat.

Kev's 'done' more Sumos than anyone, even me. DJ's are the lynchpin to a clubnight. They are the sole reason they will succeed or fail. The venue can be a shithole, the beer can be warm, the bar staff can be rude, but if the DJ's dead right, you'll be fine.

The Friday night DJ team in Middlesbrough of Kev, Dani, Craig, Ste, Henry and Fil, and the Saturday night DJs in Middlesbrough of Chris, Burnsey and Foy (and Ste again) are probably the most talented team of indie/rock/pop DJs in the entire country, and Boro is so lucky to have them.

Skid Row

Friday 16th November 2007

We got an email from an agent offering us Skid Row.

If you don't know Skid Row, they're a band from New Jersey, formed in 1986. They've sold over twenty million records and, in their day, toured the world on a rollercoaster of sex, drugs and rock and roll alongside the likes of Guns n' Roses and Aerosmith.

They're a big deal.

To come and play Sumo in Middlesbrough, something that the world never thought would happen, their fee was £2000. Usually, there's a bit of haggling on an artist fee. Both the agent and we knew this was a bit of a bargain for such a cult act.

Even though the band hadn't released anything noteworthy for over a decade, it didn't matter. I desperately wanted to book the band. Skid Row had been a massive part of my formative years as I discovered rock and metal at around age 14. The idea of these iconic rockers performing Youth Gone Wild, Eighteen and a Life and their other anthems in the Cornerhouse would be insane.

Graham and I did the math.

Skid row £2000, PA system £350, Lights £150, Load Crew £80, Rider £100, Print £100, Flyer team £100, Ads £100, Support £50. So it's going to cost three grand.

What would the good people of Boro realistically pay for a ticket to see Skid Row? About ten quid.

How many people from Boro would realistically come and see skid row? About 200?

It just didn't stack up.

But Graham, as always, had a glint in his eye *"we have to do it, we just have to"*.

So, we booked the show.

I guess it's what they call a loss leader, and luckily for Sumo and me, Graham really believed in them. Sure this gig was going to lose a thousand pounds minimum, but we made sure that the whole world knew Skid fucking Row were playing at Sumo.

The show was insane, and the band loved the "scuzzy little venue", they partied hard with the crowd into the small hours afterwards. The show became the stuff of legend, and things like this became the essence of what Sumo was all about.

We wanted to give people the unexpected, do things that no one believed we would do, hit them with surprise after surprise, and keep trying to outdo ourselves. We wanted Sumo to be cult, to be cool, and it was outlandish stunts like booking bands that were off the charts, or throwing parties that were so stupid, that people would talk about it for years to come.

Ultimately this was the reason Sumo would soon take the leap from a Rock Night with 300 regulars, to a complete beast, and a Boro institution that would reach over a thousand attendees a week.

The Glory Years (2008 - 2009)

In 2008, it felt like we were launching a zillion things, and Sumo had hit fever pitch. Through 2008 and 2009, Fridays at Sumo were THE event in Middlesbrough. Nothing came close to it in terms of electric atmosphere, flamboyant theme parties, three or four eclectic alternative music policies, and 1200 people squeezed into the 800 capacity Cornerhouse. It felt unstoppable. These were the Sumo glory years.

The Ladhar group had purchased a bar opposite the Cornerhouse called Vienna, and under our influence called it Bar Sumo. It was the official Sumo pre-bar, and we gave them Jamie and Dani as DJs, and those guys also hosted and set the venue up every Friday with a few Sumo style tweaks, to attract our crowd in for early doors drinks. Nintendo's and Playstations were strapped to the end of the bar, and the music policy was a mix of rock and indie, all the songs you wanted to request in Sumo, that were a bit too weird, Jamie and Dani would play.

We also got a little budget to book every local band that wanted a slot. The pre-bar gave the Sumo experience an extra dimension and only added to the pull and the hype of Sumo being the only destination for a night out on a weekend in Middlesbrough.

Here's the odd thing, dear reader - I know these were the glory years, everyone tells me it was prime time Sumo, and I know from records that we were putting those numbers in week in week out. I would sit every Friday at 3am counting between £5000 and £6000 door money into the safe. However – I have very few other memories of what the actual fuck was happening in Sumo each week through those two years.

As always seemed to be the way, I was pulled from pillar to post, from Empire's Saturdays to midweek Bad Medicine, to the ever-growing Middlesbrough Music Live Festival. There were plenty of things that Phil was needed for. Thankfully, I had a solid gold team of Jamie, Martin, Gary and more, keeping things chugging along through these hazy days. I was still in there most Fridays through 2008 and 2009, but we'd stopped booking so many live bands, eased off on Sumo Fests, and we began recycling our theme party ideas. So these glory years have blurred in my memory into one big mush. And what a bloody lovely mush it was.

Like A Motherfucker From Hell

Friday 28th October 2008

New Zealand's finest, The Datsuns, played Sumo. It's in my top three gigs ever. The Datsuns are not the most famous band in the world right now. But at that particular little moment in time, it felt like we had the coolest four guys on the planet, in our little clubnight, in Middlesbrough.

They'd released a couple of singles, Harmonic Generator and MF From Hell, that had bothered the UK Top 40, and recently toured with The Pixies and Velvet Revolver. The timing was impeccable; they were front-page news, clubs and radio played their songs weekly. The hype and the fervour for the show was real.

When it came to stage time, the packed out crowd was like a massive pack of baying dogs, literally chomping at the bit. The roar when the guys walked on the stage felt deafening. Three hundred mesmerised souls screaming in a concrete tunnel under Boro train station.

There were a handful of other shows at Sumo Cornerhouse that reached this fever pitch intensity, Little Boots, The Big Pink and Dan Le Sac Vs Scroobius Pip all took to that little stage at the height of their debut tracks breaking in the UK.

The thing about the Datsuns show for me, was that it was the one show that I really felt brought together all of the different clans that inhabited Sumo.

Friday's at The Cornerhouse was made up of some almost-stereotypical gangs. You had the metal heads, goths, the punks and emos. You had the drum n bass kids, electro heads. There were glamorous girls, grunge guys and a new wave of eyeliner indie boys with skin tight jeans and winkle pickers. As I cast my eyes across the crowd that were heaving up against our little steel barrier, every single one of these boxes got ticked. It was like the whole Sumo-goer family had shown up to worship at The Datsuns altar. They bounced, they sang, they crowd surfed, they were absolutely crazy. The band ended their set with a triple-barrelled blast of In Love, Harmonic Generator and MF From Hell.

All those different people, eyes fixated on the stage, no phones, no cameras, just humans, together as one, three hundred voices screaming in unison; *"LIKE A MOTHER FUCKER FROM HELL"*.

The ID Problem

Towards the end of 2009, just as we were doing everything right, the local council and local licensing police seemed to start doing everything wrong. At this time, every venue in the town was faced with a string of new rules and regulations put in place to safeguard young people. There were no discussions, they just laid down the law, it felt as though late bars and nightclubs were a major hindrance to the local council, and they placed zero worth on the local nighttime economy. In 2008 it felt like the authorities just wanted nightclubs to be shut down, and to go away. There were very very few incidents in or around The Cornerhouse, but some statistics we were presented with regarding violence, thefts and drunken behaviour meant some new rules were put in place.

Plastic glasses were introduced, which I was thankful for. The thing that caused us problems was a blanket ID policy.

Every single person that came to Sumo had to show an ID, and that ID had to be a passport or driver's licence. We were given that rule, one Friday evening, about an hour before we opened. Doormen were told they'd be fined heavily if they didn't agree to ID everyone, and the police sat over the road from the venue, watching, to make sure we did as we'd been told.

Now, as a thousand regulars arrived at Sumo, without ID (because they'd never needed ID before) we had to tell them they couldn't come in, without ID. You can imagine the scenes.

Many hopped into taxis, returning later with the ID they needed, some just headed off into the night fuming. Some understood it wasn't really our fault, some headed home, to fume and vent and call us names on the internet into the small hours of the morning.

There were quite a few things that came together and contributed to the eventual downfall of the Cornerhouse and Sumo's royal reign at the top of the game, but this ID issue, I am positive, was the first major blow.

It kick-started the beginning of the end.

A Bit About Saturdays

Saturdays are another story. I can't go deep on the story of Saturdays. The book would be twice as long and it's probably someone else's story to tell. I always felt like the babysitter of Saturdays. They were Graham's baby, and even though, over 14 years I was in there (what felt like) every single Saturday, and even though half my week, week in week out, involved sorting those damn Saturdays out, they weren't ever technically mine. So someone else can write that book.

When I was still a civilian, pre-joining the team at Ten Feet Tall I was a regular at Play. Using the Empire's myriad of rooms, Graham had about four DJs in there, so multiple music policies, plus a lineup of live bands that, at the time, were unmissable shows. I went to see everyone from The Darkness, to Kula Shaker, to Biffy Clyro, to Nerf Herder at Play.

My early days at TFT were spent learning the ropes working Play, running round after bands, getting tortured by tour managers, and trying to help entertain the 1200-strong crowd of regulars.

Around 2006, Big Barry, the Empires' owner, decided that once a month, he wanted to resurrect an old dance night called Sugarshack, and told Graham he had to sit one Saturday a month out.

Graham was not happy, and rightly so; Big Barry was crazy to rock the boat and fuck with the formula when Play did huge numbers week in week out.

However, the thought of bringing House Music back to the venue must have been just too tempting for old Baz. Sugarshack had been an institution in its own right 'back in the day' - Google it.

Graham whipped Play out from under Empire's feet and took it (weekly) to another club, Onyx Rooms on Albert rd. The whole crowd just upped sticks and moved with us, and Play Saturdays at Onyx rooms now ruled the Saturdays for over a year.

In 2008, Big Barry decided to semi-retire and handed the reins of Empire over to his son, 'Little Barry' and Barry's best mate Ash.

In April that year, their first call was to Graham and to ask Ten Feet Tall to bring their monster indie night back to Empire. As it turned out, we were just starting to have issues with the management at Onyx. We were doing good numbers, and the owners had told us they'd planned to hike up the drinks prices, and they said they needed a cut of the door. Onyx's argument was that as it was so busy their costs were higher. I think it was greed. We were out of there, and we took Saturdays back home to the Empire.

We canned the name Play and renamed it Metropolis. None of us really liked a name, but we were pushed for time and got a little stuck in a rut with it. Under Ash and Young Baz's new management, the Empire made a massive push towards live music, and they sought to re-establish the venue as the place to see bands, and the Metropolis indie night would be their big guitar-heavy clubnight offering. They booked in any live show they could, which included the likes of Idlewild, Eagles of Death Metal, The Charlatans, Saxon, Anvil and Dragonforce. We added the odd live band to our clubnight offering too, booking the Cribs and also, the biggest band on the planet at that very moment, we confirmed Pendulum to play live as a full six piece band. With a lineup like that between us, no one could doubt Ten Feet Tall and Empire's new vision.

When we launched Metropolis, the promo led with 'From The Makers of Sumo', as Sumo was the biggest thing in town. The ground floor was indie (with Burnsey, plus Chris from Durham, on the tunes), there was a refurbished cocktail lounge, and the large middle floor area was a 'rock room'. We had Sumo DJs and even live bands playing most weeks upstairs. Given Sumo's popularity on a Friday, the rock floor just didn't work out and we swapped it out for Pop DJs, including Henry, Fil and even our designer Marty jumping on the decks.

Metropolis started doing 600 people a week and everyone, including Graham and the Empire seemed, bizarrely, happy with those numbers.

Someone said, *"Well if we can keep doing 600 every week we'll be happy"*. Well, that didn't last long.

Metropolis gradually overtook Sumo as the number one weekly mixed-bag-clubnight-with-something-for-everyone. It kind of thinned Sumo out for the better, and we kept the die-hard fans and rock crowd. The indie-pop kids who were always on the hunt for the latest thing and the coolest offering, soon binned Sumo Fridays off for these new unpronounceable Met-ro-Pol-is (or was it Me-trop-oplis?) Saturdays in the grander, more demure club.

To wrap this story of Saturday that I said I wasn't going to tell...

Metropolis ran for years, peaked at about 1100 a week. It was a beast, and certainly continued the long reign that Play started as king clubnight in the North East. After we got bored of the name and the night needed a freshen up, we rebranded and renamed the Empire Saturdays' as MILK, which horrified some, but didn't seem to bother the masses, and from about 2016, the MILK Saturdays clubnight continued to pull in between 700 and 900 people a week, week in week out for years.

We'll come back to MILK.

Park it in your mind here for now.

Where Is Gary Numan?

As part of our Metropolis Saturdays, we'd booked electro legend Gary Numan to play a guest DJ set up on the first floor - an event that would surely become a career highlight for a man who had sold over ten million records.

Claire was tasked with picking Gary up from Middlesbrough train station and delivering him to the discreet side entrance of the Empire at around midnight. The plan was to get Gary up to the dressing rooms to chill before his turn on the decks.

I phoned Claire at midnight to check she was in position;

"*Hey, Have you got Gary?*" I asked.

"*Yes,*" Claire responded.

"*And where are you both now?*"

"*Er... Here in my car?*" she replied.

I hope Gary laughed as much as I did.

Bad Medicine Rock Club

Bad Medicine, or Bad Med as the locals called it, was a weekly rock night in Middlesbrough that started on a rainy Monday night, on December 8th in 2008, And eventually moved to a weekly Wednesday slot, where it trundled along, with around 150 regulars until, due to dwindling attendance, it sadly fizzled out in 2012

I include this short homage to Bad Med because it was a great rock night.

It had a hard working team with Dani as the DJ, and a girl called Cat, who we sat at the helm. Cat and Dani ran a tight ship, keeping the thing going for all that time, putting on some amazing gigs including Lower Than Atlantis, TRC, Deez Nuts, The Ghost Inside, Throats, Lavotchkin, The Departed and Max Raptor. Plus we provided Boro with a mid week eclectic offering - with DJs playing glam rock, hair metal, eighties rock and classic mosh.

Our venue was Secrets - the town's lap-dancing club - which sat above Spensleys Emporium. Spensleys was and still is, owned and run by another pair of loveable rogues, the Spensley Brothers. It sits on a corner of Albert Road, opposite the train station and the Cornerhouse. This large gothic building, a former bank, was run as a late bar at the time. The downstairs bar had a capacity of around 200-300 and a small stage in the corner.

Above this bar, part of the same large building was the lap dancing club. Secrets was small, and intimate, with purple velvet walls, a bar and a small dance floor. With a capacity of around 300, it was an ideal venue for a rock night, and Graham - who was always looking ambitiously for more opportunities - spotted this. A rock clubnight in a strip club, would surely be a unique, and maybe popular event. We needed to make it different enough to Sumo, and the venue's style lent itself to the classic rock music policy. Naming it after a sleazy Bon Jovi song made sense, and Bad Medicine was born.

Now I'd like to continue this part of the book by saying something like *"well I'm no expert on lap dancing clubs"* - but that's not strictly true. Through a random series of events years earlier, I had taken a crash course in the subject.

A long long time ago, my band Exit By Name had been paired up with a Scottish band Tennessee Kait for a two week UK tour. We started in our hometown with a gig at Stockton's Georgian Theatre, headed right down the country via Manchester and Birmingham, to London and Bournemouth, and then up into Scotland for dates in Glasgow, Dundee and Tennessee Kait's home town of Perth.

Now, Tennessee Kait were called Tennessee Kait, so they told us, after a stripper in their home town called Kate, who was half the price of the other girls, at just ten quid for a dance. Hence, a Tenner, to see Kate. This merry band of Scots told us that their personal mission, on this 14 date tour of the British isles, was to visit 14 different strip clubs. And so, after every gig, we'd pack up the van, and drive from whatever dive bar we'd just played in, across the city to the nearest strip club, following Tennessee Kait on their mission. I'm not proud of it, and I understand why it's not something one should shout about, but those two weeks were certainly an insight into a world I knew nothing about. Had I documented that fortnight well enough, it could have been a book in its own right.

One thing I'd learned from my baptism of fire through the late night land of lap dancing clubs, was the etiquette. I knew what happened, what stuff cost, and what was allowed, and what wasn't allowed. In fourteen different cities across the UK, the norm was that a dance would cost you about £20, and everyone's pants stayed firmly on. Of course, this was Middlesbrough, and I was soon to discover that people make their own rules around here.

Before we even started any promo, we met the girls. Dani, Cat and I arranged to meet all the dancers at Secrets. They had the story that new promoters were starting a rock night, and we were open to dancers working the floor, if they wanted. About half the girls turned up, some out of curiosity, and some to take the piss.

I introduced the TFT team, and explained the music wasn't going to be the smooth RnB they were used to on a weekend. I handed out mix CDs that we'd carefully made for them, and we said we knew they were the experts, and if they felt their presence could work, then we'd happily have them along for the ride. About six girls agreed to come and give it a try. I felt like it was their turf we were intruding on, and if these ladies wanted to come and hang out, I wasn't going to stop them.

We had the girls. We had the tunes. Now we needed some drinks deals to tease Boro out of the house on a Monday Night. Lee and Ste Spensley really wanted our night to succeed, so they sorted us a pretty ridiculous drinks menu, £1 Jack Daniels, £1 Jagerbombs, and beers or other spirits at about £1.70 a go. Writing all this down, I can't believe this night didn't do better than it did.

We had two receptionists working, one charging an entry fee of about four quid, and one taking ten pounds for a 'Dance Token' that customers could pocket and treasure - and when they'd plucked up the courage, they could hand it to the girl of their choice.

The mosher's minds were blown. These ten pound dances were often fully nude, and so I'm reliably informed, they were very much on the wild side. Some of the kids would save up all month then take three girls into a booth at once. They got a pretty rock and roll show for their money. I was pretty sure we had the best team of girls between Dundee and Bournemouth - and as sleazy and cheesy as this might sound, it was a professional operation, the girls and Cat honestly seemed to be having the best time, and they were always fully in control. One of the girl's husbands was the head doorman, and he made sure everything was hunky dory at all times.

Cat, our rep week in week out was an absolute diamond, all credit to her. Dealing with six strippers, four doormen, and two hundred moshers (who had been downing £1 jagerbombs for five hours) was her idea of a fun midweek night out.

So eventually, the fun police and the licensing authorities cracked down on lap dancing clubs as well as nightclubs. Anything that happened after 11pm was just treated as a nuisance that they wanted rid of.

They withheld the venue's licence for lapdancing. Here's how that happened.

The town council's licensing department had asked the venue to install CCTV, to monitor the dancers - which to be fair was a great idea. It made things very safe for the girls performing in their booths.

Of course the licensing team eventually came to collect the CCTV tapes, and watched them back. You see, a lapdancer is not supposed to come into *physical contact* with a customer. There was pretty overwhelming evidence of physical contact, right there on those tapes. And so, the licence to lap dance was revoked.

Even with private dances out of the mix, this left us with live bands, cheap booze, great tunes and a few of the girls stayed to spin on the pole - we paid them a decent fee. This was still a grand recipe for midweek mischief and Bad Med continued until 2012 when we finally called it a day for the hundred regulars that still turned up every Wednesday night.

Ain't No Party Like The Sumo Xmas Beach Party

Friday 19th December 2008

The Sumo Xmas Beach Party of 2007 had been the biggest event we'd ever done, we'd jammed a thousand into the Cornerhouse for that event, and it saw our regular numbers leap up in the weeks and months following it. It had established Sumo as the place with the reputation for parties that contained the unexpected, the wild, and the downright daft.

A mix of tacky beach decor, imported inflatables and cheap cocktails was a new twist on the traditional Xmas parties in town.

Plus, cash prize incentives to convince everyone to dress up (or down) in beach clobber in the freezing Teesside winter had been the icing on the Christmas cake. If you have a massive crowd that are genuinely up for this sort of stuff, it really adds to the atmosphere. If you have hundreds of punters in costume for any theme, it's done the job for you, and beats any expensive decor package.

We knew for this 2018 version of the beach party, we'd have to take it to another level. We'd ordered huge boxes of inflatable parrots, tiki heads, and palm trees. We'd sourced cheap plastic cups that looked like coconut shells, and we'd imported crates of fake grass skirts, all to give away free to the clubbers as they piled in for their Mojitos.

We knew we still needed that extra something.

It had become a bit of a game of outdoing ourselves, so we wanted to do something that would have people talking for months following the event.

We needed a pool.

We found an eight metre garden pool at our local cash and carry - god knows why they stocked them in December, but they did. This wasn't a paddling pool, this thing was about a metre deep, with a solid plastic frame, thick canvas sides and came with a big set of white ladders so that you could climb in and out.

It wouldn't have fit anywhere in the club, and the venue managers were worried about water making the already lethal dance floors and corridors even more of a hazard, so we figured it would have to go outside on the pavement.

The first problem was the issue of the thing being spotted by the police and taken down before we'd even opened. Solution - we'll build it an hour before doors, at 10pm, and surround it with gazebos, so it might look, to passing police cars, that we've just put some cover up for the giant queue of moshers that now sprawled up Albert road every Friday.

The next obvious hurdle was filling the damn thing. A hosepipe would take all day, and we needed to fill this thing up in under 60minutes - so we needed to think bigger. Uncle Robin and his loveable rogue pal Paul had the answer. We needed to use a fire hydrant.

Opening a fire hydrant is a tricky task. A quick Google told me it was illegal, and actually some kind of ancient law meant that it was a treasonable offence. The queen owned fire hydrants, so opening one up unnecessarily was a crime. In 2008 this is what Google told me. Or maybe it was Ask Jeeves. Anyway, we were nervous.

About a week before the event, Robin and Paul appeared in the office with a large metal rod that they told us was a fire hydrant key. They told us that they'd given £100 to the local fire station, as a charity donation, and they'd handed over the key for a week, no questions asked. I've no idea where they got that key from, and what they actually did with the £100 we gave them. It didn't matter, we had the key.

The night of the beach party came around. Our promo had been damn good, the decor looked amazing, and word on the street was absolutely everyone was coming in beachy fancy dress, despite it being around 2 degrees outside.

We added a few nice finishing touches to our plan, changing rooms with signs, stacks of free towels and even a couple of lifeguards with whistles and red shorts.

At around 10pm the crowd outside the venue was absolutely huge. Everyone was buzzing for the giant pool that filled the pavement outside the venue on Albert road. With no live social media, and very few camera phones in the world, you're going to have to take my word for it. Guys in shorts, Hawaiian shirts, flippers and even a few snorkels stood shoulder to shoulder, shivering with girls in bikinis, beach hats and aviators.

To get these people out of the cold we opened the club early, bar staff were still scurrying around filling fridges and tills with coins, our team were still gaffer taping plastic parrots to walls, and the DJ's hadn't even turned up. We needed the pavement clear to get the pool ready, so everyone just piled in, and we eventually got the party started and everyone warmed up.

Outside, myself, Paul and Robin's plan was to pop the hydrant open, attach the fire hose that they'd brought along (maybe the local fireman had actually helped out here) and then get the pool filled. We knew this was dangerous, but we just hoped to get a few people having a splash before the police (surely) landed and told us to drain the pool and pack it down.

People crowded around the pool; everyone asked when it was getting filled - we just kept telling them *"soon, very soon..."*

By 11.30pm the club had reached capacity and, ironically, due to the heat inside, people spilled out onto the pavement, all over the road. The doormen were losing it, people seemed way more drunk and chewy than usual, and there was no space outside for the security staff to deal with incidents, talk to people or get any space - we'd stacked the pavement with tents, gazebos and this bloody great big swimming pool.

Side Note : It was also Black Friday. Also known across the UK as Mad Friday or Frantic Friday, the last Friday before Christmas, Black Eye Friday. The most popular Friday of the year for some people. This was night when people, some might say older, some might say scruffier, hit the town. And hit each other. Local folklore tells me this was traditionally the day that workers in the factories, the docks, and the offices all finished for their Christmas break, so drinking would commence from the time they clocked off around 5pm. They'd crawl the pubs, and then, as it got to pub-kicking-out-time (11pm in those days), the hordes would go in search of the nearest nightclub to continue the boozing.

Before this quiet end of Albert road became a Boho Zone, infused with tech companies, award winning colleges, bars and bistros, this was the red light district, this was 'over the border', and it could be a bit of a warzone.

So as Sumo's barmy winter pool party was kicking off, the door lads and I also had to deal with hundreds of tanked-up lunatics passing by who obviously wanted to know the craic with our pool, our party, and our bikini-clad customers.

It was midnight by this point, and it was chaos.

I was outside, and Paul was at the ready with his hydrant key and the short length of hose. I remember him looking me in the eye and saying, *"Just give me the word"*.

I turned from him and surveyed the scene behind me. Jonny the venue manager was having a nervous breakdown, begging me not to do it. There were piles of glass on the pavement from customers that had brought drinks outside and dropped them, plus it was now sub zero degrees. The idea of everyone stripping off and diving into whatever type of water comes out of a hydrant seemed like a very very bad idea. Was this water even going to be safe for people to sit in?

I was devastated but I told everyone we weren't doing it. I was gutted, but I knew it was the right thing to do in the middle of that mess. An anti-climactic story, right?

After all the hype and buzz, not filling that pool felt like a total cop-out and it was one of the few times I felt like I'd let the Sumo kids down.

As much as it would have been an epic tale in the Sumo story, I still think it could have gone badly. That could have been the night where we really fucked up.

Uncle Alberts

The venue opposite Cornerhouse eventually changed its name from Bar Sumo, to Uncle Alberts. A top grafter called Simon from Ladhar Leisure sorted a refit, and a proper lovely lad called Ben was the new venue manager. They were both proper grafters and worked hard, along with TFT and Henry, to make a bar that many regarded as the best in Boro.

Henry and I (mainly Henry to be honest) booked as many shows as we could on the little Uncle Alberts stage. I set about getting every local rock, punk and metal band a slot pre-Sumo on a Friday night. Henry took care of the locals each Saturday, plus some pretty special shows that I hope Middlesbrough remembers this as a bit of a golden age of live music down Albert road.

Alt-J, Rolo Tomassi, Band of Skulls, Titus Andronicus, Tubelord, Dave House, Lemuria, Blakfish, Milloy, This Town Needs Guns, Keith Burton, The Brute Chorus, Pulled Apart By Horses, Stephen Fretwell, Airborne Toxic Event, Maximo Park's Paul Smith and Johnny Foreigner all graced Albert's little stage thanks to Henry's passion for bringing new bands to Boro.

One of my favourite events, literally ever, was a local homage to Stars In Your Eyes that Henry organised as a fundraiser for the mental health charity Mind. Raptastic played hosts, dressed resplendently as Matthew Kelly and Cat Deeley. Local bands got into costume and did cover sets such as The Pixies, The Hives, Lady Gaga, New Found Glory and my band performed as

Weezer.

We also held some cracking events in the little beer garden out the back. There were quite a few drunken punk rock shows with bands hiding under tiny Argos gazebos, playing in the rain.

It was at Uncle Alberts that I learned a valuable lesson about Facebook Events, and I suppose, e-marketing in general.

I'd booked one of my favourite bands, Poison The Well, to come and play as part of their short UK tour. It had landed on Easter Sunday, so we'd added a few local bands and set door times early so everyone could enjoy some sunshine, plenty of beers, and an amazing rock show with no work or college the following day. After we'd announced the show, to a massive buzz, we had 450 people attending the Facebook event. I figured the show was sorted. The capacity was about 120 realistically and although advance tickets hadn't really shifted, I guessed everyone was happy to pay on the door. I braced myself for an epic jam packed show, and even prepared an extra barrier for outside the venue for queues. I was assuming I'd be turning people away by the hundreds.

Sixty people showed up for the show. I hadn't flyered, I hadn't got the posters out, I hadn't spent weeks hyping the gig and I was worried about overcrowding. I'd actually downplayed the gig for over a month because Facebook told me 450 people would show up.

I never trusted Facebook event figures ever again.

Side Note : Head to payforthepiano.co.uk for an extensive list of all the gigs Henry has booked. There's an impressive archive right there.

Loving The Haters

2009

An observation from 2009.

Sumo was at the height of its fame and as commercially successful as it ever got. The Fridays were regularly attended by 1000+, and we almost gave the mighty Play Saturdays a run for their money.

However, when you read about Sumo in 2009 *online*, as I did every waking hour I had, we were loathed. The forums, the messages, the dying MySpace, and by then the blossoming Facebook page, all ran a common theme.

Hate mail.

Whatever we announced, people dissed it. Any events we threw, people trash-talked. Any bands we had on, people ripped the piss.

The more popular we got, the more haters we attracted. Maybe the adage "cool to hate" is right, the cool kids are always going to resent the popular kid.

Fat Mike said something in 2020 in a Vice documentary about Green Day. They never sold out, as selling out was changing what you did, to fit in, and gain more mass appeal. Green Day just did what they did. Then, what they *did* became popular. They didn't sell out. And that was Sumo for sure. Obviously, there was an element of everyone just wanting to be at the busiest place in town, but we stuck to our guns, and musically we were as diverse as ever. Our theme parties were as daft as we could make them, the bands we booked were as cool as you could get (from Daughters to Little Boots and anything in between).

Even when we opened the indie room, we'd decorated the walls with giant skulls, six foot boards displaying lyrics by bands like Refused. We booked local deathcore bands to play there for the first two hours before letting Burnsey play his indie rock n roll. We didn't make it easy for them.

In my frequent rambling blogs and MySpace bulletins at that time, I'd refer to the haters all the time - I'd join in, call them out, I made them part of the circus. I'd print flyers saying things like *"we've got two thousand lovers and five thousand haters, come and see why everyone's talking about SUMO"*. The lovers and the haters loved it. Every bile soaked rant from a critic was reshared and waved like a flag. We were having a blast promoting this way.

I registered two domains, sumorocks.co.uk and sumosucks.co.uk and filled them with customer reviews - positive and negative.

If I heard a local band say they wouldn't dream of playing Sumo, I'd offer them a show - a good stage wage and a bucket of ice cold beers soon meant they had the night of their lives. I was on a mission to win every person in Teesside over, even if it meant doing it one by one. On one occasion, I'd spotted a kid online that had started a Facebook group called 'Bring back the good days of Sumo'. I messaged him, took him for coffee, and gave him a job.

There's a phrase - Fuck The Haters. I disagree. Love the haters. Embrace them.

It was easy to be this confident and this brazen when the product itself was so good.

The Battle For Thursdays

It was about this time in proceedings that The Arena re-reared its head. The building, formerly Middlesbrough's legendary Rock Garden venue, had another clutch of new owners, new promoters, and they were out for blood. The new team at Arena had an aggressive promo team, who weren't taking any prisoners. They trash talked every other venue, and their message was literally - *Arena is best, everywhere else is shite.*

There was a bit of an unwritten gentlemen's agreement across Boro, where all the clubs' promoters pretty much got along. We all went out with the message that our club was the best... but we never mentioned anyone else. We kept the focus on ourselves.

The Arena team, led by a chap called Neil, were out in force every weekend, promoting their new events. Everyone that was walking to Empire got a flyer for the new Arena clubnights.

We were £6 entry, so they were Free Entry, with a free bus to take you there. Our cans of Red Stripe were £3, and theirs were £2. Our club closed at 3am, and their club was open till 5am.

Much to Neil's disappointment, the Empire stayed busy, strong, and packed. The Arena was not these things. Perhaps the club was just that little bit too far out from town, or maybe they didn't have the basics right, who knows. We stayed focused and tried to avoid the slanging match that they were desperate for us to get into.

The Arena's team developed a severe distaste for all things Ten Feet Tall, they saw us as mortal enemies, and word on the street was that they *hated* us. I had a couple of theories as to why this was so.

Firstly, The Arena, as part of their reopening promo campaign, had booked Pendulum to come and DJ. We'd booked the full live band. On the Friday when two of the Pendulum entourage were DJing the Arena club, we announced our show. The Arena event was dead, and Neil blamed us. Why would Boro go and see two Pendulum DJs, when they could see the full six-piece live band a few weeks later.

Our announcement had crushed their show, it was unintentional, but it looked shitty for sure.

The other reason I think those guys fell out with us was over the Middlesbrough Music Live Festival.

The Festival, which at the time attracted 40,000 people to Boro town centre, was an all day session of live music and drinking. It was a prime target for promoters to come and flyer and promote their events.

You had all those music lovers in one spot, so who wouldn't want to cover the place in leaflets. The council, over the years, had gotten sick of millions of flyers being dropped all over the site, and in the interest of litter, had banned flyering from the site. Now Ten Feet Tall, as festival organisers, had the privilege of flyering when no one else did, and this pissed a few people off. It wound up Neil and his promo team. On the day of the festival that year, they were pretty much evicted from the festival site, and all the flyers they had printed must have gone in the bin.

So, I reckon Neil disliked us, and the more the Empire stayed busy, and

Arena stayed quiet on a Saturday, I suspect the more his fury bubbled.

The one thing Arena did have at this point (that the Empire didn't) - was a huge Thursday Night.

Thursday's in Boro had been ruled for years by Ten Feet Tall's pop night at Cornerhouse, Sixty Nine. Now, Arena's offering "Skint" - a night that offered rock bottom drinks prices for all - took the crown, and had been packing in the crowds for months and months.

Graham and Marty had a solid gold idea for a new pop night, and had decided to host this at Empire, on a Thursday.

As you can imagine, The Arena took this as a call for war, and the battle for Thursdays ensued.

'APE' was essentially Sixty Nine version 2.0, with the Cornerhouse Thursday's DJ's playing their brand of pop and dance, in the superior venue of Empire. As the resident mosher, I was kept right out of it. Besides, I had Friday's, Saturdays, and everything else to juggle.

It wasn't long before I got roped in.

The promo for APE centred around people dressed in Ape suits out on the streets handing out flyers, free passes and all the usual 'new night hype'. The fact we were in Ape suits meant our campaign had a viral element, and our photos and videos were getting shared like crazy on social media. This is the sort of thing that happens all the time these days. But in Middlesbrough in 2009, this was all pretty wacky. Ten Feet Tall had a Segway, and two pimped up mobility scooters, spray painted bright yellow. Each day Dani and I would reluctantly climb into these ape suits and race across town, to the university campus and tear around throwing promo at people for this new night. As no one could see who we were, it didn't matter we were two old moshers pushing a cool pop night to the students.

To give the Arena lads credit, they came up with a fantastic way to ruin our promo campaign, and turn it against us. They bought no less than ten identical Ape suits, and they spent hours running around Boro, being totally anti-social. They let off air horns in Primark, scared kids in the streets, climbed on cars and jumped off bus shelters. Now, on the verge of getting served ASBOs, our Ape suits now felt like a bad idea.

Rather than taking this cheeky beating, we rose to the occasion, and we bought twenty ape suits, and recruited anyone and everyone we could find. We hired a limo for the following Thursday Night, we got everyone to the TFT office, and we got drunk.

The limo picked us all up around 10pm and we headed out on a crawl of all the open clubs, starting up Linthorpe road at The Keys and made our way down to Spensleys, with an army of Ten Feet Tall photographers with us, capturing our adventure as we went. We didn't really have a plan, we just thought twenty people in ape suits diving out of a limo was hilarious, and it was getting the APE Empire Thursday's name out there. Before we'd even gotten into the limo, we agreed that we definitely should *not* go over to the Arena. By midnight, and after everyone in The Keys and Spensleys had bought us about a hundred Jagerbombs, The Arena was definitely where we were headed.

As the limo cruised up to the Arena, we saw the huge queue of people standing waiting to get into the venue's chockablock clubnight; Skint. The limo full of apes looked to me for a plan. I said we definitely shouldn't give out any flyers, we should just get out of the limo, dance around a bit with the people in the queue, throw a few high fives, maybe pose for some photos and then we jump back in the limo and bail.

I had a feeling that the Arena would be pretty pissed off that we'd showed up to crash their party.

I was correct.

The limo pulled up; we pulled on our latex monkey masks and jumped out. I felt like a bank robber ready to pull a heist. As soon as we set foot out of the vehicle, Neil and the Arena security were all over us. They formed a line between the people in the queue for Skint and us and began screaming at us to *"Fuck off back to the fucking Empire"*.

My gang of drunken primates began dancing around and waving at people in the queue. It was all very harmless, but the Arena staff looked like they were going to flatten us. I was about four feet away from Neil when I saw him reach for his phone. My phone was on silent in my jeans pocket, under my ape suit. My phone began vibrating. Neil was yelling at all of us;

"Right that's it you arseholes, I'm phoning Phil Saunders!".

You couldn't tell through the masks, but we were all crying with laughter at this point. After a few seconds, Neil had got through to my voicemail, and I watched in horror as he left me a message.

The guy was standing close enough to whip the ape mask off my head. Thank god he didn't.

The 2am voicemail went like this:

"Phil, your dickhead monkey army is outside my club being total pricks. It is totally out of order, you need to have a word with them, I am not happy. It's Neil by the way".

I made hand signals to get everyone back in the limo. We piled in, de-masked, and basked in a glow of drunken adrenaline. We headed back to the office feeling pretty pleased with ourselves.

A few take-aways here on reflection.

I'm pretty chuffed that Neil thought I was too high up the management ladder to be out at 2am being a monkey. Also, Neil's dickhead flyer pricks were outside the Empire every night it was open, spamming our crowd with their flyers and free passes. So I don't feel bad that we rolled up for ten minutes and shook our hairy monkey butts outside his clubnight.

Ape lasted about 5 weeks before we canned it. No one came. Whether people just liked to enjoy the Empire on a Friday and Saturday, so asking them to come on a Thursday was just too much, or maybe Neil's Skint Thursdays were just too good to beat. Anyway, Skint won, Ape lost, but a great battle was fought. Well played everyone.

Bring Back The Good Old Days

After our peak and the glory days of late 2007 to early 2009, many people said Sumo had gone from great to good to bad. People used to say *"Sumo is shit now"*. People would say *"Sumo isn't as good as it used to be"*.

All these years later, I'm not in denial, but people were wrong.

Sumo didn't go bad, our standards didn't slip, the music, the venue, the effort we put in, was pretty much the same. The people who said it, were the ones that had changed. A classic line at the point a relationship breaks down; *'It's not you, it's me'*.

Well, it wasn't us. It was them.

Our regulars weren't 19 anymore, and we'd lasted so long that they'd grown up. They were 22 or even 24. All my mates in their late twenties who had loved Sumo for years were now buying houses and getting engaged. They didn't need a clubnight. They needed a comfy seat in a warm pub. This, plus the issues we had with ID, were a couple of big fat nails in the coffin that was being prepared for Sumo's proverbial death.

There's always the new influx of 18 year olds ready to pick up the baton. For every person that subconsciously realises that nightclubs are just not for them anymore, a fresh new clubber is handed their driver's licence, or a crisp twenty pound note falls out that 18th birthday card from Gran, and it's off to the clubs you go. That twenty quid is exchanged at the door for £15 in change as you enter your first clubnight, and you head to the bar, and attempt to order some awful drinks over the deafening sound system.

This new generation was hitting Boro, and being honest, they were hitting the Empire. A bigger, shinier experience with more rooms, more bands, more fun, and of course – a damn good promo team – us.

There were a few Sumos at the end of 2009 where we only had around 130 people through the door. You feel the difference when you're used to ten times that amount.

130 is a cursed number in clubland.

Graham and I knew it. *"You never come back from 130"*. Hull had started doing 130. Bad Medicine, Animals V Machines, Sumo Durham, Sumo Darlington, Holy Shit, Ape... all these events had entered a run of 130ish through the door. It spelt the end.

You never come back from 130. We needed a plan.

Rock Box Boy

When we first started Metropolis Empire Saturdays at the Empire, the entire first floor was Rock. We realised there weren't enough rock kids to fill that big first floor dance floor, so we pushed the Rock tunes into this little side room up on the same floor.

I loved Rock Box. Such a shit name. Sorry I couldn't think of a better one.

In 2008-2009, there was a little golden era of Rock Box Saturdays – it had its own MySpace, a Facebook page too, and its own photographer. There was a small but loyal following for Rock Box.

Dani was Rock Box's main DJ. He'd neck an entire bottle of JD throughout the evening. Running the Saturdays were my least favourite event to run, but popping in to see drunk Dani every so often was a highlight.

Dani and I were at the Sonisphere Festival in 2009, and a group of young girls passed us, and I heard one of them say, *"Oh. My. God! There's Rock Box Boy!"*

Referring to DJ Dani course.

Another girl spotted me and added, *"and there's that guy that stands with him"*.

From then on, when people asked me what I did for a job, I would say, *"I stand next to DJs"*.

—

Like Craig, Kev, Henry, Ste A, Ste F, Burnsey, Chris, Stubbsy, Fil, JT, Robbie and a good few others, Dani is another one of the unsung heroes of the Teesside clubnight scene. A bunch of relatively quiet fella's who (mostly) kept their heads down, and played consistently blinding DJ sets week in week out, and between them helped shape a phenomenal alternative scene of clubbing between 2005 and 2020.

It's hard to imagine Middlesbrough's Rock scene without DJ Dani - when you consider he DJ'd Bad Medicine, Rock Box, Uncle Alberts, Animals V Machines and of course, from about 2009, he became one of the key Sumo DJs.

Dani's versatility in the DJ booth saw him genre hop from the pop punk party of AVM and the rock slot in Sumo, to tackling the indie room and the pop floor too. He would also be regularly roped in to DJ alongside the other lads at events like Empire's Halloween Ball and New Year's parties.

There were a bunch of other strings to Dani's bow - a talented web designer, he was quickly drafted into the Ten Feet Tall office life back in the day, coding all our MySpace pages to look especially fancy. He'd rewrite the HTML to make our online presence appear leagues ahead of the competition. He eventually ended up taking on the task of the main TFT website and the ever-evolving string of comedy club websites. He also backed up Marty in the graphic design department, taking his share of the massive backlog of design work.

Not only a DJ and designer, Dani literally *ran the show* in many ways for a long long time. When it came to Animals V Machines each Saturday, Dani would be first on the scene at the venue, letting bands in, and sorting all the decor for the clubnight. He'd be up a ladder, hanging a banner, setting up a beer pong competition, dragging a PA system up the stairs for a few hours before then going on the DJ for 5 hours. Then at 3 or 4am, he'd take everything down again. A hell of a shift to take on every Saturday night. The same happened with Bad Medicine, and then along with others, he'd dutifully troop to Durham or Sunderland for months, helping make shit happen over there.

I don't think any of us at TFT ever thanked him properly to the degree we should have. Every one of us just dived in, mucked in, and just kept going and going, making everything happen.

—

Dani and I lived together for a few years in Middlesbrough, and I noticed that he'd go out for about an hour around midnight every Tuesday night. One day, I asked him where he went on his midnight weekly jaunts.

Now, our good pal and Sound engineer supremo Nathan provided sound systems for a clubnight at The Keys venue called Mixtape each Tuesday. Nathan was loading a PA system out of The Keys at around midnight each Tuesday, then having to load that *same* PA into Spensleys ready for Bad Medicine every Wednesday night.

Dani explained that he'd been entrusted with a key to Spensleys Emporium.

To save Nathan dragging the PA back to his lock-up in between Mixtape and Bad Med, Nathan had asked Dani to let him in the Spensleys each Tuesday night. Dani had dutifully agreed and also helped Nathan unload the PA out the van and up the steps each week.

A gentleman, and a grafter.

Dani's become a great friend over the years and he joined Kev and Craig as my groomsmen on my wedding day in 2015. Top lads. Dream team.

My First Jedward Story

In 2009 after their exit from X-Factor, we booked twins John and Edward, aka Jedward, to perform at Empire.

We were the kings of booking cool cult indie shows, so Middlesbrough forgave us for the odd so-daft-we-have-to-do-it booking. Along with a Stavros Flattley show a few years later, this was one of my favourite shows to promote and run.

We spent weeks hyping the Jedward show, we took plenty of stick online but sure enough the Empire was sold out on a rainy Thursday night. I'd spent weeks preparing the rider and on the night I made sure the dressing room and sound check went just right. One of the items they had specifically marked, in bold capital letters on the show advance documents, was a request for;

2 X STRAIGHT, ROUND BASED, MIC STANDS

I don't know if you know much about mic stands. But most stands to buy cheaply online are boom stands (they have a bend, they're not straight) and they have a tripod at the bottom to stand them up. What was specifically requested was a *straight* and *round based* mic stand - basically an Axl Rose, two of them. I'd scoured the internet and bought the cheapest round based straight stands I could find, for about £150.

In soundcheck, John and Edward bounded around the stage, checking monitor levels and practising some certainly ad-hoc dance routines. Their manager picked up the mic stands from the front of the stage and put them in the wings, out of the way of the twins' energetic stage prep.

"*Do you not want those stands?*" I asked him.

He laughed aloud and said, "*have you seen those two go? Do you think they need mic stands?*"

Next, up in the dressing room, Jedward's manager packed every single item we'd prepped for the act - a mountain of sandwiches, drinks, snacks, fruit, crisps, dips, crates of water and fizzy pop - into two bin bags and carried them into the small sprinter van outside. I got the impression that it was to be supper, breakfast and tomorrow's lunch.

John and Edward sat in the dressing room with a bottle of water and waited for the doors to open. I sat with them for a while and chatted about the tour they were doing, their plans for after the X-Factor finished, and generally, we shot the breeze.

I couldn't help but notice the seams on their matching suits were frayed, and the knees of the pants were scuffed and stained. They literally had nothing with them on this tour, just the shirts on their backs and two ragged suits - that they were clearly thrashing to the max every night across the country in nightclubs, student unions and bars. They were as happy as two Larrys.

From that point of course they signed a decent management deal, and proper tours, albums and Big Brother followed. It's great to see them still being cheeky, fun and famous to this day.

It also looks like they've now got a proper tailor. Still no sign of any round based straight mic stands.

—

After the show the twins spent an age on stage signing anything and everything that the thousand-strong crowd had brought along for them. They posed for photos, shook hands, got smothered in kisses and were perfect gentlemen for two hours while Boro had their Jedward fix.

Our press officer was there, with the local paper and a few radio station types, enjoying drinks in the lounge. He told me there was a national paparazzi hanging around, and he'd heard on the grapevine that this guy was hoping to get some photos of Jedward in compromising situations and sell the photos to national tabloids.

I don't know where he got this info from, but after knowing John and Edward for 4 hours, I felt very protective, and I asked security to escort this paparazzi fella from the building. This guy was now seriously pissed off. He protested, explaining he was free to take photos with his massive fancy camera, and we couldn't stop him. I calmly explained he didn't have an authorised press pass, so he and his camera weren't welcome. I left him outside on the pavement twisting his knickers.

After we got the show wrapped up and it was time for me to leave for the night, my paparazzi friend was waiting outside for me. *"Me and you need a talk"* he said menacingly as I turned the corner to get to my car. I turned swiftly on my heel and went back inside, and did what any wise Ten Feet Taller would do - I phoned Uncle Robin. Robin was part of the original TFT line up, a man that could fix any problem, or remedy any situation.

If you needed to fill a swimming pool on a pavement at midnight with a fire hydrant, Robin was your man. If you were about to get filled in by an angry paparazzi, Robin was your man.

So after waiting about half an hour after the Jedward crowd had filed out of the Empire, I went back out to my car, and I met Robin. There was now no sign of the paparazzi.

"*You ok?*" Asked Robin. I was a bit embarrassed. This now looked like a waste of Robin's time.

Robin said he'd been nearby anyway and was always happy to help.

"*I guess I won't be needing this then*", he grinned as he put a massive baseball bat back in his car.

Raptastic In The Powder Room

On Friday July 9th, 2010, I finally got my own way, and The Cornerhouse allowed me to put on a gig in their precious ladies' powder room. A room that was essentially an extension of the toilet, just off the long red corridor into the rock room.

Teesside comedy rap two-piece Raptastic were the obvious choice for this show. Technically I knew I could get away with a small PA System, and all Raptastic needed were two mics and an aux cable for their iPod that played their backing track. The duo had just released the video for the song The Love Bear (please go to YouTube and find this), and the hype was real.

The powder room had recently been closed down. It was graffitied and it stank of staleness, but the plush carpet, pink walls, and fancy furniture remained. The door had been permanently closed by two large screws drilled through the huge door into the door frame. We'd promoted the news that the show started at 1am, and sure enough, a big queue of people snaked down the Cornerhouse's red corridor in anticipation of the self proclaimed "Smallest show on earth". Simon and Simon from Raptasitc joined me at the front of the queue and I whipped out a massive screwdriver and undid the screws that opened the door as the crowd cheered us on. The pre-prepped room was ready to go, and Simon and Simon quickly got into character as their stage personas; Tom Bola and Alan Key - and delivered 25 minutes of faux-gangster-rap daftness to the rabid crowd of 50ish Sumo goers who had pushed their way into the 15 capacity room.

I'm proud to say I've run sold out shows for 1200 people at The Middlesbrough Town Hall, and managed a festival site of over 60,000, but these Sumo mini gigs in Rock Box, Little Tokyo and The Powder Room, were some of my absolute favourites.

Joey Jordison And The Guy From Boyzone

One Friday in 2010, The Murderdolls played a show at Middlesbrough Town Hall. After their set, they headed into town to find a rock night, and they found our rock night.

So Joey Jordison, the drummer from Slipknot (who was also drumming for Rob Zombie around that time) and his pal Wednesday 13 headed into Sumo, had a couple of beers, then left and headed back to their tour bus. That's it. That's the story. I had to include that right?

Also once Bowling For Soup went to Bad Medicine on a rainy Wednesday night following their gig at The Empire. Once Miles Kane and Alex Turner came to Sumo and danced around for hours. I should probably tell that full story later.

In another random celebs-go-clubbing-in-Middlesbrough coup, the ultra famous Boyzone hunk Shane Lynch once rocked up to Animals V Machines for drinks. I presume he thought the place was still a lapdancing club and sought some glitz and glamour after a hard day at the Speedway. We welcomed him to our little pop punk night and he even dutifully posed for photos with Kim, Dani and the door lads.

I can't believe we didn't get a photo of Joey though. God rest his soul.

A 2010 Rock Room Setlist

Fri 18th June 2010

Kev played...
   Deez Nuts – There's a Party Over Here
   Lower Than Atlantis – Far Q
   Vanna – Into Hell's Mouth We March
   Cars on Fire – Sharks
   We Are The Ocean – Look Alive
   The Lucky Nine – The Program
   Far – Deafening
   A Ghost Inside – Disintegrator
   Gallows – I Dread The Night
   Propagandhi – Dear Coach's Corner
   Much The Same – What I Know
   Strike Anywhere – I'm Your Opposite Number
   Flatliners – Carry That Banner
   Polar Bear Club – Living Saints
   Alkaline Trio – This Addiction
   Mastodon – Divinations
   Parkway Drive – Carrion
   Asking Alexandria – A Candlelit Dinner
   Bring Me The Horizon – Sadness Will Never End
   Everytime I Die – Ebolarama
   Deftones – Rocket Skates

Cancer Bats – Sorceress
H2O – What Happened
Metallica – Seek & Destroy
Megadeth – Skin O My Teeth
Machine Head – Now I Lay Thee Down
Lamb of God – Now You've Got Something to Die For
Black Label Society – Stillborn
Five Finger Death Punch – Never Enough
Awaken Demons – Here Comes The Hot (2) Stepper
30 Seconds to Mars – The Kill
The Blackout – I Don't Care
Taking Back Sunday – MakeDamnSure
Alexisonfire – Boiled Frogs
Funeral For A Friend – Roses For The Dead
Killswitch Engage – My Curse
Atreyu – Bleeding Mascara
Bullet For My Valentine – Tears Don't Fall
Slipknot – Wait & Bleed
Coal Chamber – Loco
Korn – Here To Stay
Refused – New Noise
Less Than Jake – Gainesville Rock City
Goldfinger – Superman
Capdown – Cousin Cleotis
Reel Big Fish – Sell Out
Save Ferris – Come On Eileen
NoFX – All Outta Angst
Blink 182 – What's My Age Again
Fenix TX – Threesome
Rise Against – ReEducation
Four Year Strong – Wasting Time
Aerosmith – Love In An Elevator
AC/DC – Back In Black

Kiss – Crazy Nights
Motley Crue – Kickstart My Heart
Van Halen – Jump
Enter Shikari – Sorry You're Not a Winner
Prodigy – Omen
Pendulum – Granite
Linkin Park – One Step Closer
System Of a Down – Chop Suey
Limp Bizkit – My Generation
Pantera – Walk
Rage Against The Machine – Bullet In The Head
Andrew WK – We Want Fun
Lost Prophets – Burn Burn
Paramore – Misery Business
Offspring – Kids Aren't Alright
Nirvana – Smells Like Teen Spirit
Faith No More – Easy

The Great One Pound Sumo Disaster

In August 2010, we announced an event that we hoped would inject some much needed hype and love into Sumo.

'Pound Sumo" was Graham's idea, and the beautifully simple concept had the whole town talking, thankfully, again, about Sumo.

The premise was simple. Pound Sumo was £1 to get in (instead of a fiver) and drinks were also £1. If there was one way to the hearts of the people of Middlesbrough, this was it. We planned to get everyone packed back into Cornerhouse, remember how good it was, and win over the new breed of clubbers, who had maybe not been to check us out yet.

However, Pound Sumo at Cornerhouse was a total fuck up.

As promoters, we succeeded in ramming the place to rafters, and over a thousand people turned up to party with us for Pound Sumo. I hate to put it on them, but the venue let us all down. They didn't have enough staff, no one could get served fast enough, the queues at the bars were nuts, and they just couldn't cope. Everyone was ordering ten drinks at a time, and the system fell apart. On top of that, they didn't have the stock. All the drinks on a pound offer ran out. People were frustrated and the already-stressed-out bar staff were getting yelled at by eager customers who wanted the £1 drinks they'd been promised, but they'd simply run out.

The following day, the bad press was killer. We couldn't even argue with it. We tried to roll with a party line of "it was so busy, you guys partied so hard!" but Boro wasn't having it. One-star Facebook reviews, raging emails, MySpace comments. Our name was mud.

Off the back of this, and a few other frustrations, Graham and I had had a few conversations about Sumo, moving to the Empire.

I'd told him it wasn't the right move. The moshers wouldn't like it. It was too big. It was too clean. I was nervous. Following the Pound Sumo disaster, I knew we had to seriously think about moving *somewhere*, and to be honest, there wasn't really anywhere else.

Over the next few Fridays, I experienced a few worrying things at Cornerhouse. As we were opening doors, the bar staff were arriving with Sainsbury's bags full of vodka. They told me that the regular weekly delivery hadn't arrived that week, so they had no spirits. Then, there were power cuts, the heating wasn't going on, they had no change in the tills, and hardly any staff. It felt like Ladhar Leisure were neglecting the venue to the point that it just wouldn't be able to open.

The lads that ran Saturgay, Phil and Simon, had moved their clubnight to the Basement venue down the road that they'd bought, and TFT's Sixty Nine Thursday, had long dried up. I didn't want to be the final straw that caused the legendary venue to shut down, but I was certain that if we didn't jump ship, the ship was going to sink with us in it.

I asked Rick, Kev and Craig to meet me at Empire one afternoon in the middle of the week. It was September 2010. I explained to them our concerns about the Cornerhouse, how we were down to less than 200 regulars each and every week, and we were being let down week on week by the venue. We needed a new venue, and despite all the cons, Empire was pretty much the only choice.

I walked everyone into the DJ box of Empire, which is pretty luxurious compared to the Cornerhouse's DJ box. If doing a set in the Cornerhouse was like driving an clapped out ford fiesta, hitting the decks in the Empire was like piloting the Starship Enterprise. I ran to my car to grab a CD, I can't believe I didn't have one pre-prepared for the occasion.

I don't think, in the history of the Empire, anyone had played a rock, punk, or metal song through that gigantic PA system, ever, until that moment.

The only CD I had with me was The Artist In The Ambulance by Thrice, and that did the trick. I played Silhouette first, followed by the title track, and the four of us slowly paced the dancefloor and took in the vastness of the ceiling, and epic surroundings of the Empire.

The huge riffs thundered through the venue's gargantuan speakers.

"It's big, innit," said Rick. We all nodded and agreed. It was really big.

The Final Sumo At The Cornerhouse

Friday 24th September 2010

It was the last ever Sumo at Cornerhouse. No one knew but the four of us.

Rick, Craig, Kev and I stood in the cramped Rock Room DJ box, watching the final few songs play out, and we drank our beers as the last little mosh pits dispersed. I think we played Tenacious D, or something similar, and flipped the house lights up.

In 24 hours, we would be announcing to the town our plan, leaving Cornerhouse behind, abandoning ship, and that Sumo would have a new home. We'd let everyone get talking for a few days, keep everyone guessing, and then unveil our venue of choice. That was the plan.

We knew why we had to go, we knew the place was falling apart around us, and we believed there was still life in Sumo yet. There just wasn't life in this venue, and it was dragging us down and holding us back. So we hoped.

What if we launched at the Empire, and only the same 200 people showed up?

A couple hundred Sumo regulars rattling around the vastness of the Empire would look seriously shit, and be very embarrassing.

All we could do was wait and see. We were nervous. We were excited.

As I packed down all our props at 4am, I waved bye to the bar staff, glass collectors and doormen who were heading off into staff taxis. The last two guys out of the building were myself and Johnny, the venue manager.

Johnny and I had become mates over the last five years, and we'd weathered many a storm together. From listening to me vent about quiet nights in the early days to helping me manage the madness when we'd had over a thousand a week crushed in the place - Johnny was always as calm as a rock. His level-headedness was handy when we were thinking about filling a swimming pool from a fire hydrant, or wondering how best to position a knife-thrower so no one died. We always cashed up together around 2am, in the minuscule Cornerhouse office, deep in the bowels of the building. Chugging a quick beer, whizzing through the task of cashing up and throwing five grand in coins into the safe in some sort of order.

I felt like a total twat not saying anything to him, not giving him a heads up about what was to come. He was a good guy. He'd of course get the full story, the following Monday morning.

A Cornerhouse Epilogue

The Cornerhouse ultimately understood why we had to go. With Thursday and Saturday already out the door, us taking the Friday clubnight away left them little choice. The company put it up for sale after holding a handful of their own 'farewell Cornerhouse' events. There was a great dance music event called Dusted that took place monthly there for years, and from memory, I think those guys gave the place a decent send off.

The club was bought and reopened as a nightclub. It was about six months after we'd established Sumo at Empire, and there was of course, a tiny buzz that Cornerhouse "Was Back".

I don't know this for certain, but my memory tells me that a young lad called Alan was the new owner of the club, and his dad had bought it for him as a gift/investment. His dad had something to do with Fulton's Foods in Yorkshire. I could be completely wrong about that, but I'm going with that as the tale without anyone to correct me. Alan was about 23 years old and I met him just the once. He wore a puffer jacket and a flat cap. He told me he was going to bring back the club's glory days, and I wished him the best of luck.

I remember walking past the venue and seeing the huge posters they had filled the windows with, promoting their brand new Friday night. The Clubnight was called Fingered, and the poster read (obviously), *'Come and Get Fingered, every Friday at Cornerhouse'*.

I realised this wasn't going anywhere, and wouldn't be a threat to what we were doing at Empire.

A few weeks after the venue reopened, I saw Bobzilla in town, he told me he'd been in for a look, and he said, *'It's like the black hole of Calcutta'* in there now'.

It's not a very dignified final chapter in the venue's life. Still, I'm sure almost everyone remembers the venue in all its glory as the home of the legendary clubnights, Sixty Nine, Sumo and a place where some of the biggest acts in the world came and strutted their stuff.

After that not-so-grand reopening in 2011, it lasted about nine months. It's been closed since - and now the site is owned by Network Rail, who own the train station of course. I hear it will probably turn into office space one day soon. Sadly, I can't see it ever being a nightclub again.

IV

THE EMPIRE

The Gold Standard

The Empire is a ridiculously good nightclub. I'm not just saying it. I'm not biassed. You probably think I am, but I'm not. I've been in many many clubs, venues, bars, dives. I spent four years clubbing and gigging in the city of Leicester. I did a couple of years in Portsmouth. I know my way around London. I've seen a band play in just about every place you can see a band perform, in the North of England. Also - I went to Ibiza for, erm, five days and on one of those nights, I went clubbing. For a couple of hours anyway.

So I believe I am qualified, and you will have to trust me when I say - the Empire, is bloody good.

I also watched 15 years' worth of Teessiders leave our town for Universities in cities across the UK. I would see regulars at Empire, out for their leaving parties, drunk, kissing their friends goodbye, telling everyone who'd listen, loudly and drunk, that they'd never come *'back to this shithole again'*.

I'd see them all return, I'd see them in the Lounge, I'd see them on Twitter. Back in Boro. Who's out this weekend? Can't wait to get back in the Empire. Best club in the UK. Best club in the world. That's what they do. That's what they say.

For us as the Sumo promoters, moving into the place, we loved it. Everything just *worked*. After five years at Cornerhouse, with its spit and sawdust vibe and string and sellotape technical spec, the fact that the place even powered up, was a blessing. We knew we'd struggle to fill the huge club, but we figured we'd cross that bridge when we came to it (in about a week - fuck!) but for now, we stood back and marvelled at all the bonuses that our new home came with.

Some of these features you might think should be standard, but I assure you in nightclubs, the following are not usually taken care of;

- The fridges all worked, lit with red tubes, the drinks were ICE cold.
- The stage is huge, and as a former theatre, the stage is epic, perfect for bands, with easy access, massive red curtains and a nice easy load in for drum kits and big amps.
- There are dressing rooms, and there was a shower. There are huge cavernous spaces in the cellar for promoters like me to store huge props and boxes and boxes of shit.
- It's CLEAN - The place has an army of cleaners, led by the wonderful Lynn, who whizz around every single room, bar, dancefloor, corridor, nook and cranny of the place at around 6am every Saturday and Sunday morning - and they blitz the place with chemicals and elbow grease.
- They have a Matty. Matty is awesome. Matty fixes everything that gets broken. Matty replaces every broken bulb. Matty fills every punched hole in every wall. Matty repairs every scuff and every chip each week. Matty fills a hundred fridges with thousands of cans and bottles. He does it by hand. He has huge muscles. Matty has giant machines that buff floors. Matty unblocks toilets. Matty climbs on the roof and fixes leaks. Matty paints, and paints, and paints and paints.
- The Empire has technicians. Invaluable people who know how a lighting desk works and know about things like C-Form power, in 16 or 32 amps. Whatever that is. Led by a lad called Paul, who's been there years and years, this army of techs are on a rota so you know that every Friday or Saturday, you'll have Jonsie, Tasker, Giblet, Alex, Dan,

Dan 2 or maybe even Dan 3 there to make the show come to life.
- As well as technicians the Empire has tech. By tech I mainly mean lights, and fucking loads of them. Plus smoke machines, pumping out fog, and a zillion projectors that Graham and TFT naturally had firing visuals all over the place, onto 20-foot high walls and even up into the Empire's vast cavernous ceiling.

Whatever we needed (and we planned on needing loads), we had the Empire's team on hand to help us make it happen. There was no disrespect to the Cornerhouse team and good old Jonny, who did their best to facilitate our mad whims. But in the Empire, the team helped us pull off some pretty large scale shenanigans that we couldn't have done alone.

To be honest, the Empire sometimes even made sure that our somewhat DIY ideas were brought up to a decent standard and followed some sort of health and safety regulations.

The Empire team kept (and continues to keep) the place maintained to a crazy high standard. Led by co-owner/manager Ash and his trusted deputy Peter, those guys and the team work round the clock, every single day, passionately and almost pedantically, making sure that every detail is taken care of. You can't knock them for that.

I've Not Made An Empire Map

We made a few Empire maps over the years. Marty made some great flyers for Metropolis Saturday's that folded out into a big map of the place. When we had gigs up in Rock Box on the first floor, or The Gods, up on the second floor (or third floor as some people mistakenly called it), we often made posters and flyers or handed out maps to bewildered lost souls.

Although not as dark and winding as the Cornerhouse, The Empire was as much a labyrinth as Sumo's previous home. Endless stairs, multiple ways to get to the same room, and the dark purple and deep red painted walls all tend to merge into one, after a few Red Stripes.

The fact the place still exists, and you can all go there and walk around it, I think lets me off the hook from making a map. I won't do it justice. Here's a list of the rooms we used as part of Sumo, Metropolis, MILK, and other adventures

- The Ground Floor. Sometimes, in an attempt to grandify it, we called it The Main Hall.
- The Stage. Like what it says on the tin. It's the stage. Good for bands. Good for dancing on.
- The First Floor. It became known as The Pop Floor. Once we figured out that only one type of music works up there.
- The Rock Box. Later renamed The Chapel.

- The Lounge / The Cocktail Lounge / Peter's Bar / The VIP Room / The Love Lounge - the place you'd find me around 3am necking Long Island Iced Teas.
- The Gods - at the top top of the tower. Home to Kaboom, and the occasional gig. Bands never thanked me for the load in and load out up and down 500 steps.

Sumo Is Moving

October 2010

Sumo. Is. Moving. That's what the flyer said. That's pretty much all the flyer said.

We had twenty thousand massive full colour square leaflets printed ready. Half the boxes just said that; that Sumo had moved. We smashed ten thousand of those flyers far and wide for a whole week. Alongside this, we pushed the message online to our social media following. There was no more Sumo at Cornerhouse, and we had a new home. We didn't say where.

We took a Friday off on October 1st. It was the first Friday that there hadn't been a Sumo in 5 years. We needed to let the dust settle, gather our thoughts, and of course, promote the living shit out of our new launch party date - October 8th, 2010.

The whole town was talking about the news. As always, in situations like this, you get many comments and trolling from people who absolutely must give their opinion, despite the fact they hadn't been to Sumo in forever. Everyone soon piled on the We-Love-Cornerhouse bandwagon and slated our plans before they even knew the full story. We remained focused on our plan, and stuck the blinders on. If these fuckers weren't turning up at the Cornerhouse (remember, we were down to about 200 people a week), then we weren't going to listen to them online. As much as I loved the regulars, and I really wanted to support their feedback, I knew we'd never survive with only a handful of the old guard. They'd have to join us onboard the new venue; we couldn't stay behind for them and lose everything.

With our Sumo-less weekend out the way, the Monday before launch night was upon us. We tore open the secretly stashed boxes that contained the other flyers, and loudly and proudly announced our new home - The Middlesbrough Empire.

It was totally unexpected, but pretty much everyone supported the new venue choice. What was bizarre was that everyone had incorrectly theorised all week online what the choice of our new home would be. People seemed convinced we'd be going to Medicine Bar, Basement, or perhaps Onyx Rooms. All of these venues, in my mind, were too small.

The problem we had, though, was that the Empire was big.

Empire was very very big.

The Sumo Empire Launch Party

Friday 8th October 2010

With a couple of hundred regulars, a five year old clubnight, and a slightly tarnished reputation for a few events such as Pound Sumo going tits up, I think I was right to be nervous.

For the first time ever, I didn't feel the buzz online that we used to get, and I knew we'd lose a few of the metalheads that needed to hide in the shadows of a grimy old venue. The Empire was fancy, plush, beautiful, grand and other words that we'd used for years to promote our Saturdays there.

When launch day rolled around, we'd already spent a couple of days prepping our new venue. Our feng shui tricks were out in full force as we tried desperately to close down space in the cavernous venue. We lined the Empire's humongous dancefloor with tall marble tables, we'd strung up a giant projection screen that covered the front of the ten metre wide stage, and we'd covered the abundance of internal glass windows and wrought iron railings with Sumo hoarding. We'd done our best to make the 1400 capacity 18th century theatre look like Sumo. It still looked like a 1400 capacity 18th century theatre, but with Sumo branding dotted around. And that looked pretty cool.

We'd put Burnsey upstairs on the first floor for Indie, and we had Rock in pride of place in the massive main hall. We'd put a few daft trimmings in place including our little TVs with Pac Man to play, a retro sweet shop, and some face painters.

Don't ask me how or when or why we started doing face painting in nightclubs. I've mentioned it to people from other towns in passing over the years and they look at me like I'm mad. Yes, face painting is usually something you'd expect at a seven year olds birthday party, and something that anyone over nine years old would surely cringe at. However, when 18 to 25 year olds are drunk and roll into a nightclub in Middlesbrough, boy do they love face painting. So with all our staff assembled, the venue decorated, a few hundred glasses of bubbly poured and ready to dish out, and even a red carpet rolled out and gaffer taped down on the pavement outside... It was almost time to open the doors.

There's a magical little fifteen minute window of time that occurs between 10.45pm and 11pm, every Friday, and a Saturday, in the Empire. It's an odd quarter of an hour. I don't often miss working in clubnights, although it's a slice of time that I was fond of.

At 10.45pm in the Empire, the bar staff arrive, the door staff arrive, the DJs arrive. The venue that myself and a small handful of others had been rattling around in for hours, or even days, is suddenly a hive of activity. Peter begins furiously prepping the bar staff on how to make new drinks, or running them through new prices. The DJs start setting up, and the monstrous soundsystem fires up. Usually Kev or Craig would play a couple of hip hop tracks, maybe even at half-volume, but the bass swells around the room and up the walls. The doormen are exchanging stories, laughing big deep belly laughs, and stuffing Mcdonalds in as quick as they can while testing radios and signing in. The two Pauls are running around powering up things they forgot to power up three hours ago when they arrived and chain-smoked the last three hours away. At this point my phone goes daft. I'll get a heap of guestlist requests while I try to check through all the messages from the Facebook page, the Twitter DMs and also I'll get all the texts from staff that are running late. The first floor DJs will always be late, there must be something programmed into the Boro Taxis system that recognises Burnsey or Ste's numbers, and makes sure those guys get picked up nice and late. At this point 10.45pm has very quickly turned into 10.55pm and I'm starting to sweat a little. I'll usually be found in the DJ box, flapping, stressing, and ranting about how *"I've been in this fucking venue for thirteen hours already; how the fuck am I not ready? Why are the last fifteen minutes before doors ALWAYS like this?!?"* But I love it really.

Then the magic happens. Paul's been programming lights, tinkering with patterns, focusing things and pumping the place with plumes of fog, but you don't notice until he flicks the switch that shuts off all of the Empire's powerful internal white floodlights. As these house lights are killed, the place comes alive. The projections pop, and deep red and blue moving lights sweep and swirl slowly around the room, just hinting and highlighting subtle swaths of the venue's glorious aesthetic.

Outside, on October 8th 2010, a huge queue had begun to snake around the corner of the venue, and as it hit 11pm the people piled in, the bars swelled and everyone filled the dancefloor right away. Kev and Craig DJ'd together, 3 on 3, and played an absolute blinder. I can't tell you what they played, sadly I don't think there's a record of it.

My fears of anyone being too shy to let loose on Empire's vast dancefloors were maybe unfounded. Crowds moshed, pitted, shoved, pogo'd and danced non-stop without a care in the world. From those DJ boxes in Empire, you're above the crowd and you can see every face, and watch everyone's every move. We could see how much the people were loving it. Yes the place was massive, but people used the space, they filled the place up. As cliche as it sounds, more space gave them more room to bust moves. The people who wanted to slam dance could be in the same room as people who wanted to shoegaze around a handbag. They made the size of it work to their advantage.

At around 1am, I was dealing with a couple of chewy regulars telling me, loudly and drunkenly, that the music was terrible because the DJs wouldn't play their dumbshit request of an Everytime I Die song from the first album. I was patiently explaining to these guys that the great big mass of people on the dancefloor having a lovely time dancing to Paramore would all bail outside for a cigarette if we dropped an obscure metalcore track from 2001. There's an art to DJing a clubnight, and as far as I'm concerned, Craig, Kev and Dani had mastered it. Play as many requests as possible, keep as many people as possible happy, play across the board, cover all the genres that make up rock as best as you can, plenty of curveballs, get some new stuff in, play a tonne of old stuff, and then.... *always* from 1am - It's party time, and you unleash the bangers. So I had assured my Sumo regulars that we'd played a couple of ETID tracks earlier and now they should relax and enjoy themselves, and I was heading off to find a drink when I bumped into Graham.

The boss hadn't been to a Sumo in a couple of years but was, of course, around for the big launch in the new gaff. *"Hey, cheer up, you did it!"*. I was still feeling a bit deflated from having my ear chewed off, so I took a look around, 360, and soaked in the packed mass of people around us. *"Yeah, it feels good!"* I yelled back into Graham's ear. *"Good?!"* he said, *"... it's fucking great. You did it, you mad bastard, there's a thousand people here"*.

Graham had checked in on reception and done some quick maths on wristbands. We'd hit a thousand by 1am and by the time we took the till off at 2am we'd had around 1150 through the doors. The lads played until around 3.45am, Danielle took a million photos, and the whole event ran like clockwork. At 4am I didn't have to do my decor take-down, as we knew we could sort that tomorrow afternoon. Kev, Craig, Burnsey and I sat in the foyer, with a few mates and girlfriends and drinks. Ash came out from the back office and shook our hands and thanked us. He was buzzing, we were all buzzing. Sumo was back from the edge and back from the dead, and everyone was happy, and certainly relieved.

Side Note : It was in this fortnight leading up to the launch of Sumo, that Ash was doing his best to book some big name rock and metal acts. Our idea was that if we could secure a couple of live shows from household names, it would help win the moshers over, and let everyone know Empire was a rock and roll venue that could host an alternative clubnight. Ash had dates held for Slash and Miles Kennedy, Queens of The Stone Age and Deftones. As is sometimes the case, after many many emails and negotiations, the shows didn't quite get confirmed. What an top trio of shows that would have been to announce though.

Pound Sumo Part 2

Friday 15th October 2010

There are two events that are guaranteed to go well. Your first one, and your last one.

If you're a new band, your first gig should be packed; all your mates, your supportive partners, the curious live music lovers from the scene, and even your family should be there. Enjoy it, because it's all downhill from there. Most of your mates will soon drop off, your Mum and Dad are not coming again, sorry. The next best show your little band will ever have is the last one. Your last gig will be almost as good as your first. It's everyone's final show of support and it should be a decent turnout. This also applies with life - your first ever birthday party should be a fairly over the top celebration and probably quite well attended. Your funeral, also, great crowd.

Same with clubnights.

For that first Empire Sumo, with a little hindsight, it made sense that a thousand people would show up. The first time guitars had been blasted through that venue's massive speakers was a celebration for anyone into rock music, plus we had five years worth of Sumo-goers who would certainly want to come for a nosey. It's been my job for a long long time, to manage the expectations of a venue. The Empire probably thought they now had a thousand a week, they'd been fed enough hype about Sumo, and here we were to save their Fridays.

We couldn't risk dropping to a couple of hundred on week 2, so we rolled out the controversial Pound Sumo.

It was controversial because the Cornerhouse had helped royally fuck it up the first time. As we promoted the life out of this event, people were rightly sceptical. The idea of being jammed at a bar for half an hour, to be told loads of drinks had sold out, was how everyone recalled Pound Sumo from Cornerhouse. We had to turn the facts around, and we went hard with the message that the Empire had nine bars, thirty staff, and were super efficient at serving as fast as possible. We assured everyone that this Pound Sumo would be very different from the first. It felt a bit crappy to be essentially highlighting the Cornerhouses' weaknesses as we championed the Empire's ability to actually serve drinks.

However, it had to be done, we were fighting for survival, and we weren't going to rest on the coattails of a legacy that was a week old.

Thankfully, when the night came around, the Empire absolutely nailed it. There were around fifteen different drinks you could bag for a pound, the queue was massive, the ultra-efficient Dan and Carli on reception whizzed everyone in at lighting speed and the bar staff worked like crazy to fling drinks at people as fast as people could throw cash back at them.

Twelve hundred people piled in and partied with us that night. I know it sounds obvious that if you charged £1 in, and £1 for a drink, then it was going to be crazy. Sumo had been a fiver entry for so long that putting this one-off price on it drove everyone wild. We were really careful not to milk it, and kept our future pound-parties to a bare minimum. We planned and scheduled them on nights where we knew it was a bad date. Leeds Fest weekend, Download Fest, and a couple of other quiet weekends in clubnight world were turned around by this simple tactic. As many of these ideas were, this one was Graham's. You can't say he literally invented the concept of a pound party, but for the Middlesbrough clubnight scene, where standard door fees were £4-£6, his cheeky little move woke up sleepy weekends, and it wasn't long before every other clubnight in town was printing up flyers and posters and shouting about their Pound Parties.

This was also the start of all the other clubnight's in town copycatting pretty much everything we did. If we did a beach party, they would do a beach party. If we did a pound party, they did a pound party. Competition is healthy and necessary, but certain venues and certain promoters literally took our ideas and events and copied them in their entirety. I used to joke that a particular venue probably had a folder, in their office, that contained every event flyer we'd ever printed, and when they needed a new idea for a night, they'd just flick through their 'Ten Feet Tall Ideas To Rip Off' book, and pick one out. It turned out my joke was very much a reality, and this folder was shown to me years later. Flattering really.

We tried not to let stuff like that distract us. As long as we were coming up with the best ideas first, throwing the parties the best, then that's all we could do. Pound Sumo 2 was a massive success and we had two 1000+ events in our new home.

Side Note : Dan and Carli ran Empire reception for many years. At this event they got 900 people through the door in one hour. 900 people in 60 minutes means you need to service one person every 4 seconds. That's money handed, change given, and wristband on. What a dream team. I can't imagine sitting there taking a load of shit banter from drunks for 4 hours every Friday and Saturday Night. They did it, and they did it very well. They're both incredibly hard working people and both very successful business people in their own rights these days.

An Empire Playlist

A New Ten Feet Tall Office

I'd had a decent amount of help relaunching Sumo successfully in its new home, and it was a real team effort. As nice as it was to have Graham and the TFT team all pitching in, the all-hands-on-deck approach to Sumo was pretty exhausting. Doing everything by committee takes time, and I'd been very used to doing everything Sumo my own way for so long.

As was always the case , there were many plates to spin, other clubnights to juggle, comedy clubs and other gigs. So I was left to my own devices from that point with Sumo again, which was great.

We also had the task of moving into our new Ten Feet Tall office. Graham had been exploring the town for a great office space for us all, since the news that the Royal Scientific Institute and TFT HQ had been sold. He'd asked the council if they had any rooms within the Town Hall, that perhaps we could rent. They said there was one... although it hadn't been touched for around twenty years. Graham took Marty and I over for a viewing, and we knew we had to have it.

The Town Hall Courtroom had originally been Teesside's Law Courts back in the seventies. The huge room had a forty-foot ceiling with a stained glass roof, massive ancient wooden benches, pews, a press gallery and even a dock in the middle. The room also had holding cells underneath it in a basement. The whole place had randomly been converted into a canteen in the nineties, for council workers to sit and eat their dinner in, and a large working industrial kitchen had been fitted in the back.

The courtroom would make an impressive, slightly bizarre office space for the six of us and a few weeks later me, Ted, Robin, Ste, Jamie, Marty and Graham set about lugging all our computers, desks and piles of weird party props down Albert Road (in shopping trolleys and on sack barrows) into our new home. The old holding cells in the basement made ideal storage for all our posters, flyers, props and junk.

It was the start of an amazing few years full of memories working from that grand old room.

As well as all us lads and of course Debby our accountant, we added some new key people to the crew. Charlotte became our office manager, my girlfriend Claire had come onboard pretty much full time, we had Cat and Kim for help with Bad Med and Sumo and we brought Henry in for more band booking and press. In addition, a whole host of part-time people would pop in for a few hours a week to pick up wads of flyers to hand out in town and the University, then usually muck in at the weekend too, face painting, or any other random task we could throw at them.

So now we had a large core team plus an army of DJs and photographers, plus friends and friends-of-friends, that constantly popped in to hang out in the courtroom with us as we worked.

The Town Hall continued to use the kitchen at the back of our new office for catering for their bigger touring shows. Some days, we'd be working away while a team of chefs made Van Morrison's dinner or baked bread for Jools Holland. The smells would fill the courtroom, and we'd all work late those nights, get fed on all the leftover food, then slip into the gigs from the caterer's secret entrance. The Town Hall was another labyrinth of a venue, and there were plenty of hidden doors and passages that led from our office into the town hall's many rooms and areas.

A NEW TEN FEET TALL OFFICE

Side Note : The original TFT office was on the first floor of The Old Cleveland Scientific Institute – a beautiful old building at the top of Albert Road next door to the Medicine Bar, or the Purple Onion as it was once called. The 140 year old Victorian building was sold to developers to convert into student accommodation. The building was partially listed, or some historical factors were involved in the renovation. So at 5am once Sunday morning, they flattened it. The company got a huge fine, and they were banned from developing property on the site. So now it's a car park.

My Other Jedward Story

Friday 5th November 2010

I'm not shy about booking a tribute band. If you get the right one, in the right scenario, it's a recipe for a good time. Getting the balance wrong and you could have a cringe worthy disaster of an event. I'd like to think the couple of tributes I selected for Sumo over the years made people smile, and certainly the crowd reactions were always great. Yes, there were a few arms-folded-stand-at-the-back folks huffing and puffing - but I think we showcased enough original bands, and pumped enough into championing new music to afford us the occasional frivolity of a tribute act.

Just a handful of weeks into our new home of Empire, I was itching to get some bands on that huge stage, that some say is the jewel in the crown of the venue. I booked a Blink182 tribute known as Binkl182, made up of local lads that we knew from other decent original acts. I'd known these guys a while and knew they'd deliver. The drummer Jonsie was also a lighting technician at the club, so an added bonus would be that the light show would be amazing. I still had to convince a few Cornerhouse mourners that Empire was a proper rock and roll venue, so this was going to help I was certain. As usual though, I couldn't help fuck with the format and have a bit of fun.

My old pals Jedward had recently released a horrific cover version of Blink 182's 'All The Small Things' - much to the horror of moshers and punk kids across the planet (sorry John, sorry Edward, it's not very good). I quickly circulated a rumour online that Binkl182 would be joined on stage, for one song, by some very secret guests from The Pop World. I added that security around the venue that night would be very tight, and that this collaboration wouldn't be for everyone, but it was certainly a world first, and we asked everyone in Teesside to make sure they didn't miss this spectacular event.

The rumour blew up, and many believed we were going to bring back Jedward to the venue to sing All The Small Things with our tribute. Many voiced concern that the Sumo crowd would eat Jedward alive and bottle them off. Most people just said they'd be there to witness the carnage.

Of course, Jedward weren't coming to play.

But my friends and fearless up-for-anything duo 'Raptastic' (AKA Simon and Simon) would be the pair of jokers that would take the stage, and the possible bottling. Raptastic had performed at so many of my events over the years, and when I asked them to do this, they agreed in a heartbeat. We snuck the two Simon's into the Empire shortly after Binkl182 began soundcheck, and got them into a dressing room where Claire was waiting with two blonde wigs that she applied, cut into Jedward-quiffs and hair sprayed into position.

We'd of course, bought a pair of matching suits for the guys. Plus, I proudly placed my two round based mic stands at the side of the stage for when "John and Edward" would make their entrance later that evening.

Binkl182 (no typo) hit the stage around midnight to a decent reception. Dave ('Tom') did his best American Delonge-twang accent and ripped the piss out of the crowd for a good half hour as they blasted through a frantic greatest hits set. He continued to hype the 'Special Guests' that would be joining them for the finale. As the end of the set approached the room was packed, and there was a real sense of anticipation in the air. I was reading

Facebook posts and tweets on my phone from people who had claimed they'd seen Jedweard in Boro town centre that day getting coffee. This was ridiculous. This was perfect.

Backstage the two Simons were ready, and with the radio mic's hand, they were poised, ready to spring onto the stage and meet their fate. Dave Delonge announced that this was the final song and that he'd like to welcome two very special young guests to the stage.

"Ladies and Gentlemen of Sumo.. please make some noise and welcome to the Empire stage... the one... the two... the twin kings of Pop!

Heeeeeeeere's JEDWARD!".

The crowd erupted into a sea of boos. I stood in the wings, watching hundreds of faces flash with pure fury. Simon and Simon bounded onto the stage, leaping around like maniacs, high kicking, jumping off the drum risers and waving enthusiastically to the sea of people.

It was a noise I'll never forget, the boos turned into a roar of cheers, mixed with laughter, and I watched the faces in the crowd, one by one, crack up.

It was a ten second moment, and a fairly daft joke we'd spent weeks setting up. It hinged on the Sumo masses having a sense of humour.

It also relied on everyone knowing who the hell Raptastic were.

Thankfully, they all did.

Two Bands One Stage

Ever since watching in bewilderment as a French guy played a drum kit through ten guitar effects pedals, in the corridor between rooms in The Arena in 2001, I was on a quest to create gigs that were a little different.

I'd got Raptastic to be Jedward. I'd got Avalanche Party to be Biffy Clyro. I also loved putting bands on in ridiculous places and packing them into the most confined spaces possible, almost as if to distil the electric atmosphere of a live performance down into its rawest, most intense or purest form.

One thing I'd always wanted to try was two bands playing a gig at the same time.

Now I had that big Empire stage and the captive audience of Sumo; I set about making the plan. Two of the best local acts at the time were East Cleveland melodic punks Glass Avalanche and Boro lads Lifeless, who played a mix of old skool thrash, speed metal and aggressive hardcore.

I had to sell the idea to both bands. I explained that they'd all be on stage simultaneously, so ten lads with instruments taking turns playing songs. That sounded simple enough chaos, and they were in.

Next, I talked through my plan with Nathan.

Nathan is a living legend, an extremely talented sound engineer, and the man that brings sound to Teesside. His PA systems and team of engineers are almost always the guys making any gig in Boro nice and loud. From the Town Hall and Empire, to the Westgarth, to Ku Bar. Nathan could be a novel in his own right, so I won't bang on. However, it has to be said that Nathan is also the nicest man in Teesside. Ask anyone who has met him. There is no truer or more honest man.

I explained the show to Nathan, and after talking me through the technical aspects involved (which went completely over my head), he agreed, as always, to help make it happen.

Paul and Jonesy, the Empire techs, helped me set up the stage, focus lights and build two big drum risers. The way the show would work would be that the band playing would be lit with the Empire's epic lighting rig, strobes, chases, moving heads and maybe a little pyro popping. At the end of the first song, that band, Glass Avalanche, would be plunged into darkness, and Lifeless would kick in with their song as the lights fired up around them. They'd ping pong one-on-one for about half an hour, and it would hopefully be unique and interesting.

When the day came, we soundchecked around 6pm and, as sheepish as everyone was, it looked and sounded amazing. I knew the guys would relax and bust their rockstar moves after a case or two of cold beers that I had waiting for them in the dressing rooms. I was excited for the night.

Another good reason for doing daft gigs where bands do shit differently is that their mates are much more likely to come to these gigs. Like all local bands, these bands did play Boro quite regularly, but there was a buzz on this show due to its odd format.

When midnight rolled around and it was time for the bands to take the stage, everyone played their part perfectly, and the Lifeless and Glass Avalanche fans packed the Empire dancefloor right up to the front of the stage and cheered their pals along. I knew Lifeless were fairly cheeky, and I had a feeling they would take this opportunity to show off and try and one-up Glass Avalanche.

As Lifeless were lit up for their turn to play their next number, their singer Nixon proudly swung a dead pig's head around whilst screaming through their song. After a minute or so, he launched the head into the crowd. I'd positioned myself in the crowd for the show, anticipating some hijinks from either one of the bands. As the band raged on, the pig's head became a grim game of football on Empire dancefloor. I swiftly grabbed a bin bag from behind the bar and scooped up the slimy head. I slung it over my shoulder and made my way to the bins out the side door of the venue. This thing was heavy. Call me a killjoy, but all I could think was that some poor vegan would get knocked off their feet like a skittle by this beastly bloody thing.

As the show made its way to the end, Glass Avalanche launched into a cover of Lit's 'My Own Worst Enemy'. They had the crowd singing along and bouncing around, and I breathed a sigh of relief that the pig's head was the only thing I'd had to deal with. I wasn't bothered about the shock stage stunts, I was just glad the show had worked, technically there'd been no hitches, and it looked and sounded great.

That's when Lifeless brought out their fire breather.

For their grand finale, they'd enlisted their mate Ste (*not* a trained fire breather) to come on stage and 'perform'. I knew the band well enough, and I knew Ste, and I knew this was a bad idea. I made a run for the stage and began waving my arms and shouting *"No No No"*, which was futile over the noise of the band's last song. Ste spat a mouthful of something over a lighter, creating a plume of fire that billowed over the stage. I later learned this was flour. I didn't even know that was a thing, but apparently, flour makes a perfectly fiery and utterly dangerous fire breathing effect. Do not try that at home. Please. Ste turned to the crowd and spat another gob of fiery gloop out into the audience. A blob of molten flour, still flaming, landed square on the head of a lad in the crowd. I froze with fear for a few seconds. Time seemed to go into slow motion, and I remember just thinking, *'Thank fuck he's got a shaved head, thank fuck he has no hair, thank fuck he's one of their mates'.* He pulled up his hood and patted his head before whipping the hood down again, revealing a smoking head. He was laughing and cheering his mates along - totally unphased by what had just happened.

Fun Fact: This wasn't the only time pig heads made an appearance. When Ricks' band Wraiths played years later, their stage set featured not one but two pigs' heads on spikes.

Big Barry

So...

The Empire is currently managed and owned by Ash and Barry. Its previous manager and owner is a man called Barry, the father of the aforementioned current part-owner.

If you can't follow that, think of it: The Empire was Big Barry's, and now it's Little Barry's and Ash's. I think.

Back in the day, and probably still to a certain extent, Big Barry was a force of nature. An obviously brilliant businessman and I dare say a bit of a rogue. He currently lives a stone's throw away from me, in our sleepy-ish North East village, and I give him a wave when I see him walking his dog.

Through the nineties, Big Barry ran a legendary Friday called Sugarshack that attracted the world's biggest names in house and dance music and packed the club to the rafters weekly. Judge Jules, Pete Tong, Erik Morello, Lisa Lashes, Boy George, and everyone worth their salt in that genre performed many times, and the backstage stories that go along with those years would no doubt shadow my tales of Sumo. There will be enough Big Barry stories to fill another book and I reckon The Book Of Big Baz would be way wilder than this one.

I had to include one tale. Here's my Big Barry story.

It was around 2006, The Subways were playing the Empire one Saturday, and I was stage manager. The band had two massive hits with Oh Yeah and Rock n Roll Queen, and the show was sold out to capacity.

It's no exaggeration that the atmosphere was electric; the crowd had been drinking since they woke up that day, and it was a sweaty, lairy sea of arms and legs from the moment the band had struck the first note of their set.

Let me take a moment to tell you about Mojo barrier.

Mojo barrier, is the barrier that stands at the front of the stage. It's sheets of steel, a metre square, and it's held together with giant bolts the size of fat sausages. It's the thing that the front row of dedicated super fans hug throughout a gig. It's also the thing that, if you look like you're getting squished, security will pull you over it, and walk you away from the stage - along the two metre wide space that runs between the front of a stage, and the crowd.

At this Subways show, this space between the stage and the Mojo was policed by our local security (Big Martie, Big John and Other John), who were frantically catching crowd surfers.

Towards the end of the set The Subways singer/guitarist Billy chugged out the opening riff of Rock and Roll Queen and it was as if someone had given each of the thousand punters a personal adrenaline shot. Every single person in the room, went fucking bananas.

A minute later, in the breakdown of the song. Billy had sprinted and launched himself up from the stage into the royal box that overlooked the dancefloor (a move I've also since seen Frank Carter and Rou Reynolds manage successfully). From the royal box, he marched around the Empire's circular balcony that loomed around six metres above the crowd, before launching himself onto the sea of hands below and got passed back to the stage.

It was a truly magnificent rock star move, and he was met with a roar of approval from the rabid crowd.

At that point, the Mojo barrier broke.

I was in the pit, helping catch crowd surfers with security, when I saw the middle of the steel barrier buckle, then it just ripped - right down the middle. As if it were a piece of paper.

Bodies spilled through the gap; Big Martie caught them, moved them, and luckily managed to flip down the broken piece of barrier flat to the floor, so no one was cut. The band stopped playing and in the confusion of not knowing what was really happening they walked off stage and up to the dressing rooms while we all figured out what to do.

I quickly assembled Big Martie, and the tour manager in the wings of the stage, we needed a plan. Neither of them would allow the show to finish, without the Mojo barrier in place. We needed to remove the broken piece, slide the barrier back together and re-bolt it. That would have been pretty easy, but there was no way of doing it with a thousand people pushing their weight forwards up to it.

We just needed everyone to take two steps back, and we'd be able to solve the problem.

TFT's Bryan was at the show, and he grabbed the radio mic from the DJ box and addressed the crowd. No one was listening, the fans had begun singing, dancing, and the choruses of Why Are We Waiting and Pig Bag drowned out Bryan's efforts to reason with them.

The tour manager decided we should ask Billy to try and talk to them. And by we, he meant me. *"It's your shit barrier that broke mate"* he said by way of reasoning.

I trudged up to the dressing room where a topless Billy was pouring with sweat, necking water while Charlotte, wife and bass player, sat with her head in her hands. She'd figured out what had gone wrong and was quite shaken.

Billy agreed to speak to the audience. As he took to the stage the crowd roared and cheered and after settling them down he did a pretty good job of explaining what needed to be done - if everyone didn't shimmy back about a metre, the show wouldn't be able to finish. I watched as most people tried their best to push back, but it just seemed as if the back half of the room weren't budging.

We walked back into the wings of the stage. Billy and Charlotte had their guitars ready, and the drummer was sitting at the kit, but everyone just stared at the floor. Big Martie came over and said what we were all thinking;

"That crowd ain't moving, I think it's time to call it... I think the show is over guys".

That was when I heard him.

A big booming Boro voice came over the PA system;

"Get back ya' Bastards. Everyone. Move. The. Fuck. BACK!"

It was Big Barry.

I didn't even know he was at the gig - he rarely even came to the club anymore but he'd been watching events unfold from the office on the venue CCTV system. He'd come to the stage and picked up the radio mic Bryan had tried earlier to speak to the crowd on.

Martie peered round the curtain, then looked back at us and grinned. *"They've only fucking moved back!"*. He leapt into the pit, slid out the broken barrier piece and pulled the two sides of Mojo back together and bolted it securely. After a little reassurance and convincing, the band strode back on stage and finished the set to rapturous applause.

—

After the show, around 11pm, we loaded out. As was routine on Saturdays - The band went out the back door, the front doors opened to the public for the clubnight - so I still had another five hours of work ahead of me. I was glad that gig was behind me. As we said goodbye and gave thanks to the band, Charlotte made me promise we'd scrap the whole Mojo barrier and replace it, which we did. The band returned a few times to perform, and every other gig went off without a hitch.

I never got a chance to talk to Barry about that show or thank him, Bryan or Martie properly for their help. But thanks fellas. I owe you one.

Middlesbrough Music Live

Somehow, in amongst all the madness, Ten Feet Tall managed to book, promote, organise and run a huge music festival each year. The thing started quite small and morphed into a total beast over about a decade.

The slightly un-inspiringly titled Middlesbrough Music Live is very fondly remembered by anyone who attended the event between 2000 and 2011. I wanted to give the thing a notable mention because while it lasted, it was a huge part of everyone at Ten Feet Tall's life, including mine.

MML took place on the first weekend in June each year, and from its inception in 2000, each year more stages and more acts got added. Graham pushed and pushed the boundaries of what it could be, and eventually by 2009 there were ten stages in the centre of the town, all free, each with around ten bands, and every stage was at capacity for most of the day. I'm told about 60,000 people attended the event in its later years.

The whole thing was funded by Middlesbrough Council, who stumped up about £100,000 to make the thing happen; they handed the reins (mostly) to us to do what we wanted. We called on local infrastructure hero Big Martie to sort out some massive stages (and high quality barriers), we roped the Empire, The Town Hall and all the pubs around them into hosting stages too, and we got Stubbsy and Henry to book as many mint bands as they could.

The local police force and licensing department were always against the festival. A real shame. As years went on, they insisted on wrapping the site in fences, and also tripling the police presence. The bills for these things came out of the budget, leaving a lot less to pay bands with. We focused on booking emerging talent, which were cheaper of course and, luckily, people had a decent appetite for them in those days.

Here's a few key bands that played each year, to give you a flavour of how good the thing was.

Have a Google and see for yourself how epic Middlesbrough Music Live became.

2000
Terrorvision. Eddi Reader, Pellethead, Kitachi, Loon.

2001
Shed Seven, Crazy World Of Arthur Brown, Proud Mary, The Wildcats Of Kilkenny, Space.

2002
Wheatus, The Cooper Temple Clause, Easyworld, Geno Washington, Dreadzone, Minuteman.

2003
Reef, The Darkness, Keane, Junior Senior, Biffy Clyro, Oceansize.

2004
Razorlight, Kasabian, Ordinary Boys, Kaiser Chiefs, Bloc Party, Goldie Lookin Chain, The Eighties Matchbox B-line Disaster, Reuben, Electric Six, Kosheen, Dead 60s, Alistair Griffin, The Black Velvets, Viking Skull.

2005

The Thrills, Editors, We Are Scientists, The Proclaimers, ¡Forward, Russia!, The Cribs, Nine Black Alps, The Paddingtons, Kubb, Estelle, Mostly Autumn, Queen Adreena, Towers Of London, Johnny Panic, Fastlane, The Departure.

2006

Ocean Colour Scene, Paolo Nutini, The Pigeon Detectives, Little Man Tate, Larrikin Love, The Sunshine Underground, The Rumble Strips, Bromheads Jacket, Howling Bells, Morning Runner, The Modern, Zebrahead, XTN, Skindred, Sign, Brigade, Chairmen Of The Bored, Hope Of The States, Vincent Vincent and the Villains, Reverend and The Makers, Enter Shikari.

2007

Tony Christie, The Twang, Dub Pistols, Terry Hall, Dykeenies, Drive by Argument, The Envy Corps, Elliot Minor, Newton Faulkner, The Films, Shy Child, The Ghost of a Thousand, Good Shoes, The Hours, I was a Cub Scout, Kubichek!, Amy MacDonald, Lucky Soul, Malpractice, Mancini, Mayor McCA, Middleman, Miss Conduct, One Night Only, Pama International, Priestess, Steriogram, Tiny Dancers, To My Boy, Yourcodenameis:Milo, Flood of Red.

2008

Ash, Black Kids, The Infadels, You Me At Six, Outcry Collective, We Are The Ocean, The Bookhouse Boys, One Night Only, Delays, Sam Isaac, Late Of The Pier, Noah And The Whale, Hijak Oscar, The Anomalies, Glamour Of The Kill, Natty, Parka, Slaves Of Gravity, Dan Le Sac vs Scroobius Pip, The Hot Melts, Go Audio, The Lexingtons, Royworld

2009

The Zutons, The Sunshine Underground, Tommy Sparks, Dan Black, Master Shortie, Frank Turner, Dinosaur Pile-Up, Future of the Left, Twin Atlantic, Pulled Apart by Horses, Rumblestrips, Qemists, Sounds of Guns, Noah and The Whale, Beth Jeans Houghton, Bear Hands.

2010

The Blackout, Millionaires, The Hoosiers, Example, Professor Green, Sweet Baboo, Young Guns, Exit Calm, Little Comets, Erol Alkan, John Power, The Flatliners, The Blackout, Detroit Social Club, Cate Le Bon, CW Stoneking, Hot Club De Paris, Peter Hook's Freebass.

In 2011 we had the sad news that the council's £100k was gone.

Funding cuts to the arts meant potentially no festival that year. We convinced the council to try another route, offering the town a paid festival. Typically most people complained, moaned, and the wonderful people of the internet accused us of 'cashing in' on a decade of goodwill.

It was a tenner to see a hundred bands. Despite selling 7000 tickets, the experiment was deemed a catastrophic failure. The council shelved the festival, and it never returned in any shape or form. A massive shame.

Here's my Top 6 Middlesbrough Music Live Backstage Tales

1. When The Thrills arrived on site, they started to unpack their truck onto the road. They'd blocked an entrance, so we told the driver he had to move quickly. He promptly reversed the bus and trailer right over all the band's guitars that were stacked on the road behind him.
2. Estelle showed up to perform just minutes before she was due on stage. She handed the sound engineer a 3 track CD and said she'd mime along. Graham handed her the CD back and said *"No, you'll sing live, for half an hour please, as per contract."* He added; *"You're getting £500 for this you know!"*.
3. My good friend Charlotte, our office manager, proofread the MML brochures when they came back from print. She pointed out that there was a band playing 4 or 5 times across multiple stages, and surely this was a design error. I asked her the band's name. She said *"They're*

called 'See Website For Details'".

4. Ten bands on one stage means tight turnaround times, and lightning fast changeovers. Bands would show up, load in, play, get 10 minutes to catch their breath in the shared dressing room, then get loaded out. I had the job of politely telling Donnie Tourette from The Towers Of London he needed to get out the dressing room as we needed it for the next act. *"You fucking come in here and make me get out then"* - he sneered. I went and got Stubbsy. Thanks Stubbsy. I still don't know how you got him out.

5. A hundred bands on site meant 500 rock stars that needed feeding. We converted our office into a canteen, and a fantastic lady called Suzie and her team cooked all day long. The budget was so tight we only had enough meal vouchers for band members. However, each of the ten stages came with two sound engineers, loaders, pit crew and a lighting op. So that's another hundred people working a twelve-hour day. They needed feeding, we had zero budget to feed them. Between me and Suzie we'd make sure portions were adjusted so there was enough food to go around and I'd sneak out meal vouchers to the team so everyone got fed and watered.

6. Goldie Lookin' Chain, performing on the main stage to thousands of people, made the following announcement mid-set; *"Thanks everyone, especially Jamie from Ten Feet Tall, for all the Weeeeed!"*. We were mortified, but managed to laugh about it later.

Mosh Or Die

Mosh or Die was a clubnight in which there were three rooms, and every room was a rock room.

Instead of trying to appeal to a few different groups of people and spreading our bets, I wanted to make a clubnight that was exclusively for moshers. After all, there are plenty of sub-genres within the world of mosh. And so Mosh or Die was born.

We ran the event in a few different places, The Cornerhouse, Onyx Rooms, Blue and Basement and of course The Empire. The set up usually comprised of a punk and pop-punk room, a heavier room for metal and hardcore and a third room for classic rock, hair metal and eighties rock. In essence, it was like going to Bad Medicine, Animals V Machines and Sumo all at once.

The events were few and far between, but I'm glad we did them. I feel I can pull this card out, if anyone ever tries to label me a sell-out.

Xmas In July

The Saturday nights in Cornerhouse, SaturGay, were run by two lads called Phil and Simon. They and their team would usually show up on a Saturday afternoon to dress the venue in swooshing colourful satin drapes, twinkling lights and other plush features. So our paths would sometimes cross and we tried to make sure all our random Sumo shit was out the way before they started their set up.

Each year in July, Simon and Phil would throw the wildest, most Christmassy party the summer had seen. I don't think they necessarily invented 'Xmas In July' but I'd never seen or heard of it, and these guys did it really really well. When they left Cornerhouse in around 2009 I saw our chance to continue the tradition and try to throw our own mid-Summer Xmas special. I honestly don't think I borrowed anyone else's ideas that often, if ever really, but this one I certainly pinched from SaturGay. Thanks Simon, thanks Phil.

The event became a staple of Sumo's July calendar each year and I dare say we did a pretty good job of injecting a random night of festive cheer into Boro's Summer.

I'd call on one of my tallest and broadest mates, usually Be Quiet Shout Loud bassist Big Dave or Raptastic's Simon, and dig out a Santa suit for them. We'd build a ramshackle grotto where our revellers could sit and get their photo taken with Santa. Everyone wanted that random profile pic for their socials and the queue to see Santa would snake up the Cornerhouse's long central corridor.

We'd always do a half decent job of saving as many Christmas decorations from December as we could, and each July these were dragged out from the bowels of the venue's storage zones and gaffer taped or cable tied around the place. Our July Christmas event looked like a party that had happened the night before, and been trashed by an army of drunks. That was the vibe we ran with at Cornerhouse and our crowd loved it.

When we levelled up to the Empire, most of our events had to level up too, the DIY ethic of our prop-building and giveaways had to match the Empire's grandeur and Xmas in July was taken up a few notches too. Santa's grotto in Empire took over the whole foyer of the club, and Santa was armed with giant red sacks of presents; Reindeer antlers and Santa hats. The decor we pulled out of Empire's cellar was top-grade and there were about 100 metres of fairy lights to string around the balconies. Preparation for Xmas in July became a three-day affair, all for a few hours of daft fun on a Friday night.

The Empire bars served 'Santa Shots' (red shit) and a 'Rudolph Nose' (red shit with a blob of cream on top), and everyone danced the night away to Last Christmas, Do They Know It's Christmas and Fairytale of New York - all slid perfectly in between the punk rock Sumo staples. Kev and I's cheesy covers band The Gimme Gimmicks played a couple of times, too; five drunk Santa's pogoing around the stage, playing our punk rock Christmas covers, went down a storm. Finding companies to hire me snow machines in Summer was a pain in the arse but we pulled it off.

Every year around April, Graham and Ash would roll their eyes as I had the designers prep the festive posters for the Xmas in July events. Despite their wisecracks, I knew we had messages from dozens of people already planning their outfits and even booking hotels for what became one of the jewels in the crown of the Sumo calendar.

Side Note : Big Dave continued to do an utterly first-class job of 'being Santa' for over a decade in Sumo. He's a great example of the gung-ho legends that made up Sumo's extended cast and crew. The up-for-anything attitude of the team is one of the things that made Sumo the truly special show it was.

Letlive

Friday 2nd September 2011

Around 2011, I'd started to become disillusioned with putting on bands in Middlesbrough. This was partly Middlesbrough's fault, and partly mine. I definitely have an alternative taste in music, and the bands I love, and the bands I loved to book, were certainly not that popular. Over a period of a few years I learned that putting on big rock shows was a sure fire way to lose a tonne of money. I've held my passion for local bands to this day, but in terms of booking hot up and coming rock bands, I officially resigned from that, and Graham was with me.

What we thought was a great way to help promote the Sumo brand, was a maximum-effort-minimum-reward affair. I booked, promoted, and ran shows in Middlesbrough for Cancer Bats, Poison The Well, Gallows, Daughters, Deez Nuts, The Ghost Inside and loads more. These stand-alone shows barely shifted advance tickets, and turnout was minimal. These same gigs would sell out in advance in Leeds or Newcastle. Perhaps our small town was just not big enough to play host, or maybe we were terrible promoters. I don't think it was the latter.

Don't get me wrong, at our annual Music Live festival, The Sumo Stage was always rammed from start to finish, with the likes of Frank Turner, You Me at Six or Flood of Red. Plus, we did have plenty of successful stand-alone live shows under our belts.

But, what I'm saying here is that It seemed as though our quest to bring a live music element to our packed clubnights now felt slightly futile. No one wanted to know unless the band had a decent clutch of certified bangers. The band had to be A Big Deal for anyone to care. Bands that cost a few grand like The Subways, The Cribs, Pendulum, Skindred, The Blackout, Lower Than Atlantis, Deaf Havana; this all worked a treat. Sadly, however, the days of the £500 band that would blow everyone's mind, and set the night up for a mad one, felt like something to put behind us.

We were buzzing in the office when we confirmed Letlive. Bryan had emailed me and, as usual when he had booked one of my favourite bands, I'd text the DJs and the wider Sumo team. We were all excited. Over the next few weeks leading up to the show, everything went perfectly for us as the promoters. We'd been playing their track Renegade 86 for ages, and Zane Lowe had started playing it on his prime time night slot at Radio One. After Oli Sykes told Brett Gurowitz to make it happen, the band had signed to Epitaph records. They were getting loads of UK press, and they had features running in Rock Sound and the NME. It seemed that we'd booked the hottest band on the planet.

In the days leading up to the gig, with the wind in our sails from the worldwide praise that Letlive were receiving, we hyped the show like crazy. These guys from Los Angeles were coming to play Sumo, and we hoped Boro would be as excited as we were.

Kerrang! magazine ran an issue that same week which featured '*The 50 Greatest Rockstars In The World Today*'. There he was, at Number One, on the *front cover*, Jason Aalon Butler of Letlive. A bigger rock star than Marilyn Manson, bigger than Lars Ulrich apparently. It was the icing on the cake in terms of what we needed as promoters. Surely, every person in Teesside would be at this show, right?

On Friday September 2nd when Letlive played Sumo, in the Empire, at midnight, around twenty people watched the band. It was one of the best gigs I've ever seen; the band were phenomenal, and the show was incendiary. And twenty people saw it.

There were probably 300 people in the building, and they mostly smoked outside or mooched upstairs. Once the band had *finished*, those 300 people filled the room, dancing round to their favourite songs, as played by our DJs Craig and Kev. Then by 1am, another 400 people showed up, and, as always, the night ended up packed. I was gutted and embarrassed.

Letlive loved the show. They got paid their £500 and partied with us into the small hours.

These guys had played Leeds festival on the same stage as The Mighty Mighty Bosstones and The Descendants just six days before playing Sumo, and they were super-nice and seemed genuinely grateful to perform.

Animals V Machines

AVM launched on Saturday, the 5th of March 2011

Boro didn't have a rock night on a Saturday. So we started one.

Musically I knew it had to be different to Sumo, so I was going for a pop-punk, emo, punk rock vibe. We were about ten years ahead of our time trying to tap into the nostalgia of the nineties and noughties rock scene, but there we were.

We'd planned it for an age. If we didn't do it, someone else would. Even as far back as 2009, we'd started to prepare for it. In the Winter of 2009, we had logos drawn up and a plan to launch a small intimate rock night in one of the Cornerhouse's areas. We were calling it Timebomb, after the Rancid track. We had an exploding alarm clock as the logo, and I'd worked out a time-led drinks plan, where the earlier you arrived, the better drinks deals you got, or something like that.

On parting with the Cornerhouse in 2010, and eventually the venue shutting down, our Timebomb plans were shelved.

In 2011 I was approached by my pals, the Spensley Brothers, with whom I now had a good relationship through the success of Bad Medicine and a slew of random rock, metal and hardcore shows I was putting into the venue. Even though Bad Med and those gigs didn't pack the place out, they knew me and the team were professionals, and they asked whether we fancied trying something up in the small upstairs club area above Spensleys Emporium, aka Secrets Lap Dancing club - a place that desperately needed a rebrand.

They planned to rename, revamp and relaunch the top two floors of the building as a venue in its own right. 'Spensleys Emporium' would be a ground floor late bar, and upstairs would have its own identity. They had some dubious names pencilled in for the new venue, but I managed to talk them out of those names and go with my suggestion - 'ATIK'.

Having gone off the Timebomb moniker, I christened our new weekly event, 'Animals V Machines'.

We were on a mission to make it as different as possible to Sumo. We didn't want to take anything away from Sumo's numbers and risk the Empire falling out with us (That old chestnut). At the same time, we knew we shouldn't have all our eggs in one basket. That basket was the Empire. We were on track to having the three best rock nights in the town. That wasn't a particular goal, but that's what eventually happened.

Animals V Machines, or AVM as everyone called it, played a throwback-ish mix of pop-punk and emo, and entertained the punks of Teesside every Saturday until 2016. We played songs from Drive Thru Records, Epitaph, Fat Wreck and the like - a style of punk that seemed to appeal to the slightly older crowd, and we succeeded in gathering a following of a couple of hundred people (that filled ATIK) and provided a viable alternative to Sumo. As people started to feel a bit old for Sumo, they graduated over to AVM. The rockers in their late twenties switched to ATIK so as not to rub shoulders with the giddy 18-21-year-olds that bounced around the Empire. We mixed the punk rock playlist up with some hardcore, some ska, a dash of cheesy metal, and a good dose of cheesy pop in the last half hour because why not.

On the Ten Feet Tall team at the time of AVM's launch we had a girl named Kim. Kim was a fiery Scottish stick of dynamite, who swore like a soldier, partied harder than I did, and most importantly worked like an absolute trooper. Kim fronted up the event, Dani was the DJ and between the three of us we set out on a mini crusade to make AVM as wild as we possibly could. Between us we managed to throw a completely off-the-wall theme party into the mix most weeks for five years

As I became ultimately distracted with Sumo, the Empire, the ever-expanding catalogue of club nights and infinite comedy shows, Kim and Dani took AVM and made the thing run like clockwork - something I'm eternally grateful for. I would of course, constantly stick my nose into their plans, suggest different ways of doing things, which probably wound Kim up no end, and I'd frequently roll into ATIK half-cut after an Empire shift, begging the bar staff to serve me past last orders.

One of my favourite random theme parties that we threw in ATIK was a Dexter party, which revolved around the hit Netflix show of the same name. Dani and Kim coated the walls of the club in plastic sheeting, threw fake blood up the walls, gave everyone surgical scrubs, masks and gloves, fake knives and other stupid murderous party props. Dexter episodes played from various screens around the club.

We wanted everything about AVM to feel different to Sumo, even the drinks. I asked Spenseley's to stock the bar with anything and everything they could find that was just *different* in some way. We found a Japanese beer called Asahi, which came in giant silver cans. At the time no one had really heard of it, so it became our house beer. For cocktails we would buy teapots from the local hardware shop, Boyes, fill them with Jack Daniels, Red Bull, Coke and cherryade, and sell them for a tenner.

Many bars, and especially the rock nights had gotten into Beer pong, so we wanted to follow suit but give it a twist. We'd give everyone that came in a ping pong ball. They could throw the balls over the bar staff's heads, into red cups that lined the back of the bar, to win free drinks. It was chaos, as two hundred punks crowded at the tiny bar, while the ever patient bar staff attempted to make cocktails in half cracked teapots, pour giant fizzy cans of Asahi into glasses, and dodge flying ping pong balls.

Those teapots were a nice little earner. When you took your teapot back to the bar, you got a two pound deposit refunded to you. Weirdly, no one returned their pot, they just left them scattered round the club. At the end of the night, it was quite easy to scoop up twenty teapots and bag forty quid. One Saturday on this quick pot sweep, I realised a pot that I'd picked up was warm to the touch. Some dirty bastard, I thought, had pissed in one of these pots. I carefully lifted the lid. They hadn't. They'd shit in it. A punk rock protest, perhaps. I binned the pot, and tried to keep a lid on the story (pun intended). Thankfully, it was a one-off occurrence.

The Spensleys gang were a dream to work with. Anything we wanted to do, they were up for it. The dafter the better. Drinks were cheap, they gave us keys so we could come and go as we pleased. We literally had the run of the place. Down the road at the Empire, it felt like everything was monitored, everything was done by committee, and everything had to be at a very high polished standard for it to go ahead. Quality control is no bad thing at all. But in the slightly scuzzy worn venue of ATIK, we could do what we liked. It had a real Cornerhouse vibe to it, which was accentuated on the day that the Spensley Brothers actually bought a few skips full of decor that had been ripped out of The Cornerhouse. Giant gold framed pictures, huge floor to ceiling mirrors, and even light fittings and handrails were dragged 20 metres from the ghost ship shell of Cornerhouse and up the sticky stairs of ATIK. In terms of giving the old rock crowd who had yearned the dark corridors of Cornerhouse (and never quite settled in the high glamour of Empire) this was a dream come true.

In addition to its main room, ATIK had a second tiny room, with its own micro bar, a small DJ box and a dance floor space of about nine metres squared. It felt like a new Little Tokyo for us to play with. We'd open it a few times a month and throw absolutely anything and everything in there as a side-show to the main room's punk rock party. We tried drum and bass, hip hop, thrash metal, classic rock, we showed Star Wars marathons, we held open mic sessions, and we put on gigs. This claustrophobic black box had originally been the location of the dressing rooms of the lapdancers of Secrets, and now the square room with its black carpet, black walls and blacked out windows was home to some of the most fun shows I'd done in years. We had Jame Arthur's early rock band Save Arcade play on week two, and followed that up with gigs by a whole host of great local bands with the odd out-of-town guest such as Above Them. We managed to squeeze Watford post hardcore legends Feed The Rhino into the room to play for forty die-hard fans. The atmosphere was electric. You couldn't see, you could barely breathe, and the volume was deafening.

The Empire Run

One of my fondest memories of Animals V Machines was through 2014, Dani and I created a little game we called The Empire Run.

I'd be running most of the Empire's Saturdays, usually along with a helper or a trainee member of Ten Feet Tall. This gave me the chance to hop up and down Albert Road between Empire and ATIK. I could leave things in Empire with my assistant for half an hour at a time and jog down to AVM to check out how it was going, catch a bit of a band's set, or pester Kim for an Asahi or two. Later, If things in Empire were going particularly to plan, I could duck out and enjoy the last hour of AVM, propping myself up in the DJ box with Dani - and a couple more Asahi's would certainly be sunk.

AVM closed at 3am. However, the Empire closed at 3.30am.

And so The Empire Run was born.

At the stroke of 3am, Dani and I had 30 minutes in which to; pack down the DJ kit, clear ATIK of all our decor, banners, party props and crap, and then scoop up any rogue teapots for £2 a go. By that point, it would be about 3.20am. This gave us ten minutes to sprint (and I mean sprint) down Albert Rd, dodge all the fights, taxi traumas and kebab-munching monsters outside Flares, and get through the Empire front door and to the Lounge Bar by 3.29am.

At this point, we would order a colossal amount of drinks.

The Empire Run drinks order typically consisted of four shots (to be consumed while the other drinks were being made), two Black Russians, two Long Island Iced Teas, and four cans of Red Stripe. We could then grab a plush booth in Empire's lounge and plough through our drinks before staggering out into the night at about 4.30am.

Side Note : As tragic as the spelling of ATIK is, I knew there was a shed load of clubs already called Attic, and for the purposes of claiming unique social media handles, and a decent Google result, we went with that bonkers version of spelling it. I told Spensleys "Trust me, I'm a promoter." They ripped me for saying that, but they went with it.

Bonus Rock Fact : Exit By Name's unreleased/shelved third album, that never reached public ears, was named Animals V Machines. I always thought it was a shame that big daft name never got used for anything, so when we needed a name for this clubnight, I took the opportunity to use it.

Let's Put A Skate Ramp In The Club

I don't know why we didn't just hire one, and I don't know why I thought it was a good idea to build one. It was Kim's idea to have one, and I agreed we should do it. It turned into a bit of a nightmare to be honest. (I'm still glad we did it though).

We built, from scratch, a full size half-pipe in the ATIK nightclub above Spensleys.

This is a great example of this venue letting us do whatever we wanted. The Empire would never have let us start this. In fact when Lee Spensley saw the ramp, the day after the event, he told me we'd never have gotten away with it, had he seen the sheer size of the thing before it was too late.

My nephew is Billingham Skate Legend John Saunders. In his teens John became a bit of a star in the North East and helped create the film opus that is Billog Badlands. I shall take this opportunity to apologise to John, and his mates, for dragging him into the unholy mess that was Putting A Skate Ramp In The Club. However, I did ask him; 'can you build a half pipe in here', and he assured me that Yes - it was possible. He'd just need a little time.

My nephew's day started well, with the huge sheets of plywood that they'd strapped to the roof of their cars, being whisked away by the wind as they hurtled up the A66 from the timber merchants. After an hour of foraging in lay-bys they'd retrieved all the panels, re-strapped them to the roof racks and made it to ATIK for noon. They worked relentlessly for ten solid hours building the huge framework and carefully attaching the panels and scaffolding to create the half-pipe.

There was black B and Q netting staple-gunned to the ceiling, to stop skateboards from flying off and beheading punters, and old duvets gaffer taped around the club's huge radiators to stop skaters skinning their shins. This structure was immense.

I gave the skaters an envelope of cash and a case of beers and asked them to skate till midnight to entertain the crowd.

Like many amazing nights, fate would mean the weekly photographer was poorly, on holiday or had technical difficulties. It always seemed to be on the craziest nights that this happened.

The crowd piled into the venue, bewildered by the gigantic wooden structure that stood proudly occupying half of their clubnight. Exhausted from the day's joinery, John and his mates skated their hearts out into the small hours before bailing as the moshers reclaimed their space and the half-pipe became a dancefloor.

I smiled as I sipped a beer at 3am and watched a hundred drunks sliding down the ten-foot ramp on their arses, safety net nowhere to be seen. It all seemed worth it.

We then had the task of turning up the following morning, to somehow pack it all up and take it away. We were hungover and it took all day that Sunday to clear the club. I remember my colleague Ben, hands bloodied, swinging a crow bar for hours upon hours, while I dutifully sucked up ten thousand shards of wood with the venue's ancient Henry hoover.

The main support timbers that made that skate ramp went into the walls of my first house - a practically derelict money pit that I'd recently bought, on Roman Road in Middlesbrough.

Some old pals of mine now live in that house and probably don't realise their bedroom walls were once part of a punk rock skate ramp for drunk moshers.

Side Note : There are some great photos of the build at thisclubcouldbeyourlife.co.uk

Sumo Sunderland

Some of Ten Feet Tall's greatest adventures and almost-success stories always seemed to be born in small awkward Northern towns with great scenes - but without great clubnights.

Hull, Hartlepool, Durham, Yarm. Those places had great local bands and groups of alternative kids that the likes of Sumo, Sweet n Sour, Lifesize, Betamax, Metropolis or Cannonball were perfect for. Whatever the state of the venues we found in these places, with the right DJ, the right flyer, a smoke machine and a sound system, we could Have It until 3am.

In October of 2011, we launched Sumo Sunderland at a venue called Independent, or as the locals called it, Indie-P.

Kim and I had spent the summer of 2011 wandering the city's deserted streets, trying to learn the lay of the land. We found a handful of great record shops, pubs and bars that seemed good craic, and we tried our best to blu-tac as many posters up as we could. We managed to find approximately twelve places that would accept a Sumo poster. Probably an omen that this was going to be a tough launch.

The two club owners, Ben and Paul, were perfect hosts and absolute characters. Ben looked after promo, booking bands, and seemed the night owl of the pair. He had a fairly acute stutter plus his thick Sunderland accent meant I never really understood a word he said. He also had a sheepdog that never ever *ever* stopped barking. So meetings were usually me smiling and nodding and agreeing to god knows what.

Paul was another super loveable character and seemed to run the day to day. They reminded me a little of the Spensely brothers Lee and Ste, but less gangster. Like the best club owners, they were immensely hard-working and very accommodating - they let me get away with murder every Friday night.

We threw ourselves headfirst into a Freshers based launch. We kept a strong Boro team back home to look after Empire Fridays, and the AVM team were the ones who drove up to Sunderland each Friday to run the show. Dani was on the decks, and Kim and I ran about, passing out trays of free shots, popping confetti cannons, throwing daft hats and inflatable crocodiles at people, and generally trying our best to make pals. It was hard.

There were a few obstacles in our path to conquering Sunderland. Firstly, a club two minutes down the road called Passion ran a rock night. We didn't know that when we started, and it had somehow flown right under our radar. As soon as we launched Sumo, the team at Passion upped their game. Their drinks became 99p, and the door entry went down to £1.

Thursdays in Sunderland had (apparently) always been the rock night, and they weren't going down without a fight.

We added a second room into our mix with Chris and Fashion Fil making a wonderful DJ double act. As always, we jammed plenty of live bands into the mix, and tried literally everything to make Sumo Sunderland stand out from the competition and turn people's heads. We did the theme parties, the beach parties, the £1 parties. We ran a death metal and hardcore live band all-dayers, we had The Blackout come play a sold out show, we even booked seminal skate punk legends OPM to come and perform one night, Heaven is a Half Pipe taking the roof off. For some reason I convinced local talent Avalanche Party members Joe, Jordan and Kane to dress up (or down) and perform a set as Biffy Clyro. They smashed it. Thanks again for that lads.

It took a lot of work, and in the early days there were certainly low points where I looked at Kim, and Dani and thought, I can't force them through this any more.

Eventually though, after every trick from the decade-long Sumo book was thrown into the mix, the hard alt of Sunderland finally started to warm to us. We managed to stop competing with Passion's daft discount door charges and pull our door price up to £6, and we started hitting 400-500 regulars each Friday.

In a city where we'd been told since day one...

... *The Students Won't Come, You'll Never Compete With Passion, People Only Go To Inde-P on a Saturday, You'll Never Get a Fiver Off People For Entry, No One Wants To See OPM...*

...We were absolutely rocking it.

At around this time we also scored another fantastic result in that we managed to assemble a great team of locals to help run things. We found a lad called Mickey who was really into it, got his head round the madness straight away, and he stepped up to the plate to graft the promo all week, and run the nights alongside Kim. Not having to bring a whole TFT squad up from Boro every week was a massive help.

Those first few months had been tough, a big room with 50 kids bopping about. Those long drives home, going to bed at 5am, then trying to muster a smile for the poster run on a Monday morning. The thousands of pounds sunk into bands and inflatable crocodiles. It had eventually all been worth it, and I think we finally had a clubnight in Sunderland to be proud of.

Then.

The Council told us they were going to bulldoze the club.

The news that Sunderland city council had decided to renovate one side of the road through Holmeside came as shocking news to Ben and Paul. But like the troopers they are, they quickly pulled together a plan. They also owned a bar over the road, directly opposite Independent, called Plugged Inn. They set to work bashing the insides of the new space out, ready for rebuilding and relaunching a new nightclub. A club that would sit about ten steps directly opposite the old Independent. Perfect right?

They worked tirelessly every day and night to get the new place ready. However, the time came when the Council had to lock the doors at the original space - and they just couldn't get Independent Two done in time. Each week I watched the progress, and despite all their graft, when the date rolled around, we had to prepare a promo campaign to say Sumo was on holiday... but we'd be back, in the brand new club, very soon.

There was about a three-month gap before we relaunched in the new digs. The irony was that the new club was way better than the old one; but we'd lost the crowd, lost the spark, and I dare say, Kim, Dani, Mickey and myself just didn't have it in us to launch Sumo Sunderland all over again.

We hoped that given our reputation, our social media, and our mighty fine product, those five hundred people would come to find us again. I don't know what happened to them, where they went, or how they then chose to spend their Friday nights, but we were back to under a hundred heads, discounting entry and putting more cash in to try and make it happen.

I sat down with Ben and Paul one Monday morning in 2014 and had to look them in the eyes and tell them we were out. We'd lost money week over week for months since relaunching. We just couldn't keep going. The team was tired, I was tired.

We tried - like *really* fucking tried, and we'd given Sunderland what I thought was our best, but in the end they just didn't want it.

A Live Music Empire

Through 2010 and 2012, the Empire went hell for leather booking as many live shows as they could. I think as the new gaffer, Ash aimed to establish the place as the best live music club that he could. He spent a stack of time and money on backstage, the dressing rooms, added proper power for lighting rigs and nightliner coaches, and probably blew quite a few quid on daft shows - but he just wanted people to recognise the venue on the circuit. It did the job, and he had the pick of the TFT team to help run the events too, so bands were super well looked after and would always give great feedback back to their agents. This fuelled more and more great bookings.

Wiley, CAST, Calvin Harris, You Me at Six, Puddle of Mudd, Soil, The Subways, Alkaline Trio, Miles Kane, PiL, Stiff Little Fingers, Imelda May, DJ Shadow, Professor Green, Big Country, Murderdolls, Feeder, Eagles of Death Metal and erm, Joe McElderry, all hit the big Empire stage once Ash took over.

It was no doubt an expensive process, and a big gamble, investing so much into live music, but what Ash did for the venue, and for Middlebrough, was a sweet move. It also helped bolster the credibility of our clubnights.

May The 4th Be With You

Random chapter. But - There are good dates, and there are bad dates.

Good dates are when people are most likely to go clubbing. Bad dates are when people are most unlikely to go clubbing.

Do you find a good date, like December 21st, when everyone's going out, and throw a massive party to entertain the masses? Or do you save your money and effort and enjoy the busy night without stress? Do you spot a bad date, like February 14th, and plan an event, push in a load of money and energy to try and make a bad date into a good date?

We always seemed to want to try the latter. On Valentine's night (a terrible date to try and get people into a nightclub), we would throw everything into the mix. Love song karaoke, speed dating, a local Elvis impersonator who performed live on stage then married everyone in the building, two by two in a "chapel of love" (that we spent three days building).

We tried everything on bad dates, even though Graham told us not to. Sorry Graham. We probably wasted a few quid there.

Friday the 4th of May was a good date.

Rick spotted it. International Star Wars day. I was off running something else, probably Sumo Sunderland, and Rick threw a Star Wars party on May

4th. May The 4th Be With You, get it?

Lightsabers, themed cocktails (I think there was blue bantha milk) and Kev playing the cantina band song relentlessly.

Anyway, one thousand one hundred and ten people showed up. It was double the amount of people anyone expected. And three times busier than we usually were at that point in the year. Utterly brilliant.

Anticipating and planning for good and bad dates on the calendar became a much needed skill – as we shall come back to later.

Zombie Survival Sumo

Friday 31st October 2012

In and around 2012, Rick was very much Mr Sumo, as I span the plates for other stuff. Much to Rick's annoyance, I occasionally (Ok, constantly) stuck my oar in and helped him out or did his head in. One of the two. Or both.

I love Rick, a ball of energy, always doing a hundred things. He was perfect for Sumo, a creative, hardworking creature of the night, with an unflappable positive attitude.

So in 2012, October rolled around, and the closest Friday to Halloween was, as always, Sumo's Halloween special. Always the busiest Friday of the whole year. An easy win. Everyone was always out and mad for it on Halloween Friday.

I'd done something a little bit daft. I'd booked some bands. It wasn't needed, and it was probably sadly detrimental to the event. No one wanted to watch a band on Halloween, they just wanted to dress up and get smashed. To be honest, on any given Friday, people just wanted to dress up and get smashed, but such was my desire to inflict live music upon the town. I'd taken the opportunity to have Rolo Tomassi, Goodtime Boys, and Oathbreaker play the club that night.

The bands were very cool, amazing live, and I'm glad we did it. There weren't that many people in Boro that would be bothered about those bands (sadly) but we knew they'd put on a hell of a show and entertain the masses. At least it wasn't just another generic Halloween party, right?

So Rick could have taken the easy route, and gone with a fancy dress competition, some spooky themed drinks, and not worried too much about throwing any kind of mad party, as the entertainment was already booked right?

Nope. Not Rick. Rick had his own idea of what he wanted to do for Sumo's Halloween spectacular. His idea was phenomenal, and we just had to let him roll with it. Rather than me trying to explain exactly what the plan was, here is the blurb from the Facebook event that Rick wrote. So he can effectively describe the event to you in his own (decade old) words;

Ladies and Gentlemen, please put your heads together, and try to stay alive.

The Zombie Survival Sumo

Friday 26th of October 2012

The town has been overrun – The apocalypse is nigh – The Dead are everywhere – It's kill or be killed.

Sumo will provide you with the weapons needed to survive... BUT one bite and you're on the other side and the living are your lunch.

RIGHT – Here's all you need to know – We have zombies – We have guns

The aim of the game is to shoot as many zombies as you can, OR eat as many people as you can.

CIVILIANS;

If you come as a civilian (no zombie make up) you can bring your own gun (Obviously, a water pistol, a soft toy gun, or a spud gun). If a zombie tries to get you, shoot it. Keep track of your score. When you inevitably get bitten, head to the zombification zone and note your score on the scoreboard. Then get zombied up and bite people!

ZOMBIES;

Eat everyone with a gun. If they have a gun, they are playing the game. If they shoot you, you return to the zombification zone, note your score down and start again. Feel free to lurk as much as you want, or just jump around and dance to your favourite songs and bite fools every so often.

Play nice. Have fun! – Best scores win class prizes. Best costumes also win awesome prizes!

When there's no more room in hell… The dead will walk the earth…

—

I mean, fuck knows what the bands thought of playing in an 18th-century theatre to a crowd of a thousand drunks all waving water pistols and biting each other, but surely that was the gig of their entire careers?

Sumo Darlington

It was either Oct 2012 or 2013

I'm going to keep this brief. Sumo Darlington was a little bit of a shit show.

Ash and Barry, owners of the Empire, had bought another nightclub. In Darlington. They put their hearts and soul into it, and it was beautiful. We were all a little jealous, to be honest.

The equipment was superior to that in the Empire, from the DJ kit to the lights, the bars, and the glassware. They'd gone all out on the place. When they opened, they had clubnights Thursday, Friday and Saturday, and they'd put some pretty decent big touring bands in the mix too. Frank Turner, Spector and The Courteeners did the trick for convincing Darlington that 'The Hub' as the venue was called, was a serious contender.

The Empire decided to run the clubnights themselves. They'd employed a clutch of full time promoters and rightly felt like they didn't need external people coming in to manage things.

After a couple of months, no one was coming to their clubnights, so TFT got the phone call to come in and have a go. I was pretty gutted to hear from Graham that we were being given the Thursday night on which to put on a Sumo. We were in a tricky position. As the guys that ran Ash's Fridays and Saturdays at Empire, we could hardly say no to his request for help in

Darlington. We felt sure it wasn't going to work, but we had to have a good go.

So we turned up in town with flyers, posters, our DJs, and decor and began the launch hype that Boro's biggest rock brand was here in Darlington and ready to rip the roof on Thursdays. I was very sceptical. However, we did have one thing going for us: our launch night was on Halloween.

Surely, of all the nights, Halloween would be the perfect night to launch Sumo in Darlington.

We'd spent weeks on the streets flyering, hit all the colleges, and spent a fortune on paid Facebook ads. On launch night, we had about a hundred or so people. It wasn't great. The club was huge, cold, and although the crowd was cool, the venue was in a rough corner of town, and the doormen didn't do a good job of keeping the crap out. After a few weeks of this, we didn't have to worry too much about getting the numbers up - as Ash and Barry literally closed the club down.

This should have been the end of my brief and foolish folly into Darlington, but sadly, people had other plans for me.

The next phone call that came in was Simon. Simon was the area manager from Ladhar Leisure - our pals that had owned The Cornerhouse. They also had a club in the town called Inside Out, which had a great Friday and Saturday Night going, but they didn't have a Thursday. Simon suggested, given the Hub's demise, that 'Sumo Darlo' could hop over to Inside Out and be their all-new Thursdays. I winced. Just when I thought I'd escaped Darlington, I was sucked right back in.

I'd known Simon from the Cornerhouse days so it was good to see him again. An absolute workhorse of a man, he'd been a big part of the Cornerhouse's success and the man behind transforming Bar Sumo into the infamous

Uncle Alberts on Albert Road in Boro. He gave me a tour of the club, Inside Out. It was cool, with plenty of different little rooms, nooks and crannies. It suited Sumo down to the ground. It could have been the start of a beautiful relationship. The only problem was, we were in Darlington, on a Thursday night, and no one gave a fuck.

We shouldn't have done it, and it wasn't worth the roll of the dice. All it did was waste a truckload of money, depress our DJs (sorry again Dani for this one) and take my eye off the ball in Boro.

Somehow, we ended up continuing the clubnight for months with a dedicated crowd of around 75 people turning up each week. We'd moved into the smallest little basement room in the club, known as the Pawn Shop, which looked decent with 50 people in it. The venue had this room decked out like a junk shop, with battered armchairs, tiny TVs and random scrap hanging from the walls and ceiling. It was intimate, sweaty and loud. My favourite article was an old Amstrad CPC 464 computer that still booted up behind the bar and flickered permanently on a loading screen for a broken game.

A sinister metaphor for my life at that moment.

An old relic stuck in a loop, in a clubnight that never seemed to end.

Styrofoam Crucifixes

Did I mention that the Empire's main hall was bloody big?

We were always looking for creative ways to fill the void, cosy it up, and somehow make it more intimate. It definitely used to wind Ash up, as he was obviously proud of his epic regal main hall, and we'd come along, always trying to edge the dance floor with tables, or hang drapes, banners or bunting across the dance floor.

We'd try anything to make it feel more enclosed and create an atmosphere in this vast theatre space.

The sheer size of the space above people's heads meant that even when you created huge props or pieces of decor, as we often did, as soon as things were hoisted up or strung up above your head, they seemed to visually shrink into nothing. Even the biggest creations had minimal impact.

Marty had a great idea for Halloween - to create two giant white crosses, And then fire full-colour projections onto them. He proposed buying two giant ten-foot styrofoam blocks, and with a couple of swift cuts, we'd have two ten-foot high crucifixes that we could stand up on end in the royal boxes that overlooked the dancefloor.

The blocks cost a small fortune, but Marty and I assured Graham, who as always footed the bill, they would look spectacular.

When the blocks arrived, we dragged them into the Empire and laid them out on the dancefloor.

We'd bought two new hand-saws, and we set to work attempting to carve into the styrofoam.

I don't know if you've ever tried to hand-saw styrofoam, but this shit was not cutting. After an hour of sweating, swearing and putting our backs into it, we'd barely made a dent. Marty suggested we use a hot wire that would cut through the blocks like, well - like a hot wire through butter.

I must have phoned every hire company and DIY store in the North East, but no one had such a thing. Google told me they existed, but they all would take a few days to arrive if we ordered online. It was Friday morning, and these things needed to be installed right there and then.

I drove to B and Q and bought a chainsaw. It was all we could think to do. We unpacked our new toy, powered it up, and annihilated the foam blocks. You've never seen such a mess in your life, we were coated from head to toe in tiny white balls of foam, and the Empire dancefloor had become a winter wonderland - not the look we were going for.

After about four hours of cutting and with numb arms from the saw's vibrations, we squeezed our gargantuan white foam creations up the venue's narrow stairways and into the royal boxes. We propped them up and left them looming over the dancefloor.

After rushing home for a shower and getting back to open the club up at 10pm, I soon discovered that with the house lights down, the disco lights on, and the venue's hazers chugging away, our relentlessly crafted pieces of decor were barely even noticeable.

If I hadn't had five hours of Sumo to get stuck into, I might have had a chance to laugh or cry about the day we'd had making that pair of useless props.

Sumo Was Seven

I did it again. I remember Rick's face when I told him. It was Sumo's seventh birthday party, and I'd booked some bloody bands.

Not only that, but Graham had booked some bands too.

We'd triple booked the date, and in true Ten Feet Tall fashion, the more was to be the merrier, and we didn't cancel anything. We just piled it all into one mismatched messy party.

It could have been a simple fun-packed, punter-packed event with minimal effort, but it had now become an exercise in multitasking. We had live bands in multiple rooms, tons of staff in to pull it all off, loads of extra staging, extra work and extra chew.

I don't know how we got ourselves into these situations.

Sumo's seventh birthday was a blast. Rick organised a truckload of cakes, I seem to recall seven of them, and he cut them all up and handed them out at 3am. There were balloons, clowns, confetti and everything you'd want and expect from a birthday party. All his fun little touches went down a treat. Face painting, drinking games, people loved all that.

People hated the bands.

It's not the band's fault, and they were absolutely mint. We'd booked them in good faith. Months before the event, I'd been offered a band from Surrey called Hold Your Horse Is. They weren't signed, no one had heard of them, but I thought they sounded great. What was I thinking? I think I had some sort of band-blindness. If I was offered a great band, I just had to book it. I couldn't help myself.

This occasionally worked out great. We once booked a Finnish folk punk duo called Jaakko and Jay for Uncle Alberts. One of them played acoustic guitar and sang brutal political lyrics, while the other played the drums, but instead of having drums, he mic'd up the floor and stomped on it. The Friday night drunk moshers of Boro loved it. It was a hell of a show.

As for Surrey's Hold Your Horse Is (great name) they died a death on the vast Empire stage, as the Sumo party masses hung about, chugged VK, patiently waiting for them to finish their set and go away. I felt bad for them. Sorry lads.

Meanwhile, in the lounge.

"Multi-time winner of 'Best Female Vocalist' and 'Best Traditional Jazz Artist' at OffBeat Magazine's "Best of the Beat" Awards, Meschiya Lake & the Little Big Horns are some of the finest performers in New Orleans today."

Graham had booked Meschiya Lake to perform at Stockton's ARC. He figured it would be a great move to ask them to double up and play Sumo too, later on on the same night. The band, being utterly punk rock in spirit, agreed. Graham suggested we put them in the Empire's lounge.

It was a sublime show. One of the greatest live acts I've seen. In all seriousness, the performance was Grammy-worthy.

I can't imagine what they thought as they loaded their trombones, drums and french horns out of the lounge's fire door, past people puking in the street, and into their van, at 2am, but they were extremely polite.

Rick gave them some cake to take in the van for their journey home.

Empire Sumo In 2012

Here's some of the events we did in 2012. Tick them off if you were there.

May 4th - May The 4th Be With You

May 16th - Wheatus

May 25th - Sumo Golden Ticket Giveaway!

June 1st - Sumo Royal Swindle

June 8th - Pound Sumo

June 15th - Lennox + Whalter

July 6th - Weird Shapes

July 6th - Arcane Roots & [ME]

July 13th - Xmas in July

July 27th - The Sumo Olympics

August 10th - Set Your Goals

EMPIRE SUMO IN 2012

Aug 17th - The Hitchers (+ Odessa + Foundations + All At Sea in Rockbox)

August 26th - Pound Sumo Sunday

September 7th - Seven Years Of Sumo + Meschiya Lake + Hold Your Horse Is

September 21st - Titchy Fest with Bisons + No School Reunion + Kairo + 4 Mile Drive

Septeber 28th - Enter Tha Dragon

September 28th - Deadbeats

October 12th - The Departed + Never Cry Wolf

October 26th - The Zombie Survival Sumo + Rolo Tomassi + Oathbreaker + Goodtime Boys

November 16th - Versions + The Orchard + Rituals

November 30th - Sumoustache

December 7th - TRC + Polar + Prowler

December 14th - Sumo Xmas Beach Party

Dec 21st - The End Of The World Party

The Art of Partying

We had many cheesy catchphrases and straplines. Our flyers, posters, and social media always had a little tagline to accompany the Sumo Fridays message. One of my faves was The Art Of Partying. I think that was Ricks.

Kingsize Alt Adventures was one of mine, as was The Beast Of Boro. I also quite liked Friday is Sumo Day.

These taglines were important, they were part of The Formula.

The Formula wasn't something we ever wrote down. It wasn't something we consciously invented. We just looked at these events, and studied them, studied the buildings, the environment, studied the people and how they behaved.

As I said before, Graham would spend hours at his desk staring into a flyer. This was all part of creating the formula. Unlocking the puzzle. Hunting the unicorn.

We would take hours over our clubight setups. Moving a chair or a table to five different places in the room. It was like extreme Fen Shui.

Where was the smoke machine? Was it full of fluid? Could we add essence to the fluid? Freshly Cut Grass Flavoured Smoke? Is there a timer on the smoke machine? If not, can we put it on the event plan that someone has a reminder on their phones to press the smoke machine button every thirty minutes, so the room never loses its smoky atmosphere? I know this sounds crazy, but this meticulous shit is what made the likes of Sumo so good.

What happens when people arrive? Something fun? Something nice? Give them a lolly, a shot, whatever. At Sixty Nine, the legendary Cornerhouse Thursdays, a wonderful human called Jamie Wisdom would stand by the door and shake everyone's hand as they came in. What a move.

What happens when people leave? This is your final chance to make a good impression. If your customers have had a great night, this is your chance to ice that cake. If they've had a shit time, turn it around. A slice of pizza, a badge.

"Hey, thanks for coming out".

Projectors, lights, lasers, bubbles, drapes, fake walls, fairy lights, rugs, musicians, performers, face painters, sounds, smells, visuals, art, vibes, the lot.

This was the recipe. This was The Formula.

Bands That Want Drugs

A Friday in 2012

I hated buying drugs for bands.

I'm anti-drugs. I've seen people on drugs for so long, and every time I see people on drugs, they act and look fucking stupid. It's put me off. I don't ever want to look like that. I don't ever want to act like that. They think no one can tell they're on drugs.

We can all tell you're on drugs, and you look stupid. No offence.

Rant over. Not very rock and roll, I know.

So bands would sometimes ask me to buy them drugs.

In the early days, I had no idea what they wanted. *"Can you get us some class A's?"*. What the hell is that, like heroin? I just didn't know.

I got wise and figured it out as I went along. I ended up with a few phone numbers in my phone, guys from local bands that would drive over to wherever needed and do the deals.

I mostly stayed out of it. I was convinced that if I was even a middle man, that made me a dealer, and I'd go to prison. I can laugh at that now. Towards the end of my life in clubs, I came to realise that pretty much *everyone* is on drugs. As Noel Gallagher said, it's as common as having a cup of tea.

So here's a bands-that-want-drugs story.

In around 2009, the Empire had added a wall about three-quarters of the way down the huge long First Floor part of the club, essentially creating a small room that we at Ten Feet Tall told them would make a perfect small cinema. As the Empire sometimes did, they completely ignored our ideas, put a DJ box and sound system in it - then asked us to fill it with people. Over the years, we tried everything in that room, from Thrash Metal to Dubstep to Soul. With a projector and a few sofas dragged in, it also makes a pretty good small cinema.

The room's been known by many names, but my favourite, was The Rock Box.

It was a total bitch for bands to load into - up four flights of narrow winding stairs, every band's worst nightmare. This was usually done around 5/6pm, and on this particular dark, freezing December night, it was pissing down with rain. Once all the gear was stacked into the room, which also leaked rain in, the band set about setting their kit up. The DJ box was frustratingly built right in the middle of the room against the longest wall. With an entrance and exit at each end of the Rock Box - the room felt like a glorified corridor. Despite the architecture being against us, with creative lighting, fabric slung across the ceiling and a smoke machine chugging away, we made Rock Box feel like a miniature club in its own right, with the band crammed at one end, and enough room for about forty people to watch.

The Rock Box gigs were a totally in-your-face affair. Bands became part of the crowd and the atmosphere that those shows generated was awesome. Over the years, we had Feed the Rhino, The James Cleaver Quintet, The Swellers, and a whole host of amazing local bands play to a packed crowd.

After a show, loading *out* of Rock Box was even less fun than loading in. The stairwells were filled with drunk revellers, who didn't really want to get out of the way at 2am when you needed to lug the PA system, drum kit and amps back out into the street.

Getting back to the frosty December night in question… This band of mid-twenties Americans had gotten themselves loaded in, sound checked and were tucking into the big plastic tubs filled with iced beers. The singer of the band asked me if I could get him some pot, about £80's worth would do, so he told me.

I phoned my usual guy, who said he'd be along in 30 minutes and he'd meet me at the car park at the rear of the venue. As usual, I explained to the guy from the band that I would introduce them and let them do their transaction without my involvement.

Sure enough, in half an hour, I got a text – *"here"*.

So this young American rock star and I made our way out the rear fire exit doors, into the dark Middlesbrough air.

I can only assume my drugs guy had been held up, so had sent another dealer to sort out what was needed.

I was greeted by what looked like a 65-year-old lady, whom I'd never seen before, waving an iPhone at me across the car park, offering up a cheerful *"Hey Phil, you alright?"*. I politely introduced my friend from the states, who handed over his cash and took what he needed.

The lady asked me if I could get her tickets for Dreadzone; I said I'd see what I could do. She said, *"I'll give you a call, yeah"*. I was mortified that this dealer now had my number. We said farewell and headed back inside.

As I walked back to the Rock Box, the singer from the band announced to his bandmates and crew;

"THIS DUDE GOT US WEED FROM HIS MOM!"

The band fell about laughing and proceeded to slap me in the back and tell me how awesome it was that 'my Mom sells blow'.

Silent Sumo

I'd never been bothered about Silent Discos, it looked like a good way to over-complicate our thing, for what would probably be something everyone would hate. Imagine spending all that money on headphones, and no one shows up?

This changed in 2011 when all of us on Team Sumo got to partake in one ourselves. The good folks at Kilimanjaro had recently brought the Sonisphere festival to the UK, and they'd splashed a load of free tickets to local rock club promoters. We helped them promote the festival, and we all got free tickets. Dani, Kim, Nic, Kev, Claire and I all piled down to Knebworth for the weekend. After our first full day of booze and bands, we headed to an aftershow party tent, which was a silent disco. They had two DJs, and with the flip of a switch on your headphones, you could listen to the rock guy, or the pop guy. We were very very drunk, and it had been a very long day, but in that tent, in that field, with a thousand people all singing Gay Bar, and Welcome To The Jungle, over each other, at the same time, we all knew that this was fucking brilliant.

We agreed the following morning that we needed to try this in Empire, so in 2012, after finding the right company to help us pull it off, we brought the Empire the first ever Silent Sumo. We only needed one room; our DJs took residence perched up in the royal boxes above the dance floor. Everyone that came in got headphones in exchange for a tenner deposit, and we were off.

Walking around the club without headphones on was a truly bizarre experience. The bar staff loved it. The one night of the year, they weren't getting deafened by mosh. You had to put up with the crowd's singing, and people accidentally yelling drinks orders at bar staff, but apart from that it was weirdly chilled.

Silent Sumo's were great, and we did around five of them over the next few years. The sad thing was, they cost a fortune. We paid to hire the headphones, of which we needed 1000, and we also had to pay for any that got broken. Even with the ten quid deposits, people did trash them, eat them, flush them, and pour drinks into them. People can be idiots. At this point, we were doing about 700 people a week, and when we put a much-loved, much-hyped 'Silent Sumo' on, the same 700 people showed up. So the investment didn't add any numbers to the door.

These were the brutal facts of the maths. If we were going to spend £1500 on a 'thing', ideally it would put an additional couple of hundred people on the door.

This was sadly how we started to see things more and more. Sumo costs a couple of grand to put on, on a regular week, with costs for DJs, security, whatever. We'd always been trigger happy with spending loads on bands, parties, giveaways. That's what made Sumo fun, the icing we added to the cake.

However, Graham and I did need to start keeping a watchful eye on costs. We'd thrown a few bigger parties that had ended up with smaller numbers attending, and these hurt the TFT wallet. We didn't scrimp or cut back the fun factor overnight, but we definitely started to be a lot more careful about what we booked. Our £1500 silent disco didn't put extra bodies in, so we stopped them.

But we figured there must be something out there that would have people queuing round the block, right? Pound Sumo did it. So what else was out there that we could invest in, to get more and more people through the door.

This was the start of the hunt for the unicorn.

One Pound Fish

The song One Pound Fish by the internet sensation known as 'One Pound Fish Man' was released on 7 December 2012, reaching number 28 in the UK Singles Chart, number 4 in the UK Dance Chart, and number 1 in the UK Asian Chart.

I asked Graham if we could book One Pound Fish Man to come and perform at Pound Sumo. I'd found the UK agency handling the bookings, and the fee was £1200.

That was for a three-song set, followed by an hour of meet-n-greets. Graham said no.

He said, for £1200, you could get The Cheeky Girls.

I asked Graham if we could book The Cheeky Girls. He said no.

Looking back, who can blame him.

Cannonball Claire

Sometime in 2009

I'd been dating this girl Claire (the one that swerved DJ Adam F's advances) since 2007. We'd both ended up simultaneously single, and we met at Etsuko noodle bar, next to Boro Cineworld, for lunch one day, and the rest, as they say, is history. So five years in, we lived in Middlesbrough with our housemate, the aforementioned DJ Dani.

Claire worked for the Inland Revenue, and she hated it, not just because of the random shift patterns but because she was (and is) an incredibly creative soul. She'd lived in New Zealand and worked for a local artist through her school days. She'd come back to Teesside, studied Media production at Teesside Uni, and she was a DIY genius - very handy with a drill and a hammer. I knew this, and Graham saw this, and he offered her a job. I knew working with my girlfriend would be tricky, but we needed good staff, and I knew she'd do great.

There was a clubnight called Cannonball, which took place on the fancy high street of Yarm every Wednesday Night. We'd blagged our way into the fantastic venue, The Keys, offering them a mid week student friendly night, akin to Metropolis. The Friday and Saturday were £10 entry, and bottles of bud were £4. I know in this day and age, that's not too shocking. But a Bud in our timeline in Teesside was about £2. The £4 Bud's were out of my price range, but the footballers that frequented weekends at The Keys would turn up and drink them by the case.

I'd already tried my best with these Cannonball Wednesdays. Marty had done a good job with the decor and projections; we had two of the best DJs, with JT and Fashion Fil from the Kaboom room doing a first class Indie and Pop set in the club's two rooms. We'd had bands in, daft parties, and the prices were rock bottom, especially for Yarm. However, we worryingly only had about 100 regulars.

Claire came in with a fresh pair of eyes, and she very much did things her own way. From her desk in the office she made giant colourful charts, planners and diaries. Her work zone looked like the desk of a primary school teacher, and her new ideas definitely rubbed some of the other guys up the wrong way. It's not that Claire's impatient, it's just that if she's kept waiting, she'll just crack on without you. So when she asked for the guys at TFT to help, collaborate, design, pitch in, they were just too slow.

Claire assembled a street team, used MySpace and Facebook to gather addresses, and posted out tote bags, flyers and badges. She took this little gang of "Cannonballers' out for lunch, she drove round to their colleges, houses, to drop promo gear off. She assembled an army. A Yarmy army. And, with this troop of young pups by her side, she got the word out very successfully. We went from 100 heads at Cannonball, to 900.

This was a gradual process that took a few months, but it built and built steadily. Claire suggested switching the rooms around, working with the DJs on music policies, rearranging furniture, throwing Toga Parties, and generally making the thing totally fun. It was a very old school TFT approach, but one she'd hadn't really been taught or shown. Remember, no one got training manuals; we just threw people in, and she smashed it.

With 900 kids now queuing up Yarm High street to get into the club, this brought its own problems. The residents who lived nearby were not impressed, we had complaints about the noise, and as the hyped up punters waited in line they'd occasionally fight, sing and one night a few windows got put through. Not good.

From then on, we had eight police officers patrolling the queue each Wednesday night, and after a few weeks their assessment of the situation was that we needed to bring in more door staff, to watch the crowd outside. The Keys obliged and got some big guys with high vis jackets to patrol the street each week. They then handed us the bill. With great numbers comes great responsibility, so we added the bulging security bill to our Cannonball costs. It was a big minus number to input into the spreadsheet.

Claire's hard work in Yarm was rewarded with another clubnight. Metropolis Empire Saturdays. Having lost a great employee, Mr Metropolis - Gary, some months before all this, our monumentally rammed Saturday at the Empire didn't have a leader or anyone we could trust.

We needed to keep Ash and the Empire sweet and keep the party going. We'd spent a fortune on Metropolis to turn it into the 1000-plus attended beast that it was. The days of paying Pendulum five grand to come and play had gone through, and we'd settled into a routine of face painters, confetti, balloons, free sweets, and four rooms of DJs. It trundled along doing the epic numbers week in and week out. It still needed a bit of love, and Claire was put in charge.

Behind the scenes, the Empire was (and in some ways still is) a man's world, so a few eyebrows were raised as Claire marched in, and like Claire does, took charge and did things her own way. Empire gaffer Ash knew me and trusted me well enough to know I was surely handing him a good egg, and he and Claire got on really well. She introduced a dance troupe who would rehearse on Saturday afternoons, and then on the night would spring onto the stage and perform routines along with the songs. I would crease up watching Chris the DJs face as the girls (dressed in resplendent Vegas style kit) Can-canned onto the stage to perform their choreographed routine to Lonely Boy. Even he had to admit, it was so bizarre it was pretty cool. The doormen, the DJs, the dancers and all the staff loved Claire as much as I did, and she injected a much-needed dose of fun and frolics into what was turning into a fairly laddish indie disco.

Claire continued whizzing around Yarm and Middlesbrough well into summer 2012. About this time, we also began doing grown-up things like buying a house and starting a family (pretty much simultaneously). Claire took a back seat for a while, then gracefully retired from clubnights.

Empire Sumo In 2013

Here's some of the events we did in 2013. Tick them off if you were there.

January 25th - Sumo Vs Australia

February 8th - Falling Red + Princes & Thieves

February 15th - The Sumo Anti-Valentines Day

March 1st - Sumo in Space

March 8th - Sumexico

March 15th - Sumo Russian Roulette

March 22nd - Sumo Air Guitar Championship

March 29th - Pound Sumo

March 29th - Control, Trapped Inside + Eaten Alive in the Rockbox. No School Reunion + Lessons in the Lounge

April 26th - The Sumo Scramble

May 3rd - The Empire Strikes Back

May 24th – The Sumo House Party

June 7th – Lifeless + Evil Never Dies

June 28th – The Sumo World Records

July 12th – Xmas In July

July 19th – Attention Thieves + Hey Vanity

August 2nd – Raptastic (Rockbox) + John and The Ragmen (Lounge)

August 3rd – The Damned

August 9th – Silent Sumo

August 25th – Pound Sumo Sunday Special

August 30th – The Departed + Wraiths + Foundations

September 6th – Castrovalva + Exit International + Abel Raise The Cain + Captain Disko! In the Lounge

September 13th – Sumo Vs. Jason : Friday The 13th

September 13th – Cytota + Across All Oceans

September 20th – Sumexican Birthday Bash

September 27th – Win The Sumo Car

October 4th – Canterbury + The La Fontaines

October 11th – Sumo UV

October 18th – Silent Sumo Strikes Back

October 25th – Sumo's Monsters Ball

November 1st – Pound Sumo Halloween Hangover

November 8th – Warped Tour Giveaway

November 15th – Mallory Knox

December 6th – Pound Sumo

December 13th – The Sumo Beach Party

December 20th – Sumo Office Party

December 27th – Suit Up for Sumo

Rick Sumo

We're approaching the point in this tale where Rick Sumo is about to exit stage right. I wanted to flip back to where and how this absolute superstar entered Sumo's life.

I'd half-known Rick for a long time. Like myself, a Billingham OG, Rick had skills with a video camera and was known to many as Rick Video. He also worked the counter at the Billingham branch of Blockbuster, where I'd be just about every weekend, even years before becoming Mr Sumo.

If I ever went to Blockbuster to rent some DVDs or buy second-hand PS2 games, I crossed my fingers that Rick was working the desk. As an employee he got ten free rentals a week and rarely used his quota, so I saved a fortune by getting freebies from him.

Maybe this is also why they called him Rick Video?

I think the timeline went something like this. Rick left Blockbuster after college and went away to University; while he was there, I started Sumo, and our paths began to cross again. As I became Phil Sumo, I could repay the free videos favour in guestlist at Cornerhouse. He was also playing drums in local bands, and our acts often shared a bill.

Rick is one of the most enthusiastic, dedicated, passionate, organised, honest, and nicest guys I've met.

I was buzzing when he agreed to help out at Sumo during holidays from Uni, flyering, promoting, and setting up our YouTube channel, SumoTV. It's still out there somewhere on the internet. Rick would shove his camera in people's faces while DJ-come-TV-host Ste quizzed them, holding out a glittery toy microphone. It was still early days for things like YouTube channels, but our videos were wild, and no one else was doing them for clubnights as far as I could see.

As my time started to get split between Sumo, Saturdays, more comedy shows and more Sumos in other towns, I knew I needed a wingman to help out. A good few people were well capable of running the show, and between Jamie, Gary, Martin, Kim and Cat, there were plenty of good hands on deck.

However, Sumo needed a fresh captain to steer the ship at that time. It wasn't that anyone else on the team wasn't good enough or that Rick stole anyone's job - I needed the others elsewhere too. Rick finished Uni just at the right time and he was flung right into the madness of running the super wild Fridays at Cornerhouse.

On Rick's first shift running Sumo at Cornerhouse, he got mugged.

It was summer 2008 or 2009 and I'd double-booked myself to run Sumo and a Jimmy Carr show at Middlesbrough Town Hall. Rick was back in town that night and jumped at the chance to run the Sumo for me.

The plan was, I'd be setting up and getting the party ready, then Rick's bus from Leeds came in around 7pm and he'd meet me at Cornerhouse. Then I could run up Albert road to get doors open for Jimmy at the Town Hall, and Rick could take over and run all things Sumo through till 3am.

At about 8pm Rick arrived ready for action, although he looked shaken. He filled me in - he'd been beaten up and mugged in the toilets of Boro bus station. Some coward had whacked him round the back of the head while he'd stood taking a piss at the urinals in the station toilets. He'd had his phone and wallet taken and took a bit of a kicking. He was ok, and so he told me - ready for duty.

I got Rick a glass of water and told him he should surely go home and rest, but he told me there was no way he was leaving, and he was working - he pretty much shoved me out the door down to the Town Hall.

At around midnight, I came back down Albert road to find Sumo in full swing, and Rick had everything under control. Perhaps the adrenaline and a few Red Stripes had carried him through. After that shift, the rest of Rick's six years at the helm were probably a breeze.

During his reign, he continued to add to and evolve the Sumo party-hard spirit, and it only became bigger and stronger with his influence.

Like me, Graham quickly threw Rick into many other events and shows, and he became an awesome stage manager, working on Middlesbrough Music Live Festival, running plenty of Saturdays at Empire too and also took to the DJ decks now and again. His Double Denim DJ sets of classic rock and post-hardcore downstairs at Bad Medicine were a favourite of mine.

When Claire would head off the Yarm to run Cannonball on a Wednesday night, I'd usually end up at Bad Medicine, Sinking £1 Jagerbombs and £1 Jacks with Rick and getting fairly messy.

Rick added an extra edge to Sumo. Stuff like Zombie Survival Sumo or the Sumo Redneck Backyard Bash (or whatever he called it) were events that stick hard in your memory. Rick also helped us steer the crashing Cornerhouse train into the Empire and land with the bang it needed.

The shame for Rick was always that Graham only had sixteen hours for him.

He was on a part time contract, which often suited Rick, as he pursued his other ventures and toured with his bands.

But like us all, Rick got older, wiser, and the need to pay the rent became a fundamental requirement.

Despite Sumo being the beast it was, it supported a lot. Between Sumo and Metropolis, Graham was paying for the office, bankrolling shows and the other ventures Ten Feet Tall entered into. The wage bill was pretty huge, and as Graham saw it, Sumo could only afford half a Rick. He and Rick set about on a few schemes like trying Sumo merch sites and other clubnights (including a fantastic Thursday night at Ku Bar called Riot), but nothing stuck.

There'd been a few conversations behind the scenes around *What Shall We Do About Rick*. I always insisted that he stayed, and we needed him. I was desperate to give Rick full-time hours, but I was presented budgets and spreadsheets that told me no. Sumo couldn't support me *and* another full-time body. So it was up to me to make more money, to fund the ever growing army. Apart from Sumo, I was having trouble launching anything new that might bring in more money.

So in June 2014 Graham, Rick and I sat down to dream up some new schemes, to figure out how we could get more hours for Rick. About a half hour into that meeting, Rick said he was out. Perhaps like I would eventually see it coming, Rick saw it coming, and jumped ship.

A day or so later Graham asked me who would run Sumo now Rick was gone.

"Well, I thought I could do it."

I thought Graham would say that was a lazy, unprogressive and unambitious answer. But he seemed chuffed and commended my decision to 'roll up my sleeves and get stuck back in again'. That was always the thing about Graham; you could never guess how he would react. Usually, it would be the opposite of what you'd expect.

He also probably realised he was saving a few quid.

I just knew I didn't trust anyone apart from Rick or myself to look after the Sumo show.

The Real Cost Of Halloween

Halloween was always the busiest night on the calendar and to be totally honest when the lights went down, the doors opened, and about fifteen hundred people flooded in - *all* in costume - no one probably even noticed the way the venue had been lovingly decorated.

But still, every year, the team from Ten Feet Tall descended into the basement cellar of Empire to drag out the boxes upon boxes of decorations. I'm not complaining, it was a welcome break from sitting in our office on the other side of town, staring into Facebook statistics and endless spreadsheets. Getting the decorations up was a good team building exercise and it was a few extra quid for the promo teams, which I always liked.

We'd usually start prepping for the Friday, on the Wednesday prior; three full days to dress the venue, with enough decor and daft stuff to get through Friday and Saturday. Each year when Halloween rolled around, we put about £1000 into new decor, so in the end there was a serious amount of zombies, ghouls, prosthetic arms and legs, and other large hanging Halloween props in storage under the club. I think we did a grand job of decorating that vast building as best we could.

Halloween was a huge thing for the Empire. Ash tells me he 'reinvented' Halloween in around 2007. According to him, and I think he's right, the people of Middlesbrough never left the house to go clubbing for Halloween, it was considered an event for kids. He took a leaf out of Ibiza's book and made Halloween a full scale clubnight party for adults. He filled the place with decor, drinks deals and circus performers. Ash had a great package from a local company that specialised in stilt walkers, fire breathers, little people, actors, dancers and skilled acts who wore massive bonkers costumes and performed all night long amongst the masses. He gave them a good paycheck and they took the event to another level.

Once we came onboard, the Halloween Ball became a co-promote with Ash and Ten Feet Tall, we'd share the costs and share the profit. We'd provide the fun and games, the decor, and of course the best DJs from our Fridays' and Saturdays - Ash would book his theatrical troupe, and the events were insane. You'd always get 1500 people at least, everyone totally got into the spirit and dressed up, and the show always blew people's minds.

We'd usually squeeze three events out of Halloween. An Empire Official Halloween Ball midweek, then we'd pull off a Sumo Fridays Halloween Special, and a Halloween Saturday event too.

Once the team and I had spent our three days prepping the venue. It was straight into three nights of madness, managing the heaving mass of people that packed every inch of the venue.

Halloween was hard work, and along with the promotion of the triple bill of events, they took up a big chunk of time for TFT throughout every October. Here's the crazy thing though - we never actually made that much money out of them. The Fridays and Saturdays were always decent, but the stand-alone event of the Halloween Ball always took pride of place. For that event, we were on a 50/50 deal for the door take, but that was after production costs. Those costs were sky-high.

If anyone's thinking that 1500 people paying £6 means nine grand in Ten Feet Tall's pocket, you're sadly mistaken. After costs and always giving the VAT man his share, you're walking away with a few hundred quid profit.

That's for a month's work, and the busiest event you've had all year. It's a head scratcher for sure.

It was around this point in our timeline, 2015, that my life became centred around spreadsheets. We had Excels for every event. Making the bottom line stack up became a big part of day to day life. It was an essential part of promoter life, and it was eye opening. I'd thundered through over a decade at Ten Feet Tall, and I'd not spent a huge amount of time analysing figures. I lived very much in the moment and despite planning some events months ahead, it felt like we all lived day-to-day. Like any business, there were daily fires to put out, people to keep sweet, problems to solve and hurdles to overcome. The spreadsheets of costs for each event were pretty sobering. We soon learned we were spending a huge amount of money unnecessarily. It was time to start being a bit more strategic with our spending for sure.

Twenty Four Seven

This job was all-consuming and all-encompassing. From the moment I opened my eyes each morning to the second I fell asleep at night, I was on.

On my phone, texts, emails, DMs - I was constantly replying, smoothing, sorting, all the time, day and night.

They called me the shit shield.

When things went wrong, as in life they often did, I was the guy to sort it. If someone had a problem, as in life they often did, I was the guy they needed.

I've talked a lot about spinning plates. We span many, many plates. Inevitably sometimes plates dropped.

In amongst all this, though, I managed to squeeze in a ridiculous amount of personal fun shit too. I played in two or three bands, we released albums and did small tours, I even started a record label. I also managed to get married and have two amazing kids. It's not all doom and gloom. When I look back though, I have no idea how I managed to fit it all in.

Schooled By A Strobe Light

Friday 31st October 2014

There's a room at the very top of the Empire known as The Gods. It sits above the large first floor dance floor, and you need to climb hundreds of steps to reach it.

I'm told that back in the days before Ten Feet Tall looked after the Empire, when the venue was the crown jewel of the House music heyday, The Gods was a VIP room and I can imagine the sorts of intimate stoppy-backs that took place up there.

Under our watch, The Gods hosted everything from Drum n Bass to live gigs - with the worst load-in known on the circuit. Within the original epic Saturdays known as 'Play' the Gods was the Rock Room, under the moniker Bad Habit (like The Offspring song); DJ's Dave and Lauren played punk, ska, emo and the like. When Saturdays became Metropolis in around 2008, the Gods was the home of Kaboom - a self-styled Clubnight-within-a-clubnight (we did a lot of them) and Fil and JT played an eclectic mix of left field indie, retro anthems, and Kate Bush last. Ten Feet Tall's creative accomplice Pop was the man in charge of promoting and curating that party, which he did with great aplomb.

The Kaboom parties up in The Gods raised the bar way beyond bizarre - Pop would smuggle Jelly and Ice Cream, Colouring Books and Poppers up to the room (smuggle, as the Empire disliked such silliness within their grand walls). He put a topless girl in a paddling pool dressed as a mermaid, and dressed himself as a horse in a cage. You could buy a polo from the mermaid and feed it to the horse. This was all standard practice at a Kaboom Saturday from 2008 until about 2010.

Four years later. Back to 2014

For this particular Halloween event I was in charge of, The Gods had been dusted off, re-opened, and was part of the show. The sound system had been tested and sounded barely passable, the ancient bar fridges had been powered up, the toilets mopped, and the dregs of our Halloween decor had been strung up.

It looked.... Okay.

The thing letting the room down was the lighting rig. There was a cheap Maplin lighting controller in the DJ booth, it was sticky from years of vodka splashes, and it made the crude family of lights that hung from the room's ceiling deliver a thoroughly depressing light show.

I decided that what this room needed was a strobe light.

Looking back, no one would have noticed the difference an extra strobe light would make, but I had it in my head that I couldn't tick this room off my list without adding a strobe. Rather than getting one of the venue's lighting technicians with years of experience, proper tools, ladders and insurance, I decided the job of adding a new light fell to me. I dragged one of the God's decrepit bar stools over the middle of the dance floor. It creaked and groaned under my weight as I vaulted up onto the stool with the grace of a circus seal jumping on a ball - an art I'd perfected.

After getting the strobe light plugged into one of the ceiling's 13amp sockets,

I got down from my perch and tested it. These lights came with a tiny infrared remote control on a keyring, about the size of a fifty pence piece. The kind of thing that would be lost in the vastness of the Empire after less than two events, but for this Halloween weekend at least, this room would have one decent lighting effect. A storm of white lightning pulsing above punters heads as they jumped around on the small dancefloor.

The light didn't work. I jabbed the button on the tiny remote, but nothing happened. I looked around, and laughed aloud to myself - the large 1500watt bulb was still in the bottom of the box.

I mounted the stool, unplugged the light from the mains, and flipped open the light's cover and jammed the bulb into place.

This was when I found out that strobe lights hold their charge for a good few minutes, even after you've unplugged them.

A searing pain shot up my arm; my hand seemed glued to the light, and despite the agony, I couldn't let go. It was probably only lasted about three or four seconds, but my mind flashed through the following rollercoaster story;

I would now die, right there in The Gods. Burned out and blackened on that sticky dance floor, surrounded by cable ties and shitty Halloween decorations. I would lay there until about 10pm when the bar staff would arrive to stock up the fridges. They would undoubtedly assume my charred carcass was a Halloween prop, step over me, and carry on their duties. Perhaps the club would open, and my superiors would wonder where I was, but The Show Must Go On, so the Empire's doors would open, and people would flood in to enjoy the busiest, wildest date on the calendar. Would my body even be noticed among the costumes, cocktails and frivolity? When The Gods got locked up at 4am, I'd be left there only to be discovered by the cleaners at 7am. My corpse would be bundled into a blue plastic bar caddy with the other broken decorations and set outside, ready for the bin men.

This didn't happen, of course. What did happen was I hopped around The Gods screaming '*motherfuckermotherfuckermotherfuckershitshitshit*' for a minute or so. I couldn't feel my right hand or forearm. But I had things to do.

I composed myself. I headed downstairs. I checked the team had finished the decorations in the rest of the club.

A quick drive home. The feeling started to return to my shocked limb. Shower, shit, shave. Back to the club to get doors open for 10pm.

A Bit Of A Blur

Dear Reader,

I feel like I went into much more detail about the weeks and weeks we all spent in The Cornerhouse. I find myself now jumping through a decade at Empire so swiftly.

On my watch, there were about 250 Fridays at Cornerhouse. However, there were over 500 in the Empire.

So why can't I remember a few more Empire details?

There are maybe a few reasons. I was continually distracted. I was pulled from pillar to post, or rather, from Durham to Darlington - Setting up more Sumos, more gigs, more parties.

In these hazy 'Sumo Empire' days, the team at TFT had expanded, we had loads more staff, and I essentially ran the whole show. I'm not complaining; it was fun, it was an honour.

These were crazy days. Graham went to live in France for a year. I had kids, and I got married, my Dad passed away, and I bought my first house, sold it, and moved into a second - all in ten very fast years. All through 500 Sumos.

So, I can't seem to recall that many details.

Another reason for this apparent amnesia; we'd learned to recycle events. Not in a bad way. But if you put a load of time and energy into making the perfect Grand Theft Auto party, you'll want to hold onto the event plan, save that spreadsheet, and whip it out again a year later. Sumexico, Silent Disco, A Nineties Party, A Balloon Drop, A UV Megarave, Etc, Etc.

A new crowd came to the club every new year we entered, so I don't think we were short-changing anyone.

Entering Empire, then exiting Empire a decade later, is all a bit of a blur.

New Years Eves

We perfected the art of New Year's Eve.

It was pretty easy to pull off a NYE worthy event in Empire; it had the grand scale, the stage, and the ceiling height to accommodate a midnight pyrotechnic display.

Once Ten Feet Tall had got Fridays and Saturdays established and we had Ash and the Empire's trust, we became their go-to promoters for any other events they wanted to pull off, namely, Halloween and New Year's Eve.

Since the turn of the millennium, NYE parties have come with a hefty price tag. On NYE in 2000, every nightclub charged £20 upwards for a the party, and most clubs had tried to continue the price tag into future years. Punters weren't having it and what ended up happening was a string of half baked events and half-full venues from 2001-to 2009.

We all knew we had to hit the reset button on how New Year's Eve events were planned and executed and do something drastic to reignite people's passion for partying through into the coming year. No one was buying an expensive club ticket, and house parties had become the norm.

We decided to throw the biggest NYE party Teesside had ever seen and charge £2.50 a head. We booked in the local circus troupe, we loaded the ceiling with as much pyro as we felt we safely could do. We prepped confetti cannons, a zillion balloons, red carpets and huge projection screen with a countdown animation that hit zero (obviously) on the stroke of midnight. The pyro would go boom, the confetti cannons would pop and everyone would sing, hug, cry, laugh and dance en-masse to welcome in the new year.

That was the plan. Our £2.50 NYE event needed a great name. We needed posters that would catch the eye, and huge banners on the side of the Empire.

So we named it... "£2.50 NYE". Not the most exciting name, but it got the point across, I suppose.

We sold a thousand tickets in advance, which alone was twice as many people as we'd been bringing into the place previous NYE's. We opened up at 9pm, and everyone rocketed through the doors. We served up all the explosive trimmings, and the best thing was, that we pulled another 600 people through the door at around 1am. Our early doors crowd had been partying hard from the off and had started to drift a little once they'd seen our midnight finale. This extra throng of punters piled in post-house-party and gave the event a second wave of energy and we ended up rocking till 4am.

Like the total clubnight organiser nerd I am, I'd made an action plan for the event. It had every item we'd need to buy, and links where to buy it at the best price. Every performer and their role was listed along with contact numbers and fees. There was a timeline of what happened when. What needed doing at 9am, what needed building at 12noon, what needed to be done before 9pm. Every little detail was in there, down to buckets of iced beers placed in each DJ box ten mins before doors. Happy DJs, happy crowd right?

We'd also stick a bucket of iced beers up in the top balcony too, so the guys popping the pyro and pulling the plugs on the confetti cannons could enjoy a drink and say cheers as they welcomed in the new year from the dizzy heights of the Empires ceiling, fifty feet about the thousand drunks below them. Also on this spreadsheet, you have the exact minute-by-minute plan of the event from doors opening. From wristband procedures, to doormen briefings, to countdown prep and execution. This spreadsheet, if I do say so myself, is a true piece of work. When planning and executing the once-stressful NYE plan the following year, I simply printed off the spreadsheet and followed it through, piece of cake.

I'll be honest; I fell out of love with New Year's Eve. I dreaded them. The team was well up for it, and so into it, that I'd never let my lack of enthusiasm show. I was super grateful that the people who made up the TFT team gave up their daytime to spend eight hours prepping the thing, and many gave up their whole night and the following morning to ensure that Middlesbrough had the biggest party going.

I guess to them, younger and more carefree than I, they were partying as they worked, and they were surrounded by all their mates. How did I get so cynical about New Year's Eve? Well, they were a lot of work, and they were a lot of chew. I was used to the work, I didn't mind it, but the crowd was twice the size of a regular night, twice as drunk, and twice as daft. Inevitably we had ten times as many fires to put out.

Anyway, here's my other Frank Turner story.

In December 2010 I was busy planning the bulging Christmas calendar of events for Sumo and Ten Feet Tall, which included the NYE ball at Empire. An email dropped in my inbox from Darlington Promoter Becky Stefani asking would I like to support Frank Turner at a show on NYE. The show was already sold out, and she'd been asked to add a couple of local supports. I was totally buzzing and said yes without hesitation.

I should probably add here that after playing in a few punk and metal bands for years, I'd put out a solo album (I know, cringe) and did a bunch of shows as a solo acoustic act and also with a band that included talented musicians such as TFT's Kev, Rick and Jamie.

So anyway, now I had to figure out a way to play a gig in Darlington on the same night as throwing the big party at Empire in Middlesbrough.

The timeline just about worked out. I could spend all day at Empire, start early, get the team moving, and be done by 5pm. I could then drive to Darlo, soundcheck at 6pm, play my set at around 8pm, and be back to Empire for doors opening.

My set was pretty good. I'd roped Kev in on a second guitar to fill out the sound and add some nice twiddly riffs and backup vocals. As my long term musical partner in crime, Kev's been making our musical endeavours sound 300% better for about 20 years. Anyway, we played a bunch of my songs and sprinkled the set with covers that I hoped the crowd would know. We played What's The Matter With Parents Today by NOFX and Olympia, WA by Rancid, and they had the sold out crowd singing along. After our performance, Frank collared us and said he'd had an idea.

Frank's set would take him through the turn of midnight, so his plan was to count in the New Year at 12am, and then play Auld Langs Syne to the crowd who would no doubt rabidly lap this up. Frank asked if we'd join him onstage to play Auld Langs Syne with him, and did I have time now to quickly jam through the chords?

I told Frank I had to leave.

A support band leaving before the headline act is a bit of an industry faux-pas, so I swiftly added that I had to go to work, and I was in charge of a nightclub about half an hour away, and despite really really really wanting to quit my job there and then and enjoy my four minutes of fame on the stage with him, I just couldn't bail on Empire.

I quickly thought through my options, like of who was in Boro, who could do what, and what would happen If I just phoned them and said, sorry, not coming.

Frank was already walking away.

I headed out to my car, left Kev to enjoy the gig and welcome in the new year with Frank, and I drove to Middlesbrough to get the next party started.

Sumo WK

Sumo WK was a Sumo event in which we would play loads of songs by Andrew WK. We had a photo booth where people could grab a white T-shirt, and get fake blood under their nose, thus recreating the classic Andrew WK album cover.

That was it, that was Sumo WK.

Sumo WK was great.

Sumexico

Sumexico was a Mexican themed party that we threw every year from about 2011 to 2017. In the latter years, I began to question the party narrative and became aware of the cultural appropriations. I still don't know if shit like this is cool or not; I'm pretty sure it is not. However, at the time, a good few hundred people in Middlesbrough liked drinking tequila, falling off a mechanical rodeo bull (random) and celebrating all things Mexican. We had a decent array of Mexican style decor for the venue, and the main centrepiece of a Sumexico was a gigantic handmade cardboard piñata.

We'd start piñata making first thing Friday morning in the TFT office. I think it was Laura that made the best Sumexico piñata one year, but most years I took on the task of gaffer-taping together as many cardboard boxes as we could find in the vague shape of a donkey, then painted it with glue and wrapped it in brightly coloured crepe paper. We'd then snip into the coloured paper to create a frilly edge and stick on two giant cartoon-like eyes - Hey presto, you now had a giant cardboard piñata.

Next, we'd cut a hole in its butt and load it full of sweets, cheap toys, and about twenty kilos of confetti. I'd fashion a harness for our creation from zip ties, and between a few of us, we'd carry the beast over from the office to the venue.

It was a three-person lift because this thing was super heavy. I was always surprised by how much the thing weighed once built.

The plan would be to suspend the piñata from the ceiling of the Empire and then, at about 1am, when the party was in full rage mode, lower our creation down into the crowd below where people could rip it down, smash it to pieces and claim the rewards inside.

Like so many things in Sumo, we'd spend ten hours making a party trick that would last about forty seconds.

We had a system of cables and pulleys in the Empire ceiling, which we used for balloon nets, or hanging projection screens. To hoist our piñata, we attached a cable to the piñata's zip-tie harness and hoisted it up.

There was plenty of trial and error over the years. Hoisting too fast meant you cut your piñata in half, spilling its confetti guts across the dance floor below.

So over a few Sumexico's, we'd perfected the art of building (9am), stuffing (1pm), hoisting (3pm), and lowering (1am) a piñata.

In 2014, I knew I wanted to make Sumexico bigger and better than I ever had before. We had a double rodeo bull challenge where you could ride head-to-head with your mate, loads of tequila based cocktails on the go, and free Doritos for everyone at the end of the night.

I'd spent all day on the day of this final Sumomexico building, not one but three huge piñatas. The ceiling would have two strung up on wires and I planned to launch one off the front of the stage, into the crowd, in an attempt to create the world's first crowd-surfing piñata.

As 6pm rolled around, I'd just about completed my triple cardboard donkey build, and it was time to go home for tea.

The days of just powering through to opening time at 11pm were gone. I had a beautiful one-year-old baby at home, and my wife could do with a hand. I always tried to get back home after the office on a Friday, to help get baby Sydney into bed, reading her some stories, getting her off to sleep, before heading back out into the night for the night shift of Sumo.

On this night, perhaps my daughter could sense my excitement and my desire to get her asleep fast so that I could get my arse back to Empire - I still had two piñatas to get strung up into the ceiling, so I needed to get back to the venue by 9pm. This kid was not sleepy.

I told my wife that I had an idea.

I packed my baby daughter into the car and took her for a drive; this trick always worked, and surely enough, she was fast asleep in her little car chair in no time. At this point, I figured I could get to the Empire and get the piñatas hoisted up while she slept, and the wife could have a bit of a break.

Hoist piñatas at 9pm. Take baby back home at 10.30pm. Back to Empire for doors at 11pm. Easy.

I unclipped the bucket seat with my sleeping daughter inside and carried her into the venue with me. I set the Empire's lights at a warm dim orange and set her down gently in the middle of the dance floor. I headed to the Empire's cellar and grabbed my supplies. The big ladders, wire, snips, cable ties and gaffer tape.

I whipped up two piñata harnesses for my heavy cardboard friends and hoisted piñata number one about twenty feet up above the dance floor. The piñata was loaded with bags of Haribo and confetti, and it weighed a tonne. I hoisted it slowly as always so as not to rip through the cardboard body that was wrapped in gaffer tape and frilled crepe paper.

I carefully moved the ladders across the dancefloor, and set to work getting piñata number two up.

I climbed the huge step ladders and began to attach and hoist pinata number two.

Those of you savvy readers, perhaps who have seen the Final Destination movies, have probably guessed what happens next.

Whilst up my fifteen-foot ladder, in the dim, silent nightclub, alone apart from a sleeping child in the Empire's vast main hall, I was focused on a particularly tricky knot of zip ties.

Out of the silence, an almighty *BOOM* shook my senses and nearly made me topple off the ladder.

I spun around in panic and saw that piñata number one had snapped its harness and hit the dancefloor with an epic bang. Its cardboard torso was ruptured, and confetti and Haribo had spewed across the dancefloor.

And about fifty centimetres to the right of this mess was my sleeping baby daughter, looking very sweet and cute with orange, green and white confetti in the little curls of her hair.

She was also very much un-squished and alive and well. Thank fuck.

From that day onwards, whenever hoisting a huge piñata, I made sure I didn't leave any babies on the Empire dance floor.

I would leave them in the foyer instead.

Jake Radio

How the hell do I start this chapter?

Ste (Stage Name: Jake Radio) is a legend. Possibly an unsung legend. Without him, the great walls of the Teesside Music Scene and Middlesbrough Clubnight Scene would surely wobble and then collapse. He is some kind of keystone, and architectural bedrock piece, that slots into the foundations and keeps it all very strong indeed.

I'd known Ste for years. Firstly as bass player and vocalist in The F. Then, ditching his bass for extra stage flamboyance in Secret Signal. I'd been the promoter and stage manager on a few of those shows, many of which were in the Empire at our clubnights; Play and Metropolis. Secret Signal became Be Quiet. Shout Loud!, with whom I again promoted, stage managed, and even shared many stages with, in my own bands.

I once orchestrated a (somehow) council-funded jaunt to Germany with Ste and his band to play a large free festival in Oberhausen. There could well be, and should be, a Jake Radio book. For now, please do type Be Quiet. Shout Loud! into Google to witness some of the finest stage presence and perfectly crafted indie pop known to man.

Ste gets his own chapter in this book because of all of this and because, if my theory and hazy maths are correct, he is the human that has performed the most gigs on that big old Empire stage. Ever.

Ste and I shared a love of playing music, DJing, the clubnight scene, getting pissed and generally living in the Empire, so it would only be a matter of time before he formally came on board as a Ten Feet Tall employee.

In 2014, after getting sick of the barman's iPod, Ten Feet Tall decided that the Empire's cocktail bar should be rebranded and given its own spotlight as part of the Saturday Metropolis show. Our creative-in-chief Marty christened the room The Love Lounge and drafted Ste to take charge of the tunes. Playing a ridiculous mix of eighties, nineties, guilty pleasures, and of course, classic love songs, The Love Lounge was a huge hit and quickly gained a loyal following. Guzzling colourful cocktails, necking 'Empire Special' lethal shooters, and dancing around to Ste's heady mix of bangers was a little jewel in the Saturday's clubnight experience.

Ste also wound up DJing our little Britpop Friday called Revival, which was a few hundred yards down the road at The Medicine Bar. Rick and I knew he was too good to be playing the warm up set down there so we found him a Friday home at Sumo. In Easter that year, Rick's Sumo Karaoke lounge had garnered critical acclaim making Fridays in The Lounge also the stuff of local legend. Drunk moshers stood on tables crooning pop classics was our Friday vibe, but it was missing something - A great host.

Ste stepped up to the plate (as he always did) and played the perfect host with the most. Simultaneously dealing with the nightmare that is drunk people on a karaoke, plus belting out classics to entertain the crowd, and even DJing in amongst all of this.

Now the big first floor dance floor at Sumo around this time was DJ'd each week by Fashion Fil. If you've followed the book half-closely you'll know Fil was part of the Kaboom duo and also the Cannonball guy with JT. Fil had launched his own clubnight, Creeps, which took (and holds) the crown of the biggest Thursday in Boro since 2009. Fil had DJ'd Pop music upstairs at Sumo up until this point.

Fil left DJing Sumo because the team at the Empire (not Ten Feet Tall) launched a Thursday and tried to steal his Creeps crowd. Everyone's mates now, but at the time, he was pissed. I tried to convince him to stay on at Sumo, but such was the politics in 2014, he was out.

I needed a Pop DJ. Enter Ste.

I gave Ste about four days' notice for his Sumo Pop Floor debut, and he smashed it. He arrived armed with arms full of ripped CDs; chart cheese, footy chants, love lounge bangers, nineties, noughties and one-hit wonders. He played Snoop Dogg, Steps, The Killers, Wham, and Let's Get Ready To Rumble by PJ and Duncan. Playing daft pop songs to make people laugh at and dance to wasn't a new idea. For years, Fil and Henry had done this since The Cornerhouse Room 3 days. But there was an added sense of reckless abandon and anarchy that Ste brought that just tipped it over the edge enough to make the dancefloor ignite.

Henry still made plenty of guest DJ appearances, and we added sets by Dani to the mix too - to keep everyone fresh and on their toes. The Sumo Pop Floor had found its new groove.

In writing this book, I asked Ste what his favourite night DJing on the pop floor was.

In September of 2015, Middlesbrough FC played Bretford at home and murdered them 4 - 0.

Ste had been at the match and was most definitely drunk by late afternoon. By 11pm, and most certainly much drunker, he rocked up to Empire to DJ to the pop floor to the masses and of course, an additional influx of happy, plastered Boro fans.

Despite one of the golden rules of Empire being 'don't have all your mates in the DJ box', by midnight, Ste had about thirty of his friends in there with him. The next golden rule, no drinks near the equipment. Well, Ste and his thirty pals had about sixty Red Stripes on the go between them and they entertained the crowd in a big way while no doubt sloshing the decks with lager.

Through the drunken haze, Ste spotted a gang of guys in sharp grey suits shifting onto the dancefloor. He realised that one of the suits was David Button, the Bretford Keeper. His next realisation is that this is pretty much the full Brentford FC squad before him, fresh from getting hammered four-nil by the Boro.

Ste did what any of us would have done in that situation. He broke the third Empire DJ box golden rule. He played Pig Bag.

The whole place went bananas, and everyone realised who the lads in suits were, dancing, chanting, bouncing around them, laughing in their faces.

The party of pals in the DJ box that included the BBC's Gary Phillipson went especially crackers and egged Ste on as he served up more and more footy anthems, whipping the crowd into a frenzy. The Brentford squad made themselves scarce. For a while.

Ste would spy them shuffling back onto the dancefloor every hour or so. Every time he'd drop Pig Bag *again* and send them packing to the crowd's rapture around them.

A born entertainer with nerves of steel, over the coming years, Ste became our go-to guy whenever we needed anything that involved a bit of bravado.

After Be Quiet! Shout Loud made a one-off appearance for charity as Limp Bizkit; I roped them into making the show a full-time act, showcasing their uncanny ability to pull that tribute act off once or twice a year at Sumo.

When we hired a full scale wrestling show and needed an announcer to hype the crowd, you can guess who we handed the mic too. He did such a good job, the wrestlers invited Ste into the ring to referee the match. He probably asks himself, 'how the fuck do I get myself into these situations'. I'd like to think the answer is because I facilitate them. In fact, it's also because he is a born entertainer of the highest calibre.

So Ste has handed out flyers, he's caught crowd surfers as pit crew, he's DJ'd every room there is in that building, he's stage managed shows, he's headlined shows. He's led sing-alongs with just his acoustic guitar to hide behind, and he's stood in front of a thousand people at 2am and announced a raffle prize. All the shit you'd dream of doing. All of the shit you'd never dream of doing.

Here's my final and favourite Jake Radio tale. There's many more. Just buy him a pint and ask him.

As I've detailed, we threw the biggest and best New Year's Eve parties. Now, the most important thirty seconds of these sold-out-to-capacity events, was the minute between 11.59pm and midnight. We needed a sure-fire way of counting down to the turn of the year in an explosive way, with state of the art audio and visual goings on.

For years, just before midnight, as our balloon-droppers, confetti-poppers, pyro-button-pushers waited for their moment, we'd press play on a carefully crafted countdown that played across the Empire's huge soundsystem. All our DJ's had to do was press play on a CD at the right moment. This was shoddily synchronised with a big screen projection and the whole thing got a big cheer at the stroke of midnight. We did it like that for years.

One New Year in 2015 just before doors opened, DJ Chris gave our well-used and fairly battered 'countdown' CD-R a quick test. The thing wouldn't play.

We were fucked.

Chris swiftly went onto the App Store and downloaded a NYE countdown onto his phone, he jacked it into the mixer and gave it a pre-listen. Bingo, it sounded perfect. The file was about sixty seconds long, had a great loud countdown from 30 down to 1, and then ended with some fanfare and cheering. Brilliant.

11.59pm rolled around. I was gathered in the DJ box, champagne and beer in hand, and the countdown began. Our team was all poised in various parts of the ceiling, ready to unleash our pyros, streamers and balloons as the countdown began.

A voice bellowed out the countdown, and the huge crowd swiftly joined in, the whole place counting down together, ready to erupt. As the countdown reached its final seconds, the whole place synchronised and screamed together...

'Five... Four... Three... Two... One!'

Only we hadn't fully checked the countdown download.

We hadn't pre-listened to what happened *after* the countdown.

Over the Empire's humongous PA system, a sample of Alan Partridge's voice exclaimed at deafening volume;

"*AHA!*"

People hugged. People Kissed. People fell about laughing.

I'll never forget. Chris turned to me and said;

"Fucking hell man, next year, just get Jake Fucking Radio on a mic to count it down live, alright?".

So that's what we did.

We literally replaced Alan Partridge with Ste. If you're one of the thousands of people who saw New Year in on that big Empire dancefloor, between 2016 and 2020, that voice you heard over the soundsystem that counted in your new year, that's Ste.

Side Note : I reckon between The F, Secret Signal, BQSL, Limp Bizkit, being a Wrestling Referee, hosting a daft raffle and solo acoustic performances, Ste's performed on the Empire's main stage more than anyone else. I also reckon that between all my bands, I come a close second. I had to pull the spotlight back to myself for a second there didn't I.

Baby Godzilla

Friday 28th November 2014

It had been a while since Rick left, and I was back in Sumo land every Friday with great enthusiasm. I missed Rick, but I was weirdly enjoying having Sumo back to myself. Graham hadn't been to a Sumo in years and he seemed happy I was holding the reins. I was doing whatever I wanted, and I dare say things were going well.

We'd booked Baby Godzilla on the back of their incendiary live shows. Their screamy math rock was (If I'm honest) fairly unlistenable in parts. But they had a couple of great singles and some hilarious DIY videos on YouTube that we'd been sharing like mad on social media for weeks in the lead up to the show. The main support band, Zoax, had some decent hype from Kerrang and Radio One, and I'd added my mates' band Taller Than Trees on as local support.

There was a good bustle and buzz in the club from early doors, all the band members were sound, and I had Jay with me to help run the show. So far, so good.

Baby Godzilla erupted onto the Empire's main stage at around half midnight, and no one knew what hit them. I'm not sure to this day if the band were just really good at making it look like dangerous chaos, or whether it was actually dangerous chaos. Guitars and amps were hurled around the stage, and the band played most of the show in the crowd, flinging themselves continually off the stage and into the audience, sending people and their drinks flying left, right and centre. The crowd loved it. Jay and I spent the first twenty minutes of the show running laps around the Empire's dancefloor, scooping up broken bottles, unwrapping mic cables from around people's necks, and guiding drunk randoms out the way of flying bodies.

Whenever there was a band on stage, or a mosh pit kicking off, you could guarantee that someone would be walking casually across the dancefloor holding three pints of lager, usually heading for the stairs to the pop floor. Sometimes I'd watch these people narrowly miss being sent skyward as they just missed the surge of a mosh pit. Sometimes I'd also see them knocked sideways like skittles as they ambled through the venue, totally oblivious to what was going on around them.

At this point in the show, the guitarists of Baby Godzilla had flung their 4x12 Marshall cabinets down from the stage onto the dancefloor and were sparring a guitar duel whilst straddling the top of them. The situation was all the more dangerous as the crowd was quite spread out. I'd witnessed the likes of Frank Carter or Rou Reynolds surf a sold out crowd in Empire, Frank had prowled the Empire's marble bars before surfing back to the stage.

However, the gaps in the crowd at this show meant patches of slippery wet dancefloor were exposed. As the guys from Baby Godzliia jumped up on top of their cabs, they slipped across the dancefloor into the mosh pits, and people could shove these wooden boxes back and forth like bumper cars at a fairground.

The singer from the band threw the mic at me and screamed "*SING*" as he tossed the cabs back up onto the stage over people's heads, I barked a half a chorus down the mic, then hurled it up to him. I glanced over at Jay who was stationed across the other side of the stage; his eyes were wide, and he was grinning from ear to ear. Jay was getting a crash course in rock and roll stage management and was loving it.

The next thing I spotted was the band's guitar player dragging a tall marble table from the corner of the room into the middle of the dance floor.

He'd earmarked this bit of furniture as his new podium to show off on, and I ran across to help him. Once he'd slid the table to the very centre of the dancefloor where he wanted it, my eyes met his, and I mouthed (over the deafening racket of the band) *"You can't stand on this'*. He yelled back over the noise, *"I can. I'll be FINE"*.

Now, this guy knew more about being a rock star and hopping up on tables than I. But, I knew way more about Empire tables than him, having spent five years hauling these marble and steel beasts around the venue. This wasn't the place to get into a full conversation about physics, but the skinny steel legs, the solid heavy-as-hell marble tabletop, and this wet dancefloor were a recipe for broken legs.

Both of us had two hands on the tabletop, and I just gripped as hard as I could. I kept smiling and slowly shaking my head, and I gradually moved the table back to the edge of the dancefloor. My rock star pal admitted defeat and ran off back up onto the stage.

This was the first time in my ten year career in events that I said, out loud to myself;

"I'm getting too old for this shit"...

What's The Matter With Kids Today?

I am standing in the large reception area of the Empire. I've just poured out fifty shots of honey Jack Daniels. As people come in, I'm like, *"Hey! Free Shot?"*.

The girl I was paying to stand here and do this is running late, so I'm playing host. I don't mind. Giving people free Jack Daniels is good honest work. Putting smiles on people's faces. Easy peasy. We've done this sort of thing for years.

"What's in this, please?"

"Why are these free?"

No one is taking these shots.

These kids aren't rude, and they're not squares. They're not designated drivers. They're just sensible. Until around 2010, in clubland, these fifty shots would have been gone in sixty seconds. We used to have a sign, 'one per person'. We'd have to ration them. Hide the other bottles. People were animals.

In 2014, no one wanted to neck whisky.

Whisky? Straight? That would be crazy. That's going to ruin my night. I'm out for the long haul. I've got a sesh starting at 4am at Thingy's house. Also, I'm not taking a drink from a stranger. Who is this guy? Is it drugged? What about allergies? There could be anything in that glass.

Sensible.

As the years went on, fancy dress parties went from having 90% of people dressed up, to having 0% dressed up. In the old days, you could cause a massive fuss and put a smile on everyone's face with a box of a hundred free wacky hats. Young people today (sic) do not want a wacky hat. They spent too much time and money on their hair. Fair play.

That free ice pop might drip on my £60 T-shirt mate, no thank you.

Even the once-demanded act of having your photo taken by the club photographer became a very different occasion. Up until 2010, everyone wanted to pose for the paparazzi, and no one gave a fuck where those photo's went. *It's going on Facebook? Nice one mate!*

Times changed. The *last* thing these kids now wanted was our candid snaps uploaded without their say so. The customers started having our photographers snap ten different angles, and began snatching cameras to approve which snaps made the cut.

Don't get me wrong, it's great that young people started to care about what they looked like. But I think social media gave everyone a load of pressure and unwanted anxiety. There are probably better books on that subject, so I'll shut the hell up on the subject.

It wasn't just their attitudes in the club that changed. Also, at this point, numbers through the doors started to dip.

In addition to the crowd starting to behave differently, there were literally less of them.

This, would of course, become a problem. My problem.

Empire Sumo in 2014

Here's some of the events we did in 2014. Tick them off if you were there.

January 3rd - Sumo WK

January 10th - Sumo Masked Ball

January 24th - Karaoke Sumo

January 26th - Skindred + Soil + Viza

February 14th - Sgt. Sumo's Lonely Hearts Club

February 21st - The Answer

February 28th - Silent Sumo

March 7th - Sumo Slumber Party

March 14th - Sumo's 52 Card Pickup

March 28th - Sumo Pizzalympics + The NX + Hellbound

April 4th - Brawlers + No School Reunion + Red Wolves

April 11th – Falling Red + Foundations

April 25th – The Sumo Players Club

May 2nd – UV Paint Party

May 9th – Sumo Beer Pong

May 23rd – Sumo Dank Holiday Friday

May 30th – Sumo Redneck Summer Holiday

June 6th – Sumoslam with Live Wrestling

June 27th – Sumo Sports Day

July 18th – Silent Sumo

August 1st – Sumo 182

August 15th – Hellbound + Taller Than Trees

September 24th – Dragonforce

October 13th – Sumo Human Roulette

October 10th – Limp Bizkit Y'All + Lennox

October 17th – Metallica Tribute Damaged Inc.

October 31st – Sumo Halloween Ball

November 21st – Samantha Durnan Live Lounge

November 28th – Baby Godzilla + Zoax + Taller Than Trees

December 12th – Allusondrugs + Bi:Lingual

December 19th – Deaf Havana + Lonely The Brave + Surprise Ending

December 28th – Sumo Beach Party

Definitely Too Old For This Shit

February 2015

Middlesbrough Town Hall informed me an external promoter had hired them to put on Enter Shikari. The band were now at the point where they'd sell out this 1200 cap show, and I knew it would be a great association to somehow get Sumo involved. The band had outgrown playing Sumo and perhaps even Empire as a standalone tour show. It was a scoop for the town that the Town Hall had them.

It turned out a guy called Ben, who had done a few hires at Empire, was behind the show. I called Ben and offered to help him promote the show through the Sumo social media, and promo team, if he let us get Sumo's name associated and have Sumo's photographer Eddy shoot the show. Ben was excited to have us on board. He'd made a great booking and I set about helping him as much as I could. I also offered to stage manage the show on the day, and he offered me £100 for my troubles, which I took.

The production loaded in at 8am. The band had the largest lighting rig I'd seen, and to be honest, I don't even think we got it all into the venue and onto the stage. The crew were ace, the band were in good spirits (apart from Rou had the flu, but still played a blinder) - it was a hell of a day and no one stopped running around flat out until 6pm. I'd spent hours keeping the town hall staff and Shikari's crew happy, being the middleman between endless almost-arguments about lights and sound, smoothing over the missed details from the production rider and some of the old venue's shortcomings. There were three support bands in tow, Allusondrugs, Feed The Rhino and Fatherson. I'd bounded up and down the endless staircases of the town hall, stocking dressing rooms with water, beer and food. I'd got everyone soundchecked, had everyone fed and watered, and the whole operation was running on track when 7pm doors rolled around.

At that point, twenty stewards turned up to run the pit. Not security, not trained pit crew, just a gang of sleepy stewards from a local company that Ben had hired. These guys, a mix of 17 year olds and 75 year olds, would be eaten alive by what was about to happen in the front row of this rock show. We needed people who could catch crowd surfers and deal with hauling flailing limbs over a barrier to safety. I also knew the likes of Lee from Feed the Rhino and Rou from Shikari would be undoubtedly throwing themselves into the crowd and singing into the pit. These stewards, bless them, wouldn't do the job. I set about talking the Town Hall's crew into running the pit for me. These guys had been loading heavy boxes since 8am, and would be loading the epic production out again until past 1am. They should have been resting up while the show was on, not getting thrown into the pit to deal with my problem. But they rolled up their sleeves and got on with it. Neil, Woody, Ben, John and the rest of these guys from the Town Hall were absolute heroes.

I ran around the venue for a while to finally find Ben, who was sitting on the top balcony, making his way through a bottle of Smirnoff that he'd treated himself to, to congratulate himself on booking a sold out show. I wasn't mad, he'd done well, and as the band booker, his job was done. I gave him an update on how things were going and told him we'd have to pay the pit crew a good whack, as they'd saved the day. He agreed and went back to his vodka, I left him to it.

I'd been working for 12 hours already, I still had a full four-band-show and a load out to go. I was pouring with sweat, my legs hurt, and my throat was hoarse from talking all day. The hundred quid in my pocket didn't feel worth it. I wanted to go home.

This was the second time in a couple months I said to myself - I'm too old for this shit.

Sumo Air Guitar

The premise; We'd bribe people up onto the massive Empire stage, with free drinks and other treats, and ask them to air-guitar along with the track of their choice. We had a bunch of props for them to choose from - this helped people feel a little less daft than just strumming along with thin air. Hand them a mop, a cricket bat, or an inflatable banana, and they will turn into absolute rock stars.

You'd only find ten people brave enough to get up and do this among the five hundred regulars, but that didn't matter. Everyone else could watch on in horror as men stripped, girls lip-synced, and shapes were thrown up on the stage. People were always so game and many took it way too far

It was the cheapest, most hilarious event to run - and we added decent prizes, a tournament style leaderboard (god knows how that worked, I left it to Jess and Rick to figure out), and of course, we added a host (Jake Radio, obviously) with a mic to commentate and coax revelers up to the challenge.

Sumo Air Guitar was an instant hit and the event returned many times to the calendar. You have to laugh really, that we'd succeeded in creating something out of (literally) nothing.

Grand Theft Sumo

Friday 14th August 2015

I'm not saying I invented Grand Theft Auto parties, but I'd never seen or heard of a club doing one before, so I was feeling particularly smug and pleased with myself when the idea pinged into my brain one day in 2015.

I remember rushing to my laptop and throwing the Facebook Event up, as if other clubs might see the thought in my head and someone would beat me to it.

Within a couple of hours (because back then, 18 to 25 year olds actually used Facebook), there were hundreds of people down as 'attending' the event and talking about how much they were looking forward to the night.

This was months before the actual party, and I hadn't told anyone at work about it. I had no idea what would happen at a Grand Theft Auto Party, but that's sometimes how we rolled. We'd just wing it.

In the office the next morning, I summoned a meeting with Marty, Dani, and Ste - the three people that I knew played a shit load of GTA. We assembled a plan for the huge projections and massive blown up posters that would somehow transform the venue into Los Santos. Ste agreed to DJ a GTA soundtracks special in the Lounge. We crafted a bar menu based on GTA drinks, mixing Vodka with Sprite (Sprunk), Jager with a nasty energy drink (eCola) and rebranding Becks as Pißwasser.

We added an arcade games room in the Rockbox and a Los Santos Customs zone in the vast Empire foyer, where clubbers could pick up threads and accessories. These were in the shape of fluro "pimp hats" (thanks, Amazon) and some blinging fake plastic gangster chains I found in bulk on eBay. We designed flash sheets of temporary tattoos with which to emblazon the crowds' arms and necks.

Now we had hats, tatts, visuals and the drinks sorted; we added some big prizes for best costumes. It had become a chore getting the crowd to come in fancy dress. No one was bothered, but adding some cash prizes as an incentive would drive the ambitions higher and ensure that a chunk of the punters made an effort.

The grand prize (no pun intended) for the costume competition was a fifteen inch purple dildo - probably the weirdest thing I'd ever had to buy for an event. For those who don't know, in the video game, the purple dildo is a special item you can buy or find, and use as a weapon. This was the grand prize, and it did the trick - when the night finally rolled around, a good few people did us the honour of dressing up.

I'd built a hundred "medi packs" for the first people through the door. These mimicked the health items you'd traditionally find in games to restore life. The Sumo Health Packs were palm sized green plastic cases that contained a mini Jagermeister and a stack of American candy.

Another key element of the night's entertainment was our very own Trevor Philips. Ste had volunteered his mate Kev (Not DJ Kev, this is a different Kev) to stalk the rooms of Grand Theft Sumo, in costume and in full character as the GTA V protagonist. He accosted customers and was generally obnoxious to everyone - which people absolutely loved. For the first few hours, he posed for photos with his teddy bear - Mr Raspberry Jam. He later appeared, drunk as a lord in his trademark filthy underpants, and executed his finale – stumbling onto the front of the Empire's stage at around 2am, with an enormous rocket launcher (which Marty had expertly made from cardboard). We used theatrical pyro to create the 'boom' of the launcher and played samples of gunfire and sirens over the songs to make the people on the dancefloor feel they were in the middle of a gunfight.

The centrepiece for our Grand Theft Sumo event came in the shape of a Dodge Monaco, an original American cop car that I'd rented from a guy I'd found on the internet. This full-scale eighties beast looked like something out of Dukes of Hazzard, it was perfect. I'd bought a few SWAT uniforms for the Sumo team, complete with plastic M16s. This made the greatest photo opp the Empire had ever seen. The car and crew were parked up right on the pavement outside Empire, blue lights flashing, and everyone got their photo splayed across the bonnet before entering the club.

We ended the night with another set piece from our 'actors' (people who we paid to do daft stuff). We killed the music to get everyone's attention then we staged a mock heist in the club's main hall. Four thugs in boiler suits and latex pig masks waved plastic guns at the bar staff, who handed over bags full of cash. The bar staff played their parts perfectly, and there were some oscar-worthy performances as they passed the robbers the money – Sumo Dollars that we'd printed. The bandits ran through the crowded dancefloor, pushing customers out of the way to get up on the front of the stage. We picked them out with spotlights, fired more gunshot samples over the PA system, and the crooks faked death by gunfire and fell to the ground, throwing the bags of money out into the crowd. People cheered and scrambled to grab the flurry of notes that fluttered down onto them. The Sumo dollars could be swapped at the bar for a last drink before the house lights went up on this epic event.

These theme nights cost an arm and a leg, but they usually did great numbers, and I think they hopefully cemented Sumo's reputation for throwing the biggest and best parties.

One thing that was infuriating was that whatever party you threw, however imaginative you got, you could guarantee every club in Boro would be throwing the same party a few weeks later.

Did other clubs in the town have Grand Theft Auto parties a couple of months after ours? Of course they did.

The Class of 2005

Friday 18th September 2015

Our ten-year reunion event. It was brilliant. It was packed to the rafters. People fucking hated it.

Ok, back up. So it dawned on us that we needed to throw a party to celebrate ten years of Sumo. I made the conscious decision to make it a celebration of the music. People would expect a big do, and I knew we could give them that, but I wanted to make a point that despite all the wackiness, theme parties and fancy dress nonsense we regularly engaged in, Sumo had always really been about playing the best in alternative music.

Thinking back to 2005, the music from those days was so good, a golden time in rock, punk and metal and to be honest, in 2015, we still played a decent chunk of these timeless classics that had aged well. I saw this ten year anniversary party as an opportunity to really throwback to the early noughties, and get the DJs to curate a playlist of the songs and bands that were the staples of 2005.

Down in the Empire's main hall we of course had Craig and Kev, the two DJs who started it all, playing side by side and delivering their best Cornerhouse style setlist. So we weren't playing any of the bands like Bring Me The Horizon, Mallory Knox or Don Broco that regularly filled the 2015 Empire dancefloor, and we brought back bands that had fallen off the set over the last decade; Korn, Disturbed, The Ataris, 36 Crazyfists, Atreyu, Sublime, Rancid. MSI, Glassjaw, Finch.... You get the idea.

Upstairs we axed the regular 'Pop Floor' for the night and instead went for a great big indie throwback with none other than Ten Feet Tall, Music Live, Play Rock n Roll Disco main man Stubbsy on the decks. I knew Bryan could deliver a proper naughty stack of tunes that would froth nostalgia. The Libertines, We Are Scientists, The Gossip, Fatboy Slim, Arcade Fire, Kings of Leon, The Enemy, Good Shoes, Black Rebel... This playlist in itself had people buzzing and in a world where nostalgia had recently really started to become a selling point, the idea of people being able to let their hair down and jump around to the soundtrack to their youth was something we knew would pack the venue out.

We relied heavily on the old Cornerhouse crowd finding out about the event and we spent a mighty amount of time postering the far reaches of Teesside with our Class Of 2005 posters. Facebook's super-sinister targeted paid ads also did the trick online, and that campaign seemed to be rallying the troops. Despite slight concerns that we might scare The Kids away for one night, we all felt that we could pack the club out with people who were older, and we thought they'd love it.

The event itself felt mega. Over a thousand people piled in, we'd added a couple more guest rooms, including Dani dutifully spinning a Bad Medicine classic rock room into the mix, and we'd wired up the old Pac Man and Sonic The Hedgehog machines to some cheap TVs from Cash Converters. We'd even convinced the Empire to sell some drinks in the Cornerhouse 2005 style - so cans of Red Stripe dropped from £2.80 to £1.80 and we brought back 500ml cans of Relentless with a triple shot of vodka inside - a Cornerhouse classic in its own sickly right. Surely, all of this would make a recipe for a good time?

I had a fantastic night, and the building felt amazing with that many people inside. It was so cool to hear every track in every room, just pure guitars, guitars, guitars.

It really felt like 2005, and I thought that was the point.

The following day my enthusiasm for booking more throwback events was crushed by a slew of ridiculously negative comments on Facebook.

In the present day, Facebook's not a place where the clubbing youth discuss their antics; it's a place where your Mam shares Lost Cat posts, your racist Uncle makes bad jokes or shares anti-vax memes.

In 2015, clubbers in their twenties lived for Facebook. It was where we shared every photo we took. It was where we Updated Our Status every single day. Social Media was a new-ish and exciting place where every sandwich was snapped and uploaded, and every new TV show was endlessly debated.

People's problem with the Sumo Class of 2005 event was that it wasn't *in the Cornerhouse.*

No low ceilings, no grime, no claustrophobia, no breaking your legs on slippy tiled floors, no pulling your feet up off sick stained carpet. The Empire, it seemed, was a grand, polished, cavernous event space that the nostalgic crowd of old felt a bit out of place in.

We gave them the music, the DJs, the drinks, and the decor of Sumo in 2005, but we couldn't recreate that atmosphere, that smell, that vibe. It wasn't the same, they were right, and I took that to heart a bit.

Side Note : 2022 Reflection; Sumo OGs. Don't get me wrong here, I love you guys. However, when you stop me in the street or when you drop me a comment online reminding me that *"Cornerhouse was best Phil!"* I always wonder – Was it that building you missed? Was it those condensation soaked walls? Those blocked bogs? Those bouncers? The power cuts?

Or was it just those *days?*

Think about it; you were decades younger. We all had the best times. We had more friends. We went out and got drunk five times a week. We didn't have a mortgage, or a job, or any real responsibilities. We didn't have a care in the world. Ten Jagerbombs didn't give us heartburn and hurt even more the next day; they were a chaser for the ten Red Stripes that would follow. As some band in a bad indie night might sing, You're not Nineteen Forever, right?

I miss those days too, and if you want to hold that wreck of a building up as a monument to symbolise your past life, then that's fine. I'll allow it, I guess.

They were pretty great times.

Cat Sumo

It had gotten to the point where I felt like every event we created, someone copied it less than a mile down the road. I shouldn't have let it get to me, but it was pissing me right off.

I sat down to try and think of an event that literally no one could rip off.

Was there a party we could throw, that would be *impossible* to recreate?

What if we announced an impossible event.

What if we told everyone we were going to do something so stupid or outrageous that not even *we* could do it?

I'd lost the plot at this point.

I announced Cat Sumo.

I had absolutely zero intentions of actually doing this event. I just wanted to make some noise, turn some heads, and get some attention. Maybe the other unimaginative promoters in town would attempt to copycat this (ha). I wanted to do something so very specific, that if they did follow suit, it would be obvious to all a sundry that they'd plagiarised our work.

Cat Sumo started as a Facebook event. From there, it spiralled out of control.

I told everyone we were going to fill the Empire with cats.

I told Boro that for this special event, we'd got around a hundred cats to put in the club, so that people could stroke them, play with them, and have a nice time. I explained that (obviously) the music would be very quiet for the night. I said there would be cat toys, cat themed drinks, cat fancy dress and pouches of cat food would be available to buy at the bars with which to feed the cats. To make sure people didn't think this was real (surely no one would think this was real?), I added some stupid stuff into the promo; something about a giant ball of wool that we'd lower from the ceiling. Something about no dogs: it was intentionally stupid and purposely fake.

First, the Facebook comments started, and then the tweets came in. People were excited. People were horrified. People were confused.

God bless the kids with a brain who clocked right away that this was a pointless joke and that played along. They jokingly asked if they could bring CatNip, they asked if they could bring their own cats along, they asked if we could do a Dog Sumo after Cat Sumo. All this made for great banter online.

Then came the Crazy Cat People. Some were seriously concerned, some were damn right rude. We got called names, and we got called cruel. Some people went on a mission to shut us down.

The more comments, interactions and online hate we got, the more I pushed the message; Cat Sumo Was Coming. We designed and printed posters, and we wrote lengthy blogs about how this was going to work. We added more and more ridiculous extras, while making it as obvious as we could that this thing was a joke, but we kept a straight face throughout.

On the day of Cat Sumo, the office landline rang. The office landline never rang. It was the Evening Gazette – they wanted an official word on this Cat Party that they'd heard was happening that night in Empire.

Following that call, we sat around feeling very pleased with our hype, and unpacked our boxes of Cat Whiskers and cat themed party props that we'd ordered for the night. We planned to announce at 5pm that Cat Sumo was a hoax, a lie, and sorry for the disappointment, and that we're throwing a massive Pound Sumo instead.

The office landline rang again. It was the RSPCA.

They'd had "numerous reports" that an abhorrent event was to take place in a nightclub that evening, and through an internet search for this "Cat Sumo" they'd ended up on the Ten Feet Tall website, and hence found our phone number. I assured the concerned lady that it was a joke, and she actually thought it was pretty funny.

On the day of the event, we flipped the message online from Cat Sumo to Pound Sumo, to great joy and relief from the public.

So mission accomplished – I can safely say that no other clubnight in Teesside ever threw a Cat party.

Technically, neither did Sumo.

Sumo41 and KazSumo

Sumo41 was a Sumo in which we played the entire "All Killer No Filler" album by Sum41, and also recreated the iconic album cover by taking photos of people swinging their faces side to side. That's it. That was Sumo41. It was great.

There was another brilliant idea for a simple Sumo, that never did come to light.

Long-standing Empire head lighting technician Paul was very much part of the Sumo gang and part of the venue's furniture. Paul approached me one night with a swift pitch for KazSumo.

He suggested we buy five hundred Kazoos, and hand them out upon entry to KazSumo. Throughout the night, the crowd could happily Kazoo along with the songs. I started to think about how we could get volunteers up on stage, mic them up and have them solo Kazoo along with their favourite track, to the horror or delight of the audience.

A Karaoke element to a Kazoo party. You might call that Karazoomy? So karazoomy and KazSumo. Karazumo-y?

Anyway, cheers Paul. Sorry we never got to realise this vision. Another time perhaps.

Empire Sumo in 2015

Here's some of the events we did in 2015. Tick them off if you were there.

January 30th - Up River + Taller Than Trees + Glass Harbour

February 13th - The Bloody Valentine Ball

February 27th - Sumo Air Guitar Championship

March 6th - Fell Out Boy, the Fall Out Boy Tribute

March 13th - Freaky Friday

March 20th - The Steelcats

April 3rd - Pound Sumo

April 17th - Free Sumo Shot With Every Drink

April 24th - Slipknowt - The Slipknot Tribute

May 1st - Sumo Roulette

May 15th - Sumexico

May 29th - Sumo Down Under

June 12th - Pound Sumo

July 17th - Xmas In July

July 31st - Sumo Karaoke

August 7th - Sumo Air Guitar Championship

August 14th - Grand Theft Sumo

August 21st - Who Dares Wins

August 28th - Pound Sumo

September 4th - Sumo From Hell + Wraiths

September 11th - Sumo Slumber Party

September 18th - Sumo's Class of 2005

September 20th - Brand New + Basement

October 3rd - Mallory Knox

October 9th - Sumo41

October 13th - Bullet For My Valentine + While She Sleeps + Coldrain

October 30th - Sumo's Horror Show

November 27th - Hey! Alaska + All At Sea

December 7th - Lower Than Atlantis + Moose Blood + As It Is + Brawlers

December 11th - Star Wars Sumo

December 18th - Sumo Suited and Booted

December 27th - Sumo Xmas Beach Party

Conspiracy Theory

I'd heard rumours, heard whispers. A few people had told me the Empire wasn't happy with the number of people showing up to our clubnights.

Friday's were trundling along with around 600 week in week out. I know it wasn't the thousand-strong crowd that we'd launched with at Empire five years earlier, but you couldn't fault Sumo's dogged consistency as a solid brand with a great crowd.

There had been so many nights launched and binned in Boro. Almost every rock night that had once done great guns in town was long gone, Sumo was a veteran survivor of the scene, but showed no signs of dying off.

I dug a little deeper into these rumours, and a couple of people, including some long standing Ten Feet Tall staff, told me that it was Saturdays that the Empire weren't happy with.

One of Graham's tasks for me each week was to check in with Ash at the Empire, and make sure he was ok, he was happy, and there was no sign of him falling out with us.

Hearing someone tell me that Ash would take the Saturdays off TFT, made me panic and made me worry. Graham asked me to see Ash and just ask the question directly. He laughed it off, and quashed the rumour there and then. He said he'd worked with Graham in one way or another for over so many years. If he had a problem, he'd phone Graham. He said I shouldn't worry. So I didn't worry.

Golden Hour

My favourite hour at work was 2.15am until 3.15am.

As I've said before, it's pretty hard to sum up, explain, or map out what exactly I did between 9pm and 2am, but my feet never touched the floor, my brow was never free of sweat, I never stopped talking, moving, fixing, helping, catching, whatever...

I think many people thought I was pretty rude. Mates, and mates of mates would stop me in the corridors, on the steps, out the front, or by the stage, just to say hi. I always had to run. I found myself parroting the same sentence ten or twenty times every Friday night;

"Don't think I'm rude, but I just need to go and sort this thing..."

....and I'd be off into the crowd. They'd definitely think I was rude.

Anyway, give me that 2.15am golden hour. A favourite time.

By now, everyone's drunk, everyone's happy, the drama has (mostly) burned out, and everyone's focused on having a nice time. The dancefloors are chocka, everyone's smoked all their fags, and the DJs are about the unload their very finest, biggest, most singalong songs. The tunes you've been asking for all night long, are all about to be played back to back over the next 60 minutes.

You're going to know every word to every song in the next hour.

It's going to be proper mint.

For me personally, the reception tills are off, the money's counted, the bands have loaded out, the face painters have cleared up, and the knife thrower has loaded her nine-foot solid wood rotating stage prop into the van.

For the next hour, I can slump into the DJ box, maybe to sit on a stool I stashed in there before doors opened, or maybe I just find a little space on the floor, and I sit my arse right down. I'll wave goodbye to Nic or Danielle or Eddy the photographers, they've got enough shots for the night, and I'll open an icy beer.

I might have already had a few drinks, on easier events, but on the chewy shows, this might be my first of the night, and it tastes amazing.

For the first decade of Sumo, before such things were deemed off-budget, I'd have stuck a massive plastic tub in the corner of the DJ box, filled it with beer, bottled water and pop, and covered it in ice. By 2.15am the bucket would be a lukewarm pool with the odd Sprite or Fosters swimming sadly around in it. Ste and Dena would have drank most of the beers, which I wholeheartedly encouraged. I'd probably pass on the final floating Fosters and head to the Lounge bar for a couple of ice cold Peronis, and perhaps a Long Island Iced Tea. The barman would knowingly triple up the four deadly spirits involved in that cocktail. Often in that last hour, I'd get more drunk than the people who'd been chugging drinks for the last five hours.

Around 3.30am, the door staff would politely ask the hundreds of people in the club to GTFO, and I'd merrily skate around the club, whisking down decor, snipping away hundreds of cable ties and dismantling the event that took me two days to construct. I could usually have this done in half an hour, and by that time, Kev or Dani (who rarely boozed) would dutifully drive me home to bed – thanks again guys, I owe you about two hundred lifts.

An Arctic Monkey

Fri 25th March 2016

It's 2am, and Alex Turner is dancing around the Empire lounge with his pal Miles Kane.

We didn't always have a DJ in the Sumo lounge, but on this night Henry's in. He's playing a bit of everything, and Alex has been requesting funk and soul. It had been a bit quiet in the lounge until midnight, and Henry wasn't feeling great, so I'd told him, if he wanted, he could wrap up early and head off. His partner Rachel was with him, having a couple of cans, and I think they both thought they'd be home and in bed by now. But Alex Turner is here. The room is ridiculously packed. People are losing their minds.

Whether or not you're a fan of the Arctic Monkeys, you can't argue that they are one of the biggest guitar bands of the 21st century. To anyone aged between 17 and 37, there is no more famous person in the world of British rock and roll. I don't think it's an exaggeration to say that this was the 2016 equivalent of having Mick Jagger in the club.

I'd casually tweeted, Instagram'd and Facebook'd the fact Alex and Miles had popped in for a few cans, and (from what I could read on social media) people were literally springing out of bed, into taxis and flying towards the Empire.

The Last Shadow Puppets, the hugely successful side project and super-group for Alex Turner, Miles Kane, James Ford and Zach Dawes had just performed a sold out show at Middlesbrough Town Hall. Ironically every club in town had set up an "Unofficial Aftershow Party" although we didn't bother.

Around 12am, I mentioned to Ash that I'd seen the show loading out. He'd been chatting to Miles over text throughout the day, as they'd become pals following a handful of previous Empire shows. Miles let Ash know they were all pretty tired and most likely heading home, but Ash assured them we'd put the Moet and Smirnoff on ice, just in case.

I popped my head out the fire door of the Empire and watched the Town Hall crew load the last of the equipment into the trailers on the back of the bus. Last to wander out of the Town Hall were Alex, Miles, and a few mates. I caught Alex's eye and asked him if he was coming over for a few drinks. Miles followed him, and they were discreetly bundled into the venue and made a bee-line to the office to say hi to Ash.

My first plan was to get them up to one of the Empire's royal boxes. Peter had the bar staff set up some iced drinks, and I led Alex and co. up the stairs and into the balcony box. These boxes offer a regal view over the dancefloor and certainly feel pretty plush. Still, the downside is that they're situated literally underneath one of the venue's huge speaker stacks, which are hung from the ceiling.

It is utterly deafening, and as we started to get drinks set up in the box, Kev (who was DJing in the main room) dropped an old school classic, Halo by Soil.

Now Halo is not a song we play that often, it's not a great song, and it's a bit of a weird guilty pleasure in the world of Sumo's rock setlists. It's kind of a banger – but it's shit.

Anyway, it was 100% the *worst* song that could have played at the moment, at 120 decibels, in Alex Turner's face.

I found myself yelling over the music into Alex's ear that there's a nice cocktail lounge that everyone might like to chill in – but it's *public*. He shrugs, smiles, and mouths '*yeahhhhh*' to me over the racket. We trooped down the winding stairs, across the main room's dancefloor, and into the lounge. There were no seats, no special treatments on offer, and from the moment they stepped foot in the lounge, these bonafide superstars just let loose, cracked cans, and started dancing.

It was a tad surreal. Initially people stared. But, after a few more Bee Gees songs, and a few more cans, everyone just drank, sang, relaxed and got funky, with Miles Kane and the Arctic Monkey. I think that's officially the best and worst sentence in this book; I'm sure you'll agree.

Twenty Sixteen

"2016 is going to be our year, I can fucking feel it."

Three men sit in a huge room. The walls are grey with aged white paint.

There's nothing else in the room, just three men on three chairs.

The floor is wooden, parquet, and it's thick with dust.

The room is about twenty metres square in size and ten metres high; a row of huge windows line one wall, and through them, cars and trucks hurtle past at 80mph down the A66.

This room is up on the first floor of Exchange House, tucked away in the corner of Exchange Place and a stone's throw from Boro train station. From the doorway of this cold, leaky old building, you can just about see a derelict nightclub once known as the Cornerhouse, where clubnights used to happen. Opposite the club, under the Albert bridge, is another empty unused space, once known as Uncle Alberts. You can barely see through its dark, dirty, cracked windows.

As you walk into Exchange House circa 2016, once home to local Council offices, you walk straight into an independent art gallery space known as The House Of Blah Blah. Cutting through the maze of rooms and corridors, littered with sculptures, paintings and furniture made from beer kegs, you reach a graffitied concrete internal fire staircase. This is the only way upstairs, and it's a trek through more corridors and rooms to reach the huge grey-walled room that would soon become the new Ten Feet Tall office.

The room had once been a ballroom dancing studio, then an IT suite - the flaking walls were wrapped in purple ethernet cable, and power points dotted the floor, linked by miles of steel trunking.

Marty, Graham and I sat there on those three chairs.

Marty and I listened, and Graham spoke about the future. He was brimming with positivity.

We'd lost our cosy home in the bowels of Middlesbrough Town Hall. The previous office, The Old Court Room, had been earmarked for refurbishment and there was talk of it becoming a venue, a wedding ceremony room or even a home for historical tours. The holding cells beneath the Court Room that we had filled with nightclub props, fancy dress outfits and sixty thousand old flyers were to become places of historical interest. Graham and his merry band of promoters had to be out. Luckily, due to a decade or so of great events in their venues, the council quite liked us and helped us find a home. The House Of Blah Blah was the least dusty and decrepit of the bunch we were offered.

Having the gallery and super-cool venue below us seemed like a decent bit of kudos and our 'landlady' would be gallery owner Keren, an amazing woman who made us feel right at home and told us we could do pretty much what we wanted upstairs.

I undertook the ridiculous task of getting all of Ten Feet Tall's belongings from the Town Hall at one end of Albert road down to the other. Looking back, this was crazy. We had enough shit to fill a football stadium. We had huge steel filing cabinets filled with a decades worth of brochures, posters and print; literally a physical documentation of every leaflet we'd ever made.

We had forty giant bird cages filled with plastic crows. We had twenty full-size tailor's mannequins. We had a six-foot by six-foot solid wooden crate, painted red and stencilled with "TNT" on the side. We had a set of (ironically) nine feet tall high polystyrene letters that spelt out A.P.E. There were desks, chairs, PC's and the usual stuff too. Plus, four full size ping pong tables. Everything was carted, trollied, handballed and dragged down the road. We had buckets of help from Paul and Robin. It was brutally hard work.

Paul had spent weeks painting the new office walls bright white and a retina-popping orange. The air was thick with paint particles, and we choked as we caught our breath on the infinite number of trips up and down the fire escape to get moved in. Paul had also undertaken the painful and thankless task of sanding down (four full days) and varnishing (five full coats) the vast floor in our new home. It now looked utterly magnificent, despite the fact no one could breathe in there. With plenty of help from the team, we were moved out and moved in after about ten days. My lungs and back possibly never recovered, I was a broken man, but the new place looked grand.

Apart from the herculean feat of moving office, which any sane person would have hired a removals company for, I couldn't tell you much else that happened in 2016.

Apart from, we got the apprentices.

The Apprentices

We'd had a couple of good experiences with Apprentices. Two hard working, funny, smart and dedicated lads called Jay and Mark shot up through the ranks, learned all about events and venues, and turned into cracking promoters a year later. Mark ended up pursuing a passion for DJing. Jay ran some of Ten Feet Tall's biggest events for years.

It was in 2016 that we sought out a new apprentice or two to help us fight the good fight and inject some fresh energy into Sumo and all the rest.

Along with our colossal new office, and part of Graham's speech with the three chairs, the new apprentices were very much part of 2016's Comeback Special.

Between our new orange and white four walls, we desperately needed some new blood, some new ideas, some energy and a spark. Sumo Fridays, MILK Saturdays and all that was Empire weren't exactly doing record numbers - and that had to change. The clubnights on the fringe, Animals V Machines and Revival, plus the smaller comedy nights and gigs, were losing money each week. Although none of us wanted to admit it, it was almost certainly make-or-break time for Ten Feet Tall.

Graham had executed a whirlwind promo campaign and successfully yelled from the rooftops that TFT were hiring new apprentices. The glamour and glitz of clubnight-land lured around fifty applicants, which I sifted, sorted and painstakingly whittled down to ten interviewees. I interviewed them all, and Graham gave them a second chat. When I asked him which one (or maybe two) we were hiring, he told me we should take four.

"FOUR?"

Now dear reader, you know by now that I am not exactly work-shy. However, I knew fine well that training these *four* young people would fall firmly onto my fair shoulders. Shoulders that had barely recovered from the trauma of the office move.

There would be long nights of clubnight shadowing, showing them exactly what I was doing at all times. There would be risk assessments. There would be workbooks. Ladder training. How to lift. First aid. Safeguarding. There would be a fuck-load of documenting and paperwork. That's all before even considering the day to day mental and physical well-being of four young people that we were about to expose to Teesside's dark underbelly. All of this would be undertaken whilst also trying to do my job.

Graham's pitch was that ultimately, once they were up to scratch, having a gang of four promoters that we'd shown all the tricks in the book would be an invaluable asset. Also, he added, *"If we have four, they'll all kind of look after themselves"*.

He was right, I was sold, so we gave the good news to Ten Feet Tall's new apprentices.

Adam - Tall, loves live music, knows everything about every local band.

Jade - *"Social media addict"* said the CV, just what we needed.

Izzy - Knew every detail of every clubnight in the town and beyond. Perfect.

Jacob - Would-be-designer, also draws. And ultra-ultra cool. Like, way too cool for us.

These four were also just really lovely kids, proper sound, quietly confident, and very likeable. They and I had nothing to lose, so we were about to embark on a year-long journey into the clubnights and everything that came with them.

But first, there was a fifth.

"A FIFTH?!"

At first, I thought Graham was joking, winding me up. We sat in the old Court Room. It was pretty much empty, we'd moved everything out by this point, but we had a few days before they locked the place up for the refurb.

I told him five apprentices was a mistake. It was too many.

He told me to shut up. At that point, she walked in.

"Phil, this is Dena, why don't you two go and grab a coffee".

I knew he'd already made his mind up, but I was grateful he was allowing me to do a second interview. We awkwardly walked over to Cafe Mannequin, the Polish coffee place opposite the Empire, and I sat us down with a couple of drinks.

Dena was 18 years old, a child in my eyes. She had a mop of dark curly hair, wore dungarees, and held a copy of her CV. I asked how she pronounced her name, and she told me it was like Dana, as in the lady from X Files, but spelt Dena. I asked why. She said because her Dad loved the X Files, but he wasn't great at spelling.

She had 15 GCSEs, all grades A or A-star. She played ten different instruments, some of which I'd never heard of. I told Graham that five apprentices it was, and she was hired.

Side Note : I'm still not sure if Ten Feet Tall was the best or worst thing that ever happened to Dena, but since that coffee in 2016, by 2020, Dena had become a lynchpin of the Teesside nighttime and clubnight community. Post-pandemic, Dena had become Head Of Events at the Empire, she's run dozens of sold-out events across the North East, and she was a key member of the team at Jason Manford's Comedy Clubs. Revered by everyone she's worked with, and rightly so, I'm super proud of where she got to, and how hard she works. She can also drink me and anyone else under the table. I quit trying to keep up with her years ago.

Korn Again

Friday April 15th 2016

In February 2016, I threw a Sumo party called The Big Pop Punk One. A simple premise, loads of pop punk on the playlist, and we probably made up some stupid cocktails called 'Sugar, We're Going Down In One', or 'I Drink Gins, Not Tradgedy' or whatever.

We also had a Me First and The Gimme Gimmes tribute band play called Me First and The Gimme Gimmicks. More on them later.

The night was a huge success, super busy, but we got a small handful of moans from the metal heads. I naturally, and foolishly, decided to throw a 'Metal Special' Sumo to keep these kids happy.

When will I learn?

This event was way quieter, but it gave me a chance to indulge my guilty pleasure of nu-metal and at least we were continuing to do something a little bit different most weeks. Say what you like about Sumo, but we twisted the formula as much as possible and kept folks on their toes as much as we could.

Naturally, I hired a Korn tribute for the night.

John J is an old mate and a talented soundman for Nathan and the PA crew. John's old metal band from back in the day was called Soundgate, and I'd played tons of shows with them as a kid. Soundgate had returned in the shape of a Korn tribute band out of the blue. Soundgate were talented musicians, so I knew they'd pull off the act. John was on bass and even had a wig of dreads. How could I refuse them a show?

John's Korn tribute was called Who Then Now. Which I'm told is the title of a Korn biopic. I will take this opportunity to say to anyone reading this who is thinking of starting a tribute band - PLEASE give yourselves a great, if possible pun-tastic, name.

There's so much potential for fun when naming a tribute band. Especially a Korn one.

Corn. Corny. Korny. Children of Korn. The Kornys. Korn To Do It. Korn This Way. ReKorn. Kornish.

Or my own favourite, Korn Again.

When Sumo's "Massive Metal One" night rolled around, the band were in the Empire sound checking before doors, and I was showing one of TFT's apprentices, Jade, the Sumo ropes. The band had done their soundcheck but the singer, Andy, was late. He wouldn't arrive till later, so he wasn't there to check his vocals. I was worried.

I don't know why I was so worried, but I was a perfectionist when it came to Getting-Everything-Just-Right before doors. I've sung in plenty of metal bands to know that not being able to hear yourself on stage can cause issues. So, I suggested that I hop up and sing a soundcheck song with them to ensure the onstage sound was spot on and Andy wouldn't have any concerns later. I'd seriously overvalued my vocal talents, assuming Korn songs were fairly simple to wing.

I was very wrong. As the band rumbled through Freak On A Leash, I attempted to sing it through with them, to disastrous results.

Fuck knows what Jade must have thought on her first night on the job.

Eleven years into Sumo, and I was still learning shit every day. That night, I learned that I couldn't take care of absolutely everything all by myself despite thinking I could.

Farewell AVM, Enter Holy Shit

I was running a comedy show at Middlesbrough Town Hall (I think it was Alan Carr) on this Sunday night, and my phone rang.

It was one of the Spensely brothers. He informed me that, although we'd done a fine job of Saturday Nights at ATIK with Animals V Machines each week for the last few years, he'd been offered another night by another promoter, and this night promised to fill the venue to capacity - something AVM could never really do.

I was obviously a little shocked, and a bit gutted. AVM only did a couple of hundred a week, but it was Sumo's little brother, and it was a big part of Dani and Kim's weekly wages. I couldn't let it go without a fight. I asked if there was any way I could convince them to keep us on board.

The event they'd been offered was a Pop and RnB event called Gorilla. Gorilla had been doing good numbers each Saturday at another club in town, Onyx Rooms, that was closing down. The Ex-Arena team that ran the event now had no home for Gorilla, and moving it into ATIK was a smart move. It would fill ATIK and they could also incorporate all the rooms of Spensleys Emporium downstairs, to create a multi-room event. There was no way Spenseley's would turn this down for me, there was no point in debating it further. This was a business decision that made sense, so I thanked them for their time and hospitality, and AVM was gone. No farewell party, no last night. Just dusted from the earth with a five minute phone call.

Once I'd had a night's rest to catch my breath, I strode into the office Monday morning on a mission to not just bring AVM back, but bring it back bigger and better.

Dani and I got our heads together, and I knew we could bring Boro a rock night every Saturday that felt fresh and different. Sumo was even longer in the tooth than AVM, so maybe there was space in town for a new champ.

On Saturday March 26th 2016, I launched our new rock night at The Medicine Bar, a few hundred yards down the road from Empire. Determined to make it stand out, turn heads and be noticed, I named the clubnight HOLY SHIT, and Dani came up with some of the edgiest artwork I'd seen him do. It all looked very different, but we had Dani and his AVM style DJ set as the main attraction down in the Medicine Bar's intimate cellar nightclub. I also had the pleasure of bringing Craig out of retirement to play a warm-up set up top in the upper lounge of the venue. Craig was playing Classic Rock, Dad Rock and Vintage Metal, Dani was on Pop Punk, Emo and Mosh Anthems, and we packed the club with 800 rockers on opening night.

On week two, we pulled a more-than-respectable 500 through the door. Not wanting to rest on our laurels and assume we'd cracked the promo, I blew all the profit from the first couple of nights on over-the-top performers. We had a little person dressed as a ringmaster, fire breathers, and two performers body-painted as robots pushing a tea trolley that had an endless supply of free Jagerbombs. The place was packed. The atmosphere was electric. Everyone was smashed.

At around 2am, I got called to the front door. The head doorman, a guy I hadn't met before, and hadn't taken the time to get to know yet, was arguing with a customer, who'd been thrown out for being too drunk. The customer insisted he was sober enough to be let back in, and the doorman wasn't having any of it.

I knew that once a doorman had laid out his case, it was pretty hard to change the course of events. Doormen didn't like promoters telling them what to do, and doormen didn't like being contradicted or having their orders overruled. I'd like to think I'd managed the door team at the Cornerhouse and the Empire well, and those teams always listened to me, worked with me, and I usually got my way with those guys. I was weighing up the situation here on the pavement outside the Medicine Bar, and kicking myself that I hadn't taken the time to get to know this doorman better.

I also hadn't given them any prior brief as to the crowd or the event. The Medicine Bar was the home of Creeps, a huge weekly event that had an alternative crowd. I figured if this security team could handle Creeps Thursdays, they could easily handle some emos and metalheads.

Back on the pavement, our upset drunk friend now had his phone filming and was narrating the scene, explaining on his Snapchat that the door staff at HOLY SHIT were homophobic. The idiotic head doorman yelled an utterly unacceptable homophobic slur into the phone, then grabbed it and smashed it on the floor.

It was horrific, awful, and almost deservedly so, the night never quite recovered from that incident.

The venue management trusted me enough to accept my testimony of events, and the doorman was sacked. We got a new first-class head of security, Jamie, who understood the crowd and kept things dead right. We fought on, promoting HOLY SHIT as the safe, inclusive space it now was, and we ran each Saturday at just 200 heads a week. Thankfully 200 didn't look too bad in that venue with its dark corners and low ceilings.

It was perhaps the choice of venue that frustratingly went against us as we attempted to promote Saturdays at Medicine Bar for the next couple of years. I thought the dark, intimate, low-ceilinged space, with a state-of-the-art sound and light show was the perfect space for that event. The moshers just didn't like it.

So I was constantly told they missed ATIK, and they missed AVM. I tried to get the message across that everything AVM had, HOLY SHIT had, and more - but we never got back to those big numbers we had seen in the first few weeks.

Side Note : HOLY SHIT ran for a couple more years with a small number of loyal followers. I loved Medicine Bar, and I loved the event. It was a welcome distraction from the Saturdays at Empire, and when I wrote up the weekly rota for who was repping what event each weekend, I'd usually put myself down for HOLY SHIT. I'd happily handle the reception till, taking the money and lashing on wristbands. The venue was blessed with a friendly, frantic and fearless manager called Stirzy, who was usually one step ahead of me, fixing smoke machines, adjusting lights, and tweaking sound systems - so everything ran perfectly. Sometimes there was so little for me to do that I'd spend a bit too much time at the bar. A few times, Stirzy would watch me cashing up the till, counting money painfully slowly (as I was drunk as shit), and he'd laugh and recount it all correctly for me. Thanks Stirz; I appreciated it.

Disco Load Outs

"Empire Changeovers" were no fun.

A changeover took place when a stand-alone live show had been booked on a Friday night, usually occuring between 7.30pm and 10.00pm, and then we'd have sixty minutes to get Sumo open at 11pm. Sixty minutes of pure stress.

Here's a rough list of all the shit that you need to sort in those sixty minutes.

- The band will have been told to finish at 10pm. Well, the band just played an encore. So now it's 10.30pm. Those 10pm finishes were always 10.30pm. You need to close the massive red curtains and flip the house lights on. Chop chop. The clocks ticking.
- You kick the band and their crew off the stage, politely, and tempt them up to the dressing rooms with ice cold buckets of Red Stripe, perhaps.
- Clear from the stage - a hundred cables, mics, monitors, drums, amps, keyboards and keyboard stands, drum risers, spilt drinks, sweaty towels, sleeping crew. It's now 10.40pm. Sumo opens in 20minutes.
- You need to fold up ten metres of solid steel barrier, flip it up onto the stage and drag it out of everyone's way, without trapping your toes or fingers, or anyone else's toes or fingers.
- Get a thousand people out of the venue. Some gig goers will be under 18, still giddy with gig adrenalin, some folks will want to buy merch,

some will want to hang around to meet the band, many will be drunk. Somehow, you need to get them all out. You have about 18 minutes left by the way.
- The Empire's staff are brilliant and well versed in this whole process, and Peter and Ash will be cracking the whip, restocking bars, pulling apart merch stands, shoving barriers around, and refilling tills with coins. You'll need to pitch in, go grab them sweaty stage towels and use them to soak up the 2000 spilt pints on the dancefloor.

It's 10.50pm, you've got ten minutes.

- The thousand gig-goers outside have mostly dispersed, the queue for Sumo has started. The door lads are asking lots of questions. Get them briefed. Over 18's who were gig-goers get back in free, and everyone else needs to pay. Check the wristbands. Got it? Good.
- Secure the stage, chain off some doors, and unchain others. Even though they've been at work five hours already and have five more hours ahead of them, ask the Empire staff nicely to mop and dry the dancefloor *again* because it's lethally slippery.

They're busy. Grab the mops and sort it yourself.

It's 10.57pm.

- The DJs are here. Get some tunes on. Quiet though, because there's a furious tour manager out for blood because his artists have been chased off the stage and have had no time to 'just chill'. If the gig wasn't a metal band, then you'll need to tell your DJ to play 'something nice' for twenty minutes just because on the other side of the big red curtain, some poor roadies are still breaking down a drum kit and the last thing they need is Slipknot booming into their ears.

- 10.59pm. Fresh wristbands, guestlist, face paints, kill the house lights, crank the music.
- 11pm. Open the front doors, and check the band isn't too grumpy. They're pretty grumpy.
- Head to the lounge, and buy twelve ice-cold Red Stripes and a load of full fat cold cokes. Stick one of each in your back pockets and head to the stage clutching the rest.
- Give the stage crew that arm full of cold drinks, find a quiet corner and neck the ones in your pockets. Deep breath, now - get to work.

It was at that point in the night I'd always say to myself, *"I am one hundred percent getting another pair of hands in for the next changeover"*.

And so, Dena, Ella, Adam, Jade, Rick, whoever, would eventually get roped into the changeover world. I think they ended up doing them solo plenty of times, and probably didn't stress it as I did. I didn't enjoy them.

The bands didn't enjoy them either. It was always good to let a band know as soon as the show was booked, that they were doing a 'disco load out' - as they called them.

'From The Jam' did not know that they were doing a disco load out. They didn't know when they were booked, and it wasn't mentioned to them at all throughout the day, and even up until they walked on stage at 9pm, I don't think they knew. From The Jam featured one or two gentlemen who were rightly superstars from their time in 70's legends - The (actual) Jam. Notably, From The Jam's founding member was Bruce Foxton, Jam bassist, co-songwriter and occasional actual vocalist. He's the bloke that sings News O'The World!

Side Note: From The Jam were already in a bad mood since their afternoon soundcheck had been interrupted by the rain. The Empire's roof was so damaged by a torrential rainstorm and leaked so badly that it pretty much rained in on the band. Through fear of electrocution, they'd walked off in a huff. At that point, Dena had to don the Empire's big yellow waterproof suit (always on hand for such situations) and climb up into, and *onto* the venue's roof to fix the leak. True story.

Once the roof was swept of waterlogging, leaks were patched and the rest of the day had finally got going; From The Jam were already pretty pissed off.

Bruce, his band, his crew, and his very grumpy tour manager, considered themselves almighty rock royalty. Therefore, when we politely tried to get them the-heck-off-the-stage at 10.30pm that evening (as we needed to get the Sumo party started within thirty minutes and counting), they politely told us, to fuck off.

It got to about 11.30pm. No music, no smoke machine. No one was even closing those big red curtains. Team Sumo stood and bit their lips as our crowd waited patiently in the cold outside.

It was no fun. So I was told.

I wasn't there, I was home, in bed.

Dena sorted all that. Thanks Dena, owe you one mate.

—

These pre-Sumo gigs, with their chewy changeovers, occasionally gave me the option to have a little fun. You see, Nathan's amazing array of PA equipment was all plumbed in for these early-door gigs, so rather than us waiting for Nathan to rip it all out before Sumo kicked off, we sometimes left it in, and used it for a live band of our own, as part of the clubnight.

A little less hassle, an extra few quid for Nathan, and an excuse to cram a band into the clubnight.

The Empire had Norfolk's finest Deaf Havana booked in for a sold out show one December. I'd hyped the crowd that the Sumo that followed the gig would include very special live guests, playing live at 2.45am. The poor fuckers probably expected Deaf Havana to spring back on for a set before the end of the night, but we had other plans. Boro's own tribute to Limp Bizkit were prepped behind the big red curtains.

Led by Sumo's DJ Ste as Fred Durst, the Bizkit boys were scheduled to bounce on stage to close the clubnight with a short sharp bombardment of Bizkit hits. Who wouldn't want to end their Friday Night / Saturday Morning with such a thing, right?

Without getting bogged down in the technical details, I needed the lads to set up and check-in their equipment with Nathan at around midnight - once Deaf Havana had politely shifted their shit.

By 1am there wasn't any sign of the Bizkit band and I'd put a few calls in to the lads to see where they were. They'd actually had another gig, as Be Quiet Shout Loud, in Leeds that night and were flying up the A1 as quickly as they could. They eventually rolled through the Empire's stage door, absolutely trollied, wide-eyed, off their collective tits on adrenaline, road beers, and perhaps some other bits.

Ste was hoarse but assured everything would be just fine as the band quickly built drum kits and threw amps on stage.

2.30am came around quickly, and I had the pleasure of slowly creaking open the big red stage curtains to reveal a darkened stage, pumped with ten tons of smoke. Kev had killed the house music, and loaded up the Intro track from Chocolate Starfish and The Hot Dog Flavoured Water.

About seven hundred Sumo-goers turned to face the stage. If they'd paid attention to our social media hype, they'd be expecting a surprise. Most of them probably just wondered what the hell was going on.

Whos in the house....' croaked the deafening robotic voice over the PA. *'Limp Bizkit... is in... the house'* continued the teaser track.

People started to figure out what was about to hit them and gathered around the front of the stage. Ste burst onto the front of the stage, Red cap flipped backwards and bellowed into the mic;

'LADIES AND GENTLEMEN!'...

You get the idea, the lads took the roof off the venue, and everyone left that night with a big fat smile on their faces.

—

In another Boro-Tribute-Band escapade, me and some mates from local bands got our heads together and formed a ramshackle tribute band too. We paid homage to the California supergroup Me First & The Gimme Gimmes. A very niche choice, but this band that featured members of Lagwagon, NOFX and Foo Fighters played an all-covers melodic punk rock set of classic songs from the sixties, to the noughties. Basically, they were the perfect party band, and we wanted to bring that party to the North East. We carved out a pretty good career from it, playing moshers weddings between 2010 and 2020. Our tribute band name, coined by our pal Rob, was Me First & The Gimme Gimmicks.

Naturally, we'd played the Empire a few times. Why wouldn't Kev and I put our own band up on that big stage to entertain the punks, right? Ash had used us a few times for private parties too, St Patrick's Day, that sort of thing.

In 2019, I'd heard that a massively popular local band had hired the Empire for a show, set for Friday December 13th. I took the opportunity to arrange for our tribute, The Gimme Gimmicks, to play the Sumo that would follow the early-doors gig.

The gig was arranged by Ku Bar owner, super nice guy and local live music kingpin Jimmy Jukebox. The band in question were his good friends, Young Rebel Set. Jimmy and the band sold the show out, a thousand tickets, and it was set to be a hell of a show.

In the weeks leading up to that Friday, I'd planned for the Gimme Gimmicks to land around 11.30pm, and as was now its own little set-piece of logistics, Young Rebel Set would haul their kit off once they'd finished their show at around 10.30pm, we'd set up, and crank out our set of Christmas covers at around Midnight, right in the middle of Sumo. Christmas carols had been rearranged in a punk style, and elf costumes were ironed. As was Christmas custom, the Empire hoisted up its forty foot Christmas tree, and I'd installed snow machines into the ceiling.

Young Rebel Set were a truly special local act, having garnered huge success in the UK and Europe, fronted by their enigmatic singer-songwriter Matty. I didn't know Matty that well, but we'd shared a couple decades worth of stages and dressing rooms. I'd had the pleasure of booking and promoting stacks of shows for him, under his solo monikers Billy The Kid or Matt Wilde, and of course, with the lads in his bands The Romance and Young Rebel Set. Matt lived around the corner from me, and I'd see him walking his dogs across Norton Green most days. We'd wave and say hello.

A couple of weeks before the sold-out Christmas show at Empire, the news hit everyone that Matt had tragically died.

Everyone who knew him was deeply shocked, and I just felt so so sad. I can't even imagine how his close friends and family could have been feeling.

Or how they continue to. Emotional tributes poured in over the next few days, and the family released statements to the local press.

The Young Rebel Set show was cancelled. I chatted through the notion of closing Sumo for the night, but ultimately everyone thought the clubnight should go on. A couple of weeks later, the date rolled around, and it was Friday, and Friday was Sumo Day, so we dutifully prepped that day for the clubnight.

A couple of hours before doors, Nathan loaded the PA system into the Empire and The Gimme Gimmicks and I set up, and performed a short soundcheck in the empty venue before the 11pm Sumo show got going.

We ran through a couple of songs and tweaked our rendition of Fairytale Of New York. The band headed up to the dressing room, and I tidied up a few cables on the front of the stage before realising the time. I had a few Sumo-prep bits to do before the doors opened.

It was 10.30pm.

As I stood at the front of that grand stage, something dawned on me, with the vast empty venue in front of me.

In a different timeline, what should have been happening in that moment, was that Matt would have stood right where I was, saying thanks and goodnight to a thousand smiling faces in front of him. It felt wrong standing there. It felt totally and utterly unfair.

That was the last time The Gimme Gimmicks played together. I don't remember the show much, but I'll never forget that moment standing on the stage.

Matt was an incredibly talented young soul, a superb songwriter and an amazing father and he is obviously sorely missed each and every day by all that knew him.

Double Dad

Claire and I decided to have another baby. I prayed for a girl. No offence lads, but men are fairly awful, right? Our first daughter Sydney was absolutely perfect in every way. Smart, beautiful, the apple of my eye. Claire and I wanted her to have a little mate, someone to play with, someone to have her back, someone to share her life with. Claire and I were incredibly efficient event planners and everything pretty much went as planned and expected and we brought another little girl onto the planet. Hey Piper.

We were so happy, and everything was perfect. Well, except we were broke.

If my memory serves me right, when I gave Graham the news that we were expecting a second, he said;

'Well you'll want to make sure you're making plenty of money to pay for this second baby huh?'

Fair enough.

The Graduates

More good news in 2017.

All five of Ten Feet Tall's loyal, funny, hard working apprentices 'graduated' with flying colours. It was a lot of work, getting all the paperwork right and documenting all the on-the-job training that we'd done over the previous twelve months.

These five had ultimately made my life way easier for a year, and I thought of them all very fondly. I don't know if they thought of me as a mentor, a pain in the arse, a nuisance, or a mate, but I was proud as fuck to see them pass and have a shit-ton of real life skills to pile into their CV's.

Marketing, PR, promotions, event management, copy writing, graphic design, photography, video making, social media, paid ads management, first aid and even some stewarding and security training was crammed under their belts. Izzy went on to Uni, and Jacob too. Adam started his own events company and continued to DJ and stage manage events for us. Jade went into digital marketing, and Dena was given that full time job at Ten Feet Tall.

Mrs. Sumo

Throughout that year-long task of training apprentices, we'd been trying out all sorts of new crazy shit, and we had a small clutch of tried and failed projects under our belt. Our big regular weekly clubnights, which were still the cash cow for the whole business, still weren't quite doing the best numbers ever. Despite all this, we tried to remain in good spirits.

I'd ventured into a slightly bizarre Promoters-Training-Camp project with Graham's encouragement. The government-funded project meant we could 'teach' a class of young unemployed under 18's for about eight weeks, give them some hands-on experience, and the result was these kids got a qualification in events.

I'd hastily assembled a DIY classroom at the back of the TFT office and spent my days talking nonsense to this room of wide eyed teens. I had help from the TFT apprentices in delivering this course that I'd somehow written, and the outcome was a couple of great events that these kids organised, promoted and ran. The training body, which I think was East Durham College, sent evaluators to check out the course, the results and the events. They were really impressed and commended us on the project.

At the time, it felt like a huge amount of work, a fantastic learning experience, and I was grateful for a change of pace and scenery. However, I can't help feeling, looking back at the project, that the whole thing existed to make money. In one of the meetings with the college, a guy told me there were *"Wheelbarrows full of cash"* to fund courses like this. The more kids we got qualified, the more money we got. I don't know whether this was a valuable community offering that we had curated, or something slightly shadier.

Something didn't sit right for me personally.

I mention all of the above because it was another giant plate that needed spinning, another epic distraction from the job of getting the clubnights busier. It felt that I was stuck in a balancing act, being pulled from pillar to post between trying new things to make money, and keeping the old things from not losing too much money.

Thankfully, that's when Ella came along.

I'd stumbled into work one Monday at 10am, such was our start time, and I was pouring my first of twenty cups of coffee of the day when Graham asked me to pop through to the meeting room.

Graham introduced me to Ella, an incredibly smartly dressed young lady who had recently graduated with a law degree and wondered if we had any work.

Graham suggested we give her Sumo.

I wasn't sure that this person, dressed in beige and cream, would be any good, but I knew there was nothing to lose. I also knew that any help was better than nothing. I also had started to have a very *slight* feeling, somewhere in the back of my mind, that perhaps I didn't want to do this anymore.

So you shouldn't judge a book by its cover. The beige and cream were most certainly Ella's job interview clothes, and thankfully she was, and is, a fully fledged raging mosher. On her first day, I handed Ella the Sumo Socials, and she smashed it. The content was funny, smart, edgy, and engaging. I'd enjoyed steering the ship since Rick had previously departed, but it felt great to hand someone the wheel. She was a natural.

Ella shadowed me over the next few Friday nights, learning the ropes and the ins and outs of what we did between 10pm and 4am every Friday night. She seemed into it. On her first shift, we had a live band shoe-horned into the Cocktail Lounge. Much to Peter and Ash's horror, I often jammed noisy bands in there. Having a thrash metal or a hardcore punk band do their thing on the plush carpet between the gigantic marble pillars that was the Empire's fancy little chillout room was utterly discombobulated, and I loved it.

Ella and I stood shoulder to shoulder along with about eight other people getting deafened by the lads from Strange Bones. Their singer, half naked, stood on the bar and dived over our heads onto the waiting hands of the tiny crowd.

After about four Fridays on the trot, we gave Ella a Friday off. She of course, ended up in Sumo with her mates, and I saw her being carried out by the doormen, blind drunk, at about 1am. She had graduated with flying colours, and as far as I was concerned, she was permanently hired.

I now had two top grafters starting to take hold of the many reins. Ella with Sumo, Catch 22 Comedy Club and plenty of other bits. Dena had the Empire's Saturdays under control, plus all of the Big Mouth comedy clubs and all the touring comedy too. Over the next few months I found that I was emptying everything I knew onto spreadsheets.

It wasn't just everything Ella needed to know for her role in Sumo or that Dena needed to know for Saturdays; it was absolutely everything I'd learned in my time at Ten Feet Tall. Every detail was filed, catalogued, organised and stored in my battered TFT laptop.

It was almost subconscious at first, but I think it became clear to me that I was building a manual. I was creating a set of documents that anyone could use to run the show, the clubnights, the comedy, the works.

It felt like time for someone else to spin the plates.

Side Note : A short while after we'd started that events training course, East Durham College discreetly offered me a full time job, which I turned down, because I was a fucking idiot.

Mrs. Milk

Let's talk about Saturdays at the Empire - Known firstly as Play Rock n Roll Disco, then Metropolis, and then MILK.

To be honest, it's someone else's story to tell. Saturday's weren't my thing, but there came a point where I guess I was the last man standing. As much as I wanted to be Mr Fridays, there wasn't a Mr or Mrs Saturdays for a good while, so it eventually fell to me. The numbers on a Saturday were two or three times those of a Sumo. For that fact, they frequently took priority, whether we liked it or not.

In terms of a multi-music-policy event for the masses, the Saturdays DJ line up was the strongest I think the North has ever seen and possibly ever will. Indie was the main draw in the big downstairs room. Since the Metropolis days, DJ Chris had spent years building a set that shoehorned a bit of everything (pop, dance, rock, hip hop, soul) in amongst the staples of Arctic Monkeys, Kasabian and Libertines. It was wonderful to see Chris's journey since we met on the cold streets of Durham trying to figure out how to get a Sumo going, seeing him play to a handful of kids in the Sumo Durham Indie Room, to seeing him DJ to thousands of regulars every single Saturday in the big room of the Empire.

The double act of DJs up on the first floor was Foy and Burnsey - another two GOATs of the Middlesbrough scene. Between them, they were Sumo Cornerhouse regulars in the Indie and Poprooms, Foy was instrumental in

Uncle Alberts having such a great vibe, they've done the infamous Mixtape Tuesdays, Kongs in Darlington, and been part of the Sumo/Metropolis journey from day one. Despite them being able to DJ *any* room on *any* night of the week extremely well, those Saturday's on the Pop floor were like Foy and Burnsey's own private house party and they proved to be an inimitable duo. They took the Empire's first floor to bursting capacity over a period of a few years.

The final player in the Saturday Night Dream Team is of course Ste (aka Jake Radio). Ste played host, DJ and grand master of ceremonies in the Lounge. Not to be recognised as purely a sideshow, the Saturdays in The Lounge were made of epic stuff, and Ste's larger-than-life personality carried them. Where at Sumo, we'd have Ste dressed up as Fred Durst, or playing some madcap character - On a Saturday, Ste could be himself - and his set pieces in the Lounge were an extension of his glamorous personality.

You can attribute the success of those big Saturdays to many things - the beautiful venue, the promoters did a hell of a job promoting it, and the artwork, visuals and ideas were world class. However, I can't help feeling that (just like Sumo) the cornerstone of those Saturday's success was the perfect blend of those DJs personalities and their playlists.

It was like a set of ingredients that got thrown together and coincidentally tasted wonderful - the blend of music they all brought to the table and delivered, was the lynchpin of that night, and they deserve infinite recognition for it.

—

By this point in my thirteen-year journey I was weary and feeling my age.

It was a blessing to me that we had assigned our new full timer Dena, to that big Empire Saturday.

I made sure Dena had an infinite amount of Phil Saunders Spreadsheets to meticulously guide her through every aspect of those Saturdays. Each minute from setting up at noon (or about 3pm by the time Dena got there) until 3.30am when the lights came up was noted down, so she could learn the ropes and eventually put her own spin on it. After all, she was way younger and way cooler than I was. I happily handed over the torch of Saturdays, and let Dena carry it her way. She put her own unique stamp on things, the staff, the DJs, and the management absolutely loved her. I was very happy to step away and leave her to it.

There must be ultimate respect and a lifetime of thanks to Dena, for not only running those Saturdays but also putting up with the mountain of shit that came along with them. Dena is mature beyond her years and comes across as a worldly wise soul. It was easy to forget just how young she was.

Like Ella, and like Cat, Kim, Jess, Claire, Hannah, Charlie, Laura, Charlotte and every Ten Feet Tall woman before her, I'm sure she also had to deal with harassment, demeaning comments and all the awful situations that sadly came with being a woman in the events industry. She was in charge of over a thousand people each weekend. There were bound to be a few bad apples to deal with, not just in the general public but within the venue's internal teams too.

I'd Rather Smash My Face Into That Wall

Monday 7th August 2017.

2017 continued. 2017 was not going good. Graham sat Marty and I down in the office's meeting room.

He said *"I'd rather smash my face into that wall, than have to talk about Sumo and Milk"*.

He was frustrated. We were frustrated.

Numbers weren't *bad*, as such. But they weren't stacking up. We had about 300-400 a week at Sumo. And 600-700 a week at MILK. That meant we were just about breaking even.

We had the two biggest weekly club nights in town, busier than anyone else, and here we were, the promoters, not making *any* money from them.

We tore our hair out over budgets every Monday morning.

After you'd paid everyone's wages, a cut for the venue, and the tax man, there was nothing left.

This was a problem. This was my problem.

Sumo Sauce

For my honeymoon, Claire and I jumped in our car and drove south. That was the sum total of our plan, and it turned out to be an amazing road trip to (eventually) the Isle of Wight and back, with some random stops overnight on the way there and back. One night, we ended up in a pub in Southampton with my old Uni pal and podcast legend, DJ Antman. Ant was working on a cruise ship and lived near the port with his then-finance, an ex-Corrie star if I remember rightly.

The pub Ant took us to was a perfectly cosy hobbit hole of a place, decorated and tailored to appeal to first-grade nerds. They had an insanely long menu of cocktails, all named after Star Wars planets or characters from Game of Thrones. These alcoholic treats came in all the colours of the rainbow and were served in a pint glass over crushed ice. They were beautifully simple, loaded with booze, and got you utterly wrecked in an instant.

I wanted to pay homage to (or perhaps steal) this notion and take it to the Empire. The idea that people could be trollied on just one pint wasn't the Empire's idea of a business plan, but they allowed me one of these follies.

Peter and I experimented one hazy afternoon and came up with a big purple pint of pure sugar and booze that tasted phenomenal. I wanted to call it something terrible, probably some crappy pun. Thankfully, Dena said, *"just call it Sumo Sauce."*

SUMO SAUCE

½ Pint Strongbow Dark Fruits

1 x shot Hot & Cool Cinnamon Aftershock

1 x shot Cool Citrus Aftershock

1 x Cherry Sourz

Top with lemonade, serve over ice

Toxicity

Thankfully we now live in a world with a huge emphasis on mental health and employee well-being.

Just a few years ago, though, no one talked about mental health at work. Phrases such as 'Toxic Workplace' didn't really exist. Not to my knowledge anyway.

We all worked daft hours. We all burned the candle at both ends. It wasn't anyone's fault, it wasn't the boss's fault. Everyone just got on with it. We had a common goal. If nights were busy, we were all happy, we all got well paid. When nights were quiet, we took it personally, it made us sad - and we tried to work harder and come up with good ways to get the night busier again.

I didn't know what burnout was but looking back, that's most certainly what I had.

Ten Feet Tall had been the coolest place in the world to work, but around this time, the pressure of meeting the targets and not slipping into the red was immense. To amplify this stress, I had a couple of manipulative colleagues that made it almost unbearable.

I should have manned up, I should have taken control of the situation, I could have and should have called everyone out.

I didn't. I just put up and shut up.

There was no sexism, no racism, nothing like that. But, the conversations around "taking Ten Feet Tall down" from *within*, were becoming daily.

It felt like knives were being sharpened for Graham's back.

Everyone would come to me for every problem. I didn't mind at first. The Shit Shield. I'd deal with everything that no one else wanted to. I was good at it. But shit gets heavy.

I was the leader of the gang, someone who everyone could lean on and vent to. At the same time, pockets formed, and those who faced me each day with a smile, I learned, were also trashing my name and reputation.

I tried to talk to Graham. To warn him. It was almost surreal how it didn't work. He confronted individuals. They told him not to be daft. He asked people who had told me they were miserable, if they were happy? *"Yes boss, all good here boss".*

So, now *I* looked like the crazy person. Now *I* look like the troublemaker.

Clever. Manipulative.

My suspicions were, that a coup was being planned. But I just kept my head down.

What if everything came crumbled down. Many of my friends worked here. What would happen to them? What would I do? How would I pay the mortgage?

I put up and I shut up.

My drinking got almost to the point where I lost control. Ten coffees during the day. Ten beers every night.

Home time on the weekend was 4am. Monday Morning was a 10am kick off, into the spreadsheet, into the bitching. All that mattered was the bottom line on the spreadsheet.

The club nights now felt like giant weights chained to my ankles.

On a Friday night and a Saturday night I stood proudly looking out from the DJ booth, I could see a vast sea of smiling faces in the club, electric atmospheres, hundreds of people singing and dancing together.

Then Monday morning – Profit margin zero. It felt pointless.

Was there something I was missing?

The numbers did add up. They just didn't add up to very much at all.

OK, Time For Plan B

Was this a nervous breakdown? *"I'm not one of those people"* I would tell myself.

Keep it together.

Steady.

I remember a crystal clear night.

Claire needed picking up from the pub, so I drove over to Boro, and met her and the girls. They'd just won the pub quiz. Everyone was buzzing. I bought a shandy and sat with them for a while. I just felt so sad.

My damn skin. This is how I know I'm stressed. Because I don't *feel* stressed, but psoriasis will let you know.

I'm always stressed; that's how I am. I thrive off stress! Right! Right?

You need a break.

I never wanted a day off. I didn't need one. Always got to be switched on, logged in, online, available. It's not even the job's fault. I didn't know how to switch off. I didn't know how to hand it over. I didn't want to miss a trick.

Ok, time for Plan B – what's Plan B?

—

I was at one of those Wacky Warehouse places, on a Saturday morning, for someone's kid's birthday. Possibly Craig's son Freddie's 5th or 6th, and my mate DJ Mal asked me how it was going;

"*How's work Phil?*"

"*I hate it.*" I replied.

I'd never said it out loud.

He asked why. I said I didn't know, but I had to get out.

Mal added, "*I always thought if we cut you in half, it would say Ten Feet Tall right through you, like a stick of Blackpool rock*".

I laughed; it was funny. But also, fuck that, I really needed a Plan B.

The Unicorn

Around this time, Graham and I had many meetings. So many meetings.

We sat and stared into spreadsheets. They showed us how much money we spent. How much money we earned. Sumo and MILK were especially depressing reads. I could understand his frustration.

To get more people to attend these events, we potentially needed to spend a load of money. It was a gamble. Spend X to pull in Y. But what if Y didn't turn up. You do the maths.

We couldn't afford to lose that gamble. Graham tasked me, and the team, to think of, create, and dream up some events that would reignite the fires of Teesside's nightlife.

What could we say, what could we do, what could we showcase - that would have 1500 people queuing around the block of Empire?

An exciting task! Let's get to work!

Grab a pen and paper - a bit of blue sky thinking!

Turn off your phones, and stick your email autoresponder ON!
WE are going to think up the best idea ANY of us has ever had!

Every meeting we had, the ideas didn't come. Or, no ideas that got any of us excited. Had we simply *done it all?*

There must be *something*? There must be a THING, that one magic EVENT that would send people bananas?

Fridays' were now around 300 a week, and Saturdays on average were around 500. It was a good dip down since the glory days.

Graham still thought there was a trick we were missing, a party we could throw that would flip our fortunes. I told him politely that the one truly magnificent event that would see a thousand people tripping over themselves to sprint into the Empire... just did not exist.

I told him he was chasing a unicorn.

That didn't go down too well.

I needed a Plan B.

Two Weeks In The Wilderness

Graham suggested I had a few days off to clear my head.

I knew he wasn't impressed with my unicorn craic. Plus, we both faced the fact that if these two clubnights, Sumo and MILK, the last two great clubnights standing in Teesside, were going to dry up completely, then we needed another revenue stream.

Ten Feet Tall needed a Plan B. Ten Feet Tall needed a cash injection, something like a miracle. Something like a unicorn. Otherwise, Graham informed me;

"*Otherwise, we're all going to hell in a handbasket.*"

I told Graham I needed two weeks. I said, give me 14 days, and I'll be back with a plan. He agreed.

This was my plan; I would spend seven of those fourteen days creating a plan for the up-turn of income within Ten Feet Tall, a list of carefully planned creative schemes that would enhance and add to the company's portfolio. I would lock myself away, summon inspiration, and deliver a plan to Graham that he would be proud of and inspired by.

My plan for the second half of this excursion was to get *myself* a solid list of possible options for life-after-Ten-Feet-Tall.

Because, dear reader, whether my list of unicorns was to work or not, I didn't plan on staying around to find out. I was fucking done.

Week One.

That Monday morning, I packed my rucksack, said goodbye to Claire, and drove to a Costa Coffee that had good WiFi. I flipped open my laptop and got to work. I didn't want to stress Claire out or panic her, so for all she knew, I'd gone to work. In those first few undistracted hours, I came up with twenty ideas that I genuinely knew would be easy for the team to execute, and would make money.

I was pleasantly surprised at how much work I could actually get done without an office full of back-stabby whinging in my ears. It took a couple more days, but I felt that the Ten Feet Tall Plan was done. So I moved on to the next plan, The Phil Saunders Plan.

Week Two.

I didn't know where to start. I did a job search.

B and Q were hiring. £26,000 a year salary. 37 hours a week. I filled in the application form. Fingers crossed eh? Next, I opened my phone and scrolled.

My phone list of contacts was a healthy and lengthy directory that included some of the best people in the business. I had ten days left. I picked out ten people, and I sent each of them a text. I asked them if they'd meet me for a cup of tea. For the next ten days I drank tea, and coffee, and ate cake with friends and acquaintances. We chatted, reminisced, talked about life and business, and we shot the breeze.

I told each of these ten wonderful people that if they ever wanted to collaborate on a project or needed support and assistance on anything, I was there for them. It was a subtle pitch.

I didn't really know *exactly* what I was doing. I was winging it, as always. A couple of these guys took the bait I'd clumsily laid out.

"Are we talking about collaborating with Ten Feet Tall here, or with Phil Saunders"?

I was loyal, and I was careful. *"Well, either, I guess"*, I responded coyly.

It was the end of my 14 days in the wilderness, foraging for a scrap of a future to cling on to. It was time to head back to work, back to the office, and present my boss with my Word Doc full of bright ideas.

It was a good job the list was pretty great, because B and Q had just emailed me – I didn't even get an interview.

I Look Like I Feel

After returning from my Two Weeks in The Wilderness, I was welcomed back to TFT towers with open arms. Quite literally, I was hugged. I don't think that had happened before. Everyone loved my ideas, everyone believed they could work. We chatted through them in more detail and we plucked out two or three that we felt we would actively pursue and put into action. Graham seemed genuinely excited by these random events and micro-businesses I'd brought to the table.

I sat at my desk in the corner of the office, looking out the massive windows at the trucks whizzing past on the A66 at 80-mph. I pondered over my plans. I had plans for Ten Feet Tall, and I had plans for myself. I felt a little lost, but somehow at the same time, I knew I'd put myself at a crossroads with two paths. One of those paths led me away from that desk, that place, that life.

I felt like shit, and I looked like shit. I didn't realise to what extent I'd punished myself mentally with a gruelling none stop routine.

I'd also recently contracted what I believe was a proper bad case of man-flu, but having just had two weeks "off", I could hardly pull a sickie on my first day back.

I loaded myself with Lemsip Max Strength tablets and cracked on with the day.

Ten Feet Tall had ended up talking shop with Boro businessman and all-round-geezer Salvin. Salvin owned a stack of businesses, many barbers, and the town's biggest and most successful Tattoo establishment, Skins and Needles. He was expanding into the world of bars, gigs and events for his latest venture, a bar/bistro launch, and he'd sought out the talents of Teesside's finest promoters, Ten Feet Tall. Today was the day all these fellas were coming to the office to talk to Graham about the launch campaign for the new bar, Ta Moko.

Graham was delighted I was back so that I could join the meeting. The project wasn't going to be anything to do with me, but I was asked to join them around the table anyway - perhaps as I was the only guy with tattoos, something Salvin and his pals had loads of.

I sat and listened to everyone talk excitedly through the plan. I kept quiet in the corner, which was unlike me, but I had nothing to add, and I felt absolutely dog rough. Also, from what I can recall, TFT's bistro launch plan was actually pretty weak, to be honest.

Graham spun in his chair and fired a few questions my way, and I suddenly seemed to have the eyes of the room. My head felt like it was going to pop, the painkillers hadn't done their job, and my body seemed to be running at about 100 degrees.

I hesitated for a millisecond before answering, but Graham cut me off anyway;

"Are you OK Phil, you look terrible, like really bad, like a, like a... Heroin addict or something ha ha ha".

His attempt at banter perhaps. No one else laughed.

"Yeah, erm, I think I've got a bit of a cold".

Fuck this, I thought.

Fuck this shit.

Into The Upside Down

Friday November 24th 2017

To thoroughly poster-up the whole of Sumo (be it in Cornerhouse or Empire) it took a good hour.

We'd poster every toilet door, every toilet wall, behind every bar, on each fridge, on the walls of the stairs, on the doors that interrupted the winding corridors. We would put Sumo posters up advertising future Sumos, Sumo posters that advertised upcoming gigs, and Sumo posters that just said "Sumo".

We did this purely for the craic and just so that people would pull these posters down and take them home. From a little snooping on Instagram, you could see people's bedrooms, living rooms and kitchens were covered in them, and they came fresh from the sweat-soaked walls of the club.

I did my fair share of postering the walls. The team and I took turns with this monotonous weekly job.

I was postering-up on this Friday in November 2017 when my phone rang.

I think I was onto the fridge doors - an excellent place for a poster. When everyone's waiting for their drink, they're looking right at all the lovely cold drinks in the fridges. The fridge door is a prime spot for a poster you want everyone to see.

So the phone call was from the director of a local digital marketing firm, offering me a full-time job as Head of Operations, with regular hours and a nice proper salary.

I said Yes.

He said he'd put it all in writing, in an email for me.

I hung up the phone, and I skipped and hopped around the club, whizzing up the last few Sumo posters with great gusto.

That was it. I was finally out. My career in events was officially over.

Over the previous few weeks and months leading up to that moment, I'd tried to imagine how I'd feel should I ever receive a phone call like that. It felt pretty much how I'd imagined it would. It felt fucking great.

—

On this particular Friday, our Sumo special was a night dedicated to my favourite TV show of that time, Stranger Things.

"Stranger Sumo", as we called it, paid homage to the Netflix phenomenon as it hit its frenzied initial peak. Everyone at that time watched the show, and the Sumo regulars seemed to buzz at the thought of us somehow turning the Empire into the cursed town of Hawkins - and delivering a supernatural Sumo special.

I'd had a feeling, or hope, that this might be one of my last ever Sumo events, so I'd gone all-in and put what was left of my heart and soul into the promo and the prep.

If you want to throw a Stranger Things party of your own, here's some of the stuff we added into the mix that night;

1. Eleven Yourself - We had a barber chair and a barber to shave your head, we provided some fake theatrical blood to add under your nose (to mimic the nosebleed that follows a psychic attack) and hospital gowns to give that real "escaped patient" vibe. People literally queued up for this look.
2. Fairy Lights - Just like Will's Mom, Joyce, we strung fairy lights across the venue, even spelling out Stranger Sumo in coloured lights, which flashed and twinkled erratically on the wall.
3. We offered prizes to anyone that dressed up. We had a few great Dustin's arrive with curly wigs and trucker caps.
4. We bought a shit load of our own trucker caps and curly wigs and enforced them on people who didn't bother dressing up.
5. We found a bulk load of cheap lab coats online and gave them out to add to the mad scientist vibes on the night.
6. Dani made some epic visuals and projections - so shadowy demons stalked the sides of the dancefloors.

I set about recreating what I considered to be the perfect Stranger Things Empire entrance decor; a hand-drawn crayon mosaic of psychically illustrated drawings depicting the interdimensional tunnels under the town of Hawkins.

In season 2 of Stranger Things, our protagonist Will Byers frantically and repeatedly scrawls out hundreds of sheets of drawings in crayon in his room. Later in the series his mother (along with loveable boyfriend Bob) realise that all these pictures can be stitched together to form a map of the upside down underworld where Will has become imprisoned by the Demogorgon. Still with me? Good.

There's a triumphant scene as Bob plasters the walls of Joyce's house with all of Will's drawings. Together, they to reveal the giant map.

To recreate Will's map, and completely cover the walls of that gigantic Empire entrance hall, I was going to need about 250 posters. If this was to be my final coup de grace within that venue, I was determined to make it epic and do justice to the show itself.

I took twenty-five A3 sheets of paper, and I drew out, in coloured crayons, twenty-five different versions of roads, forks in roads, left turns and right turns. I took these to the copy shop and asked them to run me ten copies of each poster. I now had 250 sheets and armed with four packs of blue tac and two sets of step ladders; I set about the monumental task of attaching all 250 posters to the entrance hall walls in a twisting turning map that would make Will, Joyce and Bob proud.

I was about halfway through when Ash wandered through his beautiful club's hallway. He paused, looked up, and politely asked;

"What the fuck is this then Phil?"

"Hi Ash. It's a replica of Will Byers hand-drawn map of the upside down – the alternate reality he is trying to escape from" - I replied.

"*of course it is*" - Ash had seen way more random shit in the decade we'd worked together.

I was pretty pleased with myself that the place looked so cool, and that I'd gotten one last big eye-roll out of Ash.

I Quit

Monday Nov 27th 2017

I asked my boss to meet me for coffee. I told him I was quitting.

I could have told him that I'd grown to hate certain elements of my job, and that certain aspects of my day to day and certain people's actions had made it impossible to find joy in something I'd once loved so much. I thought about warning him, telling him to be careful, that there were people lurking in the shadows with knives ready for his back.

But I didn't say anything like that. I kept it simple.

I'd been offered a job. A job that finished at 5pm every day. A job where the weekends were all mine, to do with what I pleased. I said I started my new job in 1 week, and this was my one week notice.

He said that people in management roles usually gave two *months'* notice, and that me giving one week's notice was shitty. I handed him an A4 letter that I'd typed and printed. It was my resignation letter, a paragraph I'd copied and pasted from a Google search; *"how to write a resignation letter"*.

He probably deserved more than that.

I assured him that I'd spent a great deal of time documenting absolutely every bit of information and knowledge I had into a Google Drive, which was ready to hand over to Dena and Ella. I had done what I considered an outrageously over the top job of leaving no matter unaddressed. They had 'The Manual'.

It was up to them now, and he and I knew they'd do a decent job.

I was, of course, sad to leave Sumo behind. I cared very much for it, all my pals worked there, and it had outlived and outshone pretty much every other clubnight I'd ever known. There was nothing quite like Sumo; despite many pretenders and contenders who came and went, Sumo had stood the test of time – that was certain.

I hoped Sumo would continue for another ten years, even without me.

And it did, carry on. For a while.

This Is My Last Sumo

Friday December 1st 2017

This was my last Sumo.

Interestingly (or not that interestingly), the first Friday in December was always a bad date. I have a few theories why.

Mainly, it's because people wake up in December with the realisation they must buy hundreds of pounds worth of gifts for their friends and family. Also, there will be a slew of events at the end of this month; Christmas nights out, The Works Do, New Year's Eve, and such. Therefore, most sensible kids stay home and save their money on that first frosty December weekend.

And thus, to ruin their plans of saving their precious wage packets, we would usually unveil a Pound Sumo event at the last minute. And hey presto; instead of a couple of hundred punters rattling around the old Empire, there would be a thousand.

Like many successful Pound Sumos before it, my last Sumo, this Pound Sumo, was everything it needed to be.

No frills, no bands, no chewy bits of decor to cable tie to ceilings, no guest DJs or entertainers to run after. It was a pound in, a pound a drink, a great setlist, a great crowd, and it went off without a hitch, like clockwork, like the spreadsheet said it should.

To be honest, I don't remember that much about it.

Perhaps I should have made a note of the last song. Perhaps I should have told my friends and colleagues it was my last one, and there could have been a fanfare. But I kept it to myself, kept it low key. At 4am I headed out into the night and drove myself home to bed.

It certainly didn't seem that emotional. Perhaps deep down, I knew I'd be back.

V

THE END

Life After Death

So this is the ending of Sumo's story. It's also the end of my story.

It is, in itself, a bit of a long, drawn-out, complicated tale.

I guess if you got this far, maybe you'll be interested in what happened next.

—

I'd took the job at a digital marketing company that specialised in social media. As the operations manager, I did a little bit of everything. I had a room of twenty 20-year-olds looking at me for the plan. I didn't have a clue what I was doing, but as the king of wing, I figured it out and got stuck in.

I almost feel bad saying it. But I didn't look back. I didn't miss the old life. It just didn't enter my head that much. Weird right? I just seamlessly slipped into a 9-to-5. I sat at a desk. I worked from a computer, I had meetings, and I wore a shirt.

Live music, live comedy, clubnights, rock and roll, backstage, on the stage, spinning all the plates, putting out all the fires, carrying the shit shield, catching pig's heads, whatever.

I certainly didn't understand this at the time, but I'd been suffering from burnout for so long. I had gotten sick. When I started my new job, I thought the lighting in the office must have been affecting me. My vision was constantly blurred, my ears rang, my head span. All while I was attending marketing meetings, PR planning sessions, and talking to my new clients.

I was trying to get my head around a million-pound campaign for Domino's Pizza or how Costa Coffee could best use Instagram. I was swimming with the big fish. I loved it, but I felt awful and looked awful.

The sickness soon passed. A few weeks in, I felt great. Amazing even.

My eczema fully cleared up, and I binned the dozens of steroid creams in my bathroom cupboard. I went to see my optician, and he ran some tests. He said I didn't need to wear the glasses he'd prescribed me six months ago. He said that was a bit weird. How mad is that?

My hair grew back. A little bit. Not a lot. But a little bit. New job, new me, huh?

I remember New Year's Eve rolling around. I was ecstatic. I had nothing to do. There was no high-pressure sold-out event for 1500 people. I did literally nothing. The kids went to bed early. We watched TV. Bliss.

Dena did keep me posted on how the Empire's NYE party was. It went without a hitch. They followed the spreadsheet.

—

After my exit from Ten Feet Tall, Graham placed Sumo in the more-than-capable hands of Ella.

She continued to do an amazing job. I'd sometimes take a peep at the Sumo socials and laugh out loud, in a good way. The events, the craic, and the memes were always bang on. I'm still unsure where the hell Ella came from, but she just really *got it*.

Dena continued to graft and took over the Empire Saturdays. She'd also inherited the monstrous amount of live comedy as well as the biggest clubnight in the North East. She was only 21, and she just dived in and dealt with it.

All the plates got span between those two people, and I don't think they ever really dropped one.

—

At this point in our timeline, Ella called me, mildly panicked. She needed advice.

Some senior members of the Ten Feet Tall team had approached Ella to ask if they were to *"hypothetically take Sumo off Ten Feet Tall..."* then would she leave TFT and board the good ship Empire and help run the show, essentially, without Graham.

I should have told Graham. However, I'd been there before.

I'd told him years ago that this would happen. If I'd grassed, everything would blow up. I was out of it. It was nothing to do with me. Why should I be the guy that pushed the big red button? I would be responsible for killing the relationship between Ten Feet Tall and the Empire. I'd essentially kill Sumo with one phone call and put a load of my mates out of a job. No thanks.

Also, I still really cared about the thing. I hoped it would last forever.

A few months later, the "*coup*" Ella had heard of never actually happened.

Maybe it was all just talk. Surely, the Empire would never do that to Graham? Kev, Dani, and Ste started to take the reins as Ella left Teesside for London. Life resumed, Sumo rolled on, and I decided I'd done the right thing - by not saying anything. I'd have looked crazy, like I was stirring up shit for no reason.

Meanwhile In Team Sumo

When Mrs Sumo moved on, TFT didn't bring anyone new in to take the reins. Luckily Sumo had a team of passionate individuals that seemingly took control and tried to make the thing work.

Dani still was DJing and taking care of the design, and Ste was DJing and had loads of experience as a promoter. Plus, long-standing original DJ Kev was still onboard. Between them all, they planned rota's and events, sent ideas and wish lists over to Graham, and made the thing happen week in and week out.

There were another couple of key figures in the mix here. Ross had worked for TFT for years. As a jack of all trades, he had booked bands, built stages, ran clubnights, and dabbled with social media accounts. Ross had been in some successful local bands, and he knew his way around Facebook, Instagram and Twitter. He took over the Sumo socials after Ella's departure and did a fantastic job.

There still needed to be someone to physically run Sumo each and every Friday night.

Despite the lads planning Sumo shenanigans to a tee, someone had to execute everything on the night. There was no Phil, and now there was no Ella. The job fell to Dena.

I think despite having Sumo dropped in their laps, Ste, Dani, Dena, Ross, and Kev felt more passionate than ever before about this ancient clubnight. It was their responsibility now. Ash and the Empire's eyes were on them, and they were determined to keep the thing going and do a grand job.

Within this Team Sumo 2018 version, you had the perfect mix of experience and new blood.

Kev and Dani had years and years of Sumo under their belts. Kev was the musical curator since day one, and Dani had come through the ranks from Uncle Alberts to Rock Box, to Bad Med to AVM to secure his place as another worthy main-room-Empire-guy. Ste had a wealth of experience in events and live music and knew that venue like the back of his hand. Ross proved quickly to have the golden touch with the socials. I'd occasionally text him, telling him how much I loved his posts, encouraging him. It was a pleasure to watch him work.

Dena, as she always does, also rose to the Sumo challenge. Dena's one of the hardest working people I've ever met. She'd now inherited pretty much everything and anything Ten Feet Tall did. The comedy clubs, the clubnights, and any stand-alone events usually involved Dena getting roped in. I'd say she'd become the new Phil Saunders, but that's not true. She was now way more than that.

She didn't have a big team of event managers to back her up as I'd always had. She was more like a one-woman-army, to be honest.

So Sumo rolled on without me, and I hadn't even set foot in the place since I'd walked out of the building in December 2017.

The Last Of The Gang

Cafe Mannequin is located right opposite the Empire on Corporation road. It's fantastic. They serve perfect Pierogi, Polish desserts and cakes. They also nail a full English breakfast. They do amazing ham and cheese toasties, and the coffee's bang on.

After quitting Ten Feet Tall, I'd often meet Dena for coffee and a catch-up. We didn't talk about work that much. We just shot the breeze, and I was chuffed she'd kept in touch. We'd spent plenty of time in the war zone, and we would occasionally regale the bizarre old days.

She let slip that Graham had taken the news that we hung out, badly. That's an old bit of the TFT code - you're either in the gang, or you're not in the gang.

I wasn't in the gang any more, and I guess Graham didn't like the idea of Dena and I getting a coffee every so often.

I don't know what he thought we'd be plotting.

It turns out, it wasn't us that he needed to be worried about.

Some Kind Of Meeting

In July 2018, I was asked to pop into the Empire for a chat. I had no idea what they wanted.

They told me Saturday nights weren't doing great. Numbers-wise, it was down to 400 a week.

I didn't say it, but I knew what that spreadsheet would look like.

More worryingly, there was no sign of a rescue plan. The Empire were worried, and allegedly, TFT hadn't shown any signs of coming up with a proper action plan to get numbers back up.

Ash and the Empire were not only worried about Saturdays. Fridays too were "*lame*", down to 200 a week, with no evidence of promotion or any decent parties to bring the thing to life. I'd also heard this from my friends, who all still worked hard to keep Fridays going as best they could.

I never mentioned this to Ash of course. At this point, I just listened, I kept my mouth shut.

The in-house Empire team seemed very much concerned about Saturdays. That's where the conversation was focused.

Summer was always hard on clubnights, numbers-wise. The good news was; Summer would end, Teesside University would fire up, and the freshers would land. The Empire, it turned out, had made a pretty sweet deal with the university. The main university bar was to be relaunched as the official 'Empire Pre Bar'.

Therefore, TFT and the Empire could promote directly to the students from within the university's grounds. This was something that had never happened before. Ash was pretty chuffed with the deal he'd secured, and he seemed confident it would solve the possible problems he was worried about facing.

He told me that the last thing he wanted to do was bin-off his promoters.

He had enough to worry about, running the venue and everything that came with it, without worrying about being the promoter.

He seemed to genuinely hope that TFT would get their act together, freshers' would help, the numbers would steady, and everything would be fine.

But.

Ash told me that he had given Ten Feet Tall an ultimatum.

That if numbers continued to drop...

Ash would have no choice but to take the Saturday in-house.

I sat and listened and digested what Ash was saying. I mean, it sounded fair enough. As much as I was close to TFT and Graham, anyone could understand Ash's predicament.

As Ash said - how could he continue to allow less and less people to show up? Does he wait until there's *no one* showing up, and then have the conversation?

So - a date was set, at some point after the freshers had been in town for a while, if things did not improve by then, TFT, would be 'out'.

It was at that point, after listening carefully through all of that, I spoke.

"So... why am I here?"

The Empire seemed confident they could run and promote a Saturday. They were trying to figure out how things would play out with Fridays.

So I heard them out. Here's how the Empire envisaged the chips could fall.

1. TFT might stay on as Friday promoters and the Empire just run their own Saturdays.

2. TFT would take Sumo to another venue.

3. TFT may throw the towel in, and leave the Empire to do what they want.

They wanted my opinion, and I offered it up.

I told them number 1, would never happen. That's not going to work.

I told them that number 2 *could* happen.

However, The DJs had been telling me for a while that Sumo was so unloved and numbers were so low that the idea of trying to relaunch and take the following elsewhere seemed very unlikely. The problem was that there was no following. Plus, no offence to the other venues in town, but anywhere other than the Empire would be a serious downgrade. I just didn't think a relaunch at a fresh venue was something that would work.

I actually thought maybe TFT had just about had enough of clubnights. They only had two left, Sumo and MILK, and I was the guy that had done the costings week in week out for years. I knew they didn't really make *that* much money.

If you recall, the last time Graham and I had spoken about Sumo he told me he'd *"rather smash his head into a wall"* than even think about it.

The idea of TFT relaunching a Sumo felt like something they just couldn't be arsed to do. The whole reason everyone was in this situation was that (it seemed like) the seniors at TFT didn't care anymore.

So option 3.

The Empire, along with having to run their own Saturday, would potentially have to run their own rock clubnight on a Friday.

Ash asked me, hypothetically, if I'd run it.

I said, *"I don't know."*

Here We Go Again

Sometime in October 2018

It had been months since I'd heard from Ash.

I was asked to come to the venue for another chat. Fucking hell, I thought, here we go.

Nothing had improved in terms of bodies through the door. The guys at Empire seemed genuinely disappointed, a bit gutted. I don't think they really wanted to do what they were about to do.

And so, the new plan for Empire Saturdays was underway. Ash was taking them in-house. He would talk to Graham soon and explain it was happening.

Ash informed me that Marty (Sumo, MILK, and TFT designer-in-chief) would be joining the Empire full time to oversee and execute these new Saturdays. A new name, new branding, and a strong launch campaign had been planned.

So this basically left Ten Feet Tall with one full-time member of staff, Dena.

Dena had confided in me around this time that she'd been applying for jobs left right and centre.

The idea of working a 37hour 'regular' week becomes very tempting. Dena had lined up a job at the prestigious Wynyard Hall as the events manager. Nice venue, nice job, one role, decent money. It was a no-brainer for her really.

Ash then told me he was going to offer Dena a job, as Head of Events at the Empire. He was putting a lot of people in difficult situations. What would she do? What would I do? Ash knew exactly what he wanted and needed to do with the Saturdays.

None of us really knew how Fridays' would play out.

We The Rats

Monday 5th November 2019

Just like he said he would, Ash sat Graham down and told him that the Empire would be taking the Saturday clubnight in-house.

Is it my place to tell this part of the tale? Are these the details of a private business conversation between two men, essentially none of my business?

But how else am I supposed to end this book?

At the time, there was so much gossip, rumour and theory around what had happened and what was going on between the Empire and Ten Feet Tall, it feels like a good idea to me, to put it down here.

To be honest, writing it down, it doesn't feel like that crazy an episode. At the time, this was a volatile and hostile situation. Later, it got daft, it got nasty, and it got personal.

The problem with Saturdays was a simple one. The Empire wasn't happy with numbers. They needed more bodies. The promoters couldn't do it. So they were going to try to sort it themselves.

Simple as that, I guess. Then it gets complicated.

What about Fridays? What about Sumo?

Neither of these guys, Ash and Graham, *seemed* like they cared too much about Sumo. That's how it looked, at first. The Sumo team generally had the feeling that Graham had had enough of the thing. The Empire themselves never felt any real love for Sumo. They didn't like the music. They didn't get the crowd.

"So, what about Sumo?".

However that conversation went, it concluded, with the Empire saying they would continue to provide Middlesbrough with a rock night each Friday.

Like the best Avril Lavigne song, what happened next, is complicated.

The Empire asked the Sumo team, DJs, photographers, the social media team, the person that put the wristbands on wrists, the people that painted faces, and everyone else... if they'd all like to work each Friday at the Empire's new rock night.

What did this team of people do?

Well, they asked Graham - did *he* have a night for them to work on a Friday, did he have anything for them?

He did not.

With rent to pay, and because they wanted to work, and because they loved the Empire very much, the team stayed on.

—

As the crew that ran this vessel, should they have jumped ship and followed the captain?

The captain had been asked to leave. And the ship continued to sail. And the crew liked the ship very much – they'd put their hearts and souls into making that ship what it was, and they weren't leaving.

A cheesy, salty, sickly analogy, but you get the idea.

Reflection

Sumo felt like everyone's afterthought. It *was* an afterthought. It felt like no one wanted it.

It seemed like Kev, Dani, Ste, Ross, Dena and everyone working on it were the only ones who cared, and they really fucking cared. Now the Empire wanted me in the mix.

I knew that if I didn't do it, someone else would. It was happening with or without me, and it felt like without me, there would be some bad decisions made. If there was one thing I was skilled at, it was putting out fires.

I do think the Empire genuinely wanted and hoped that normal service would resume, that TFT would have pulled a campaign out the bag. Perhaps they would release a unicorn.

Did I want to go back to events? No.

But... All I had to do was oversee and consult. The Empire needed someone who knew the crowd, knew the music, knew how to promote this shit. I could do this with my eyes closed.

Did I want to be running around until 4am every Friday? No.

But... I had a great team, Ash only expected me around *most* Friday nights, and his main priority seemed to be having a safe pair of hands to cash up and make sure the money was right. Again, easy.

Did I want this to happen to Graham and TFT? No.

I was actually convinced he wouldn't be that bothered. Would shedding these ill-performing events be a weight off his shoulders? I know for a fact two hundred people at Sumo does not make money. It loses money. So perhaps the Empire wasn't taking anything from anyone? The people I considered to be Team Sumo were Kev, Dani, Ste, Ross, Dena and Eddy. They would all stay on and deliver this new thing and wanted me to be part of it.

Should I have told Graham this was coming?

I'd heard this story a few times over the years. Years back, when a senior member of TFT *literally* told me he was going to orchestrate a coup with Empire and *"take that fucking Saturday night off him"*, - I'd told Graham. I'd literally told him. It always went the same way, people backtracked, talked, smoothed, reassured. And life went on.

I was made to feel like I was the crazy one. No one believed me.

Yet here it was.

This thing was happening whether any of us liked it or not.

Sumo Sumo

All credit to the team that the Empire assembled to pull off their grand rebrand and relaunch of Saturday Nights.

They turned it around in 5 days, and they nailed it.

MILK seemed to be forgotten in an instant by the people of Middlesbrough.

The all-new 'Shangri-La' Saturdays landed with an eccentric, over-the-top, flamboyant bang.

It was beautifully executed, and over the next few months, Shangri La went from 500 heads each Saturday, to 1200. Who'd have thought it?

The first Friday came around quick.

With Sumo, none of us really knew how the chips would fall post-November 5th, and we didn't really have too much of a concrete plan.

Unlike Shangri La, we didn't even have a name. We didn't think that would matter.

Of course it mattered.

There was a lingering feeling in the air, that Ten Feet Tall just gave such little of a fuck about Sumo, that a few of us genuinely thought they'd just drop it, for us to pick up.

Would Graham even care about his old rock night in the end?

Would he even care, if we just opened up the following Friday, and just... called it... Sumo?

Yeah he cared. Quite rightly, he went ape shit.

—

What followed next can only be described as a shit show. A bizarre and bitter war of words that was played out publicly on social media. It probably only went on for a few days. But it felt like forever.

We had Sumo social media accounts. By 'We' I mean everyone who'd worked on Sumo for the last few years.

Rule number one in business folks, make sure you know exactly who knows your passwords. It turns out that pretty much everyone knew Sumo's passwords.

The Empire had access to the Sumo Facebook page, and Graham didn't.

Team Empire told everyone that Sumo was 'on', on Friday Night, and we continued business as usual. Behind the scenes, we were making plans, and needed to get our shit together to sort a rebrand. But for now, what you had was Sumo's venue, Sumo's DJs and everything else that made up a Sumo, taking place at 11pm Friday that weekend.

It shouldn't have been called Sumo that weekend. That was probably a bad call.

Using the Sumo socials like nothing had changed was a very bad call. It shouldn't have happened. We rolled through a couple of Friday nights, just opening the doors, playing our songs, and seeing what happened. That shouldn't have happened either. People showed up, and had a nice time.

Every day people phoned me, asking what the plan was, what statements should we put out? Did we need new social media accounts? Should we print posters? What should we *say*?

I assume Graham reached out to Facebook, and they handed the social media accounts back to him. Everyone on the Empire side was locked out of these online tools.

So Graham could go online as "Sumo", telling everyone that we were arseholes and we'd stolen his clubnight.

Natch.

To the outside world looking on, it was all a bit confusing. Internally, a passionate team of creative individuals wanted Friday Nights at Empire to rock. They truly cared; they had a fire in their bellies, and they wanted to give the few hundred regulars a night to be proud of and take it to the next level. They wanted to do their jobs. This team of people were the same people who had run Sumo for a long time.

I know I'm labouring this point but, if it's Friday, and it's the Empire, and it's these DJs, playing these tunes and doing this thing. Well, it's *just Sumo*. Isn't it?

Had these people stolen Graham's clubnight? Not as they saw it. They were *saving* his clubnight. They were the only ones that cared, or so they felt. After years of doing it themselves, they now had to... do it themselves. It was confusing. It was emotional.

What are we going to call it?

Who cares? It's just Sumo.

Yeah, but it needs a new name.

Why? Everyone's just going to call it Sumo.

Yes. But we cannot call it Sumo.

Ash had a few suggestions.

"We should call it Sumo 2." he said. *"Or why don't we call it... SumoSumo."*

I don't know if he was joking. I think he was joking. At this point, it was hard to tell what the hell was going on any more.

What's In A Name

The Sumo situation felt like a runaway train that just gathered speed every day, and since November 5th, more and more carriages caught fire. I was busy helping the team put them out and also trying to make sure the club, the music, the drinks, the decor and most importantly the promotion - was dead right.

I got distracted from what was obviously the main problem that needed addressing right away - the name.

Some of my favourite bands of all time come under the category; 'anything-to-do-with-Frank-Carter'. Be it Gallows, Pure Love or his latest venture, The Rattlesnakes; they're all rock and roll incarnate.

The Rattlesnakes' debut single, and a real comeback moment for Frank had been the song Fangs. I loved the song, I loved the lyrics, I just loved the word; Fang.

'...I can't help but want to feel your teeth against my skin
  If you got fangs them sink 'em in, If you got fangs then sink 'em in'

It seemed to feel right, and after all, when you're naming your clubnight, it's important not to overthink it - all you need is a word.

So now, we were Fang.

It's Fang Now

Friday November 19th 2018.

At 11pm, on this dark November evening, we did not open as Sumo. We debuted as Fang.

There was no pre-announcement. No fuss. After the online drama of the previous fortnight, we just kept it casual. We had our new decor, giant projections, wristbands, staff shirts, everything everywhere in the club was Fang, Fang, Fang. We'd made a point of making those four letters as huge as we could all around the club. We did a grand job of making the Empire look like a club night called Fang.

So after all the madness online, we finally had the new name. The first few people in the club would be the first to know it. We weren't setting all the Fang socials live until midnight. We opened, and Kev played the first song at the first Fang. We were off. I went for a piss.

I headed to the ground floor gents. I passed the ten poster boards that lined the toilet wall and admired the new Fang artwork, our first poster. Like most shy guys, I chose to pee in the cubicle rather than the communal urinal and bolted the door behind me.

I heard a lad walk into the toilets and stand at the urinal. He was on the phone.

From where he stood, our new Fang poster would have been directly in front of his face, about two inches from his nose. I could hear his phone conversation. It went like this;

> "Yeah I'm already here. I'll just see you when you get here....
> ... I'm at Su... <pause> ...I'm at Fang.
> <muttering on the line>
> Yeah Fang, er, it's Fang now....
> <more muttering>
> ...I don't know, just come to the Empire. I'll see you when you get here."

It was as simple as that, I guess.

Years and years and years of Sumo, gone - in a shrug.

The kids are fickle.

It was Fang now.

Sumo On Ice

The next thing surprised us all.

Ten Feet Tall, did some Sumos.

A string of pop-up Sumo's, across Teesside. They did a Sumo at an ice rink in Billingham. They announced and promoted a Sumo in a tiny vintage shop. They did a Sumo with a wrestling tournament. It was all pretty random, and kind of cool.

However, people got very confused.

Many assumed Fang was Sumo, rebranded. So if Fang was just Sumo? Who was this new Sumo? Was Fang Sumo? Was Sumo Sumo?

We all just cracked on. The mission was to promote Fridays well, play great music, and throw great parties. We did our thing, and they did theirs. We didn't talk about them anymore, and they stopped talking about us. A vague truce had materialised.

The sporadic Sumo pop-up events ran for a while and then seemed to suddenly stop.

It appeared that Sumo, had literally, gone on ice.

Job Done

I'm not being clever here, and I don't want to sound like a dick, but Fang was great. It was really really good.

It was hard work, everyone pulled their weight, and we delivered what was needed.

The task that Empire set, was to take 200-a-week to 600-a-week, and that's what we did. It was a great event, week in week out, for over a year. We had a proper good time.

But I've written enough. You've read enough. But just for the record; me, Dena, Kev, Dani and Ste, absolutely smashed it.

Conclusion

At around 4pm, on Friday March 27th 2020 the Prime Minister of the United Kingdom announced that bars, pubs and clubs must be shut by midnight.

He gave everyone in the hospitality sector a few hours' notice.

I didn't want to go to work that night.

Coronavirus was at its mighty initial peak. The bad news poured in around the clock. Death rates and infection rates were horrifically high. There were mass PPE shortgages. There weren't enough ventilators. Supermarkets had empty shelves. There was no sanitiser anywhere. There was no toilet roll anywhere. People were dying. It felt like everyone was dying.

Fang, the Empire, Clubnights - Things like that didn't seem so important anymore.

The DJs, photographers and the Fang team didn't want to go to work that night.

On the evening of March 27th 2020, the Empire did open. I'd found them a stand-in DJ. I didn't go in.

After that night, the venue wouldn't open its doors for almost a year and a half. Covid-19 ravaged the planet. It destroyed lives, annihilated the economy, turned modern life as we knew it upside down, and it pissed all over the events industry.

Epilogue

I guess this means the last Fang was March 20th 2020. For me, that's where this story, finally, ends. I thought Fang was great. It was great because, essentially, at its core, it was Sumo.

And so, in that March of 2020, it was all gone, in an unceremonious twist of fate. A bit like Animals V Machines went out without a bang, a bit like when we whipped Sumo out of Durham, or Darlington, or even out of the Cornerhouse - discreetly and without a fuss.

A bit like me at 4am each Friday night, or should I say Saturday morning.

No fanfare, no emotional farewell. Just quietly clicking the fire escape door shut behind me, and heading off into the frosty Teesside darkness.

How swiftly it was taken away. How quickly it was gone - considering it was there for so long.

It was more than a club, or a poster, or a playlist, or a group of people.

It was more than a clubnight.

It was an institution, and it was a way of life.

TL:DR

(Too long, didn't read it)

What's Sumo?

A clubnight that took place every Friday night in Middlesbrough from 2005. It started at the Cornerhouse, then moved to the Empire. The main music policy was rock and alternative, although it also had rooms that played indie, drum and bass, metal, pop and sometimes hosted live bands, theme parties and other novelty items. It was run by a small independent promotions company called Ten Feet Tall, who also did many other things in the North East.

Why did Sumo leave Cornerhouse?

The venue was falling apart structurally, financially and credibly at the seams. Ten Feet Tall didn't have any choice. The venue would have been sold or closed down, with Sumo in it. Whether Sumo moved out or not, it was always sadly going to close its doors.

Why did Sumo go to the Empire?

It was the best club in Middlesbrough. It didn't have the Cornerhouse's rustic charm, but the Cornerhouse was no longer an option.

Who were the DJs?

Rock, Punk and Metal : Kev (2005-2020), Craig (2005-2012), Dani (2008-2020)

Indie and Pop : Burnsey (2007-2016), Henry (2009-2017), Ste A (2009-2020), Fashion Fil (2007-2016), Dani (2012-2020)

Plus loads of other great DJs that hopped in for dnb (Bobzilla, Rob Fod and friends), dubstep (Lee Bushido and friends), K-pop from Dillios and live visuals from Phil (Last Knight). Plus some great sets from Eddy, Robbie, Jamie and even a few nights with the tunes by wannabe DJ Phil Saunders.

Who designed the artwork?

A team led by Marty (aka Turtledust) in the early days. Followed by a few wild years with Pop, and then from about 2013, Dani took the reins.

Who is Ten Feet Tall?

Since about 2003, Ten Feet Tall, a company started and ran by a guy called Graham Ramsay have organised, promoted, and run events in the North East. If you've been to a gig, seen a comedian, went to a local festival, or been to any of the best clubnights in Teesside in the past twenty years... Ten Feet Tall were most probably behind it. Blame them for all those hangovers.

Who invented Sumo?

Ten Feet Tall. In 2005, when The Cornerhouse asked them to do a Friday night in addition to their massive pop Thursdays, Sixty Nine.

Who ran Sumo?

I, Phil Saunders, had the pleasure of running the show for many years, with a seriously hard-working, passionate team of individuals by my side.

No one else wanted to be in charge, so I guess it ended up being me. As I got distracted by all things TFT, including trying to launch Sumo's in Durham, Darlington and Sunderland, the Sumo ship was expertly steered by (chronologically) Jamie, Martin, Gary, Rick, Hannah, Ella and Dena at various points. They all did a grand job. Thanks for holding the baby.

Why was it so successful, and why did it last so long?

I think we had a great event, at a great time. It was a golden age for guitar music, and as much as we grafted and put so much thought and care into the thing, it was also the right place and the right time.

Then, just as we peaked and hit a decline, and people grew up a bit and started to get a little bored of those four walls, we shifted to a fancy new crib. Down the line, things in Empire got a bit tired. Another pivot, and a rebrand of sorts to 'Fang', and a change in management that relit everyone's fire. Thus, we got away with it for another couple of years.

"Clubnights have a life expectancy of about five years"... We rewrote that old adage.

Will Sumo come back?

If you want to go to a Sumo, it depends on what you mean by a Sumo. It returns us to the question of what exactly makes a clubnight. Let's not go back there.

The Empire is a beautiful building, a simply unsurpassable place to host a clubnight. I'd wholeheartedly recommend attending one of their clubnights. They do them, really, really well. But they don't have a Sumo for you to go to.

Ten Feet Tall still organise, promote and run a vast plethora of events.

The sheer variety on offer at their main venue, Base Camp, is astounding. There's nothing else like it in Middlesbrough. Base Camp occasionally run an event called 'Sumo'. It's really great - although it might not quite be the old Sumo you're looking for.

Sumo was a place and a space in time - that I think has sadly gone.

But man, it was good while it lasted.

Thanks

I was, and still am, eternally grateful to every single individual who worked alongside me at TFT through all of this. There was an army of us, too many to mention, too many to remember. So don't take it personally if you got missed out. We couldn't have done it without you. That means you Foz, Big Dave, Louise, Anneka, Rachel, Emily, Ste O, Simon W, Mark, Karlos, Jess, Shona, Bee, Laura, Danni, Olivia, Liam, Becca, Fyfe, Melissa, Reece, Hannah, Steph, Woody, Alex, Annabelle, Neil, Faye, James, Nic, Aaron, Si & Bex, Connor, Millie, Lana, Courtney, Kesia, Pooley, Snowy, Carla, Emma, SJ, Amanda, Ryan, Steph and Ben. And all the rest. Most days felt like we had the best job in the world, and we'd often laugh and pinch ourselves that we were getting paid for this. Some days it felt like a war, slogging through a never-ending onslaught of... stuff. The most overused analogy in this book, we span plates. I couldn't have spun them without you. Whether you served years in the madness, or just answered my call one day to carry a speaker cabinet up a flight of stairs for £20 and some beers, I thank you. I think we all gave this little town a good time, for a long time.

I also need to thank Ashe and the team behind Haxed. That's *haxed.co.uk/- forum*. At some point, you made the decision not to delete Haxed. Thank you. The endless boards that make up that long-forgotten forum are wondrous, and they made the creation of this book a good bit simpler. It is a goldmine of Teesside music scene history. Clubnights, bands, events, setlists, reviews, photos, allsorts. It's all still there. Please keep it there for all to explore. From 2005 to about 2010, absolutely everything I planned and promoted went on Haxed. To my shame, I stopped posting on Haxed when Facebook came along - so a massive thank you to my mate Simon, who continued to copy and paste the Sumo Facebook promo, onto Haxed, for a couple of years after I stopped.

Thanks to the Sumo photographers. The fifteen year journey of Sumo is documented in glorious technicolour on the internet thanks to the efforts of this talented team, who risked their kit every Friday night, getting amongst the madness. Dannielle, Eddy, Trudie, James, Nicola and Ben - This book was made so much easier by being able to wade through the thousands of photos in our weekly galleries. You unlocked memories and helped me fulfil the mammoth task of pulling the story together. Most of the photos are still online, and easy to find. Hence, we don't need photos in this book. (It was long enough, right?)

Thanks to Ben McQueeney for great advice on how to publish an independent DIY book. If you need such advice, Ben's the expert in that field. I didn't take most of his advice. That's why his books sell thousands of copies and mine won't.

Special thanks to Claire, Kev, Aarron and Dena for reading the book before anyone else did. I'm sure the public will catch all the typos we missed. Thanks to Jonny for the amazing cover, Eddy for the crowd shot on the back, and Callum, for the zine design skills.

An extra special thanks to Claire, my ever-patient wife. You have endured years and years and years of my projects, whims and asides. Ten bands, ten clubnights, multiple career changes, and now a book. I love you so very much. I hope you like the Cannonball chapter.

And sorry for nearly squashing our firstborn child with a giant pinata.

Printed in Great Britain
by Amazon